# Literary Theory
## The Basics

This accessible guide provides the ideal first step in understanding literary theory. Hans Bertens:

- leads you through the major approaches to literature which are signalled by the term 'literary theory'
- places each critical movement in its historical (and often political) context
- illustrates theory in practice with examples from much-read texts
- suggests further reading for those especially interested in a particular critical approach
- shows not only that theory can make sense but also that it can radically change the way you read.

Covering all the basics and much more, this is the ideal book for anyone interested in how we read and why that matters.

**Hans Bertens** is based at the University of Utrecht, the Netherlands. He is the author of *The Idea of the Postmodern* (Routledge, 1995).

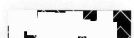

**Also available from Routledge in this series:**

**Language: The Basics (Second edition)**
*R. L. Trask*

**Philosophy: The Basics (Third edition)**
*Nigel Warburton*

**Politics: The Basics (Second edition)**
*Stephen Tansey*

**Shakespeare: The Basics**
*Sean McEvoy*

**Sociology: The Basics**
*Martin Albrow*

LONDON AND NEW YORK

# Literary Theory

## The Basics

Hans Bertens

ROUTLEDGE

First published 2001
by Routledge
11 New Fetter Lane, London EC4P 4EE

Simultaneously published in the USA
and Canada
by Routledge
29 West 35th Street, New York, NY 10001

*Routledge is an imprint of the Taylor &
Francis Group*

© 2001 Hans Bertens

The right of Hans Bertens to be
identified as the Author of this Work has
been asserted by him in accordance with
the Copyright, Designs and Patents
Act 1988

Typeset in Times by Taylor & Francis
Books Ltd
Printed and bound in Great Britain by
Clays Ltd, St Ives plc

*British Library Cataloguing in Publication
Data*
A catalogue record for this book is
available from the British Library

*Library of Congress Cataloging-in-
Publication Data*
Bertens, Johannes Willem.
Literary theory: the basics / Hans
Bertens.
p. cm.
Includes bibliographical references and
index.
1. Criticism – History – 20th century.
2. Literature – History
and criticism – Theory, etc.
I. Title.
PN94 .B47 2001
801'.95'0904–dc21

00–065328

ISBN 0–415–25061–7 (hbk)
ISBN 0–415–18664–1 (pbk)

*To my colleagues at 4 Mint Street*

# Contents

# CONTENTS

# Preface

There was a time when the interpretation of literary texts and literary theory seemed two different and almost unrelated things. Interpretation was about the actual meaning of a poem, a novel, or a play, while theory seemed alien to what the study of literature was really about because its generalizations could never do justice to individual texts. In the last thirty years, however, interpretation and theory have moved closer and closer to each other. In fact, for many contemporary critics and theorists interpretation and theory cannot be separated at all. They would argue that when we interpret a text we always do so from a theoretical perspective, whether we are aware of it or not, and they would also argue that theory cannot do without interpretation.

The premise of *Literary Theory: The Basics* is that literary theory and literary practice – the practice of interpretation – can indeed not very well be separated and certainly not at the more advanced level of academic literary studies. One of its aims, then, is to show how theory and practice are inevitably connected and *have* always been connected. The emphasis is on the 1970s and after, but important earlier views of literature get their full share of attention. This is not merely a historical exercise. A good understanding of, for instance, the New Criticism that dominated literary criticism in the United States from the mid-1930s until 1970 is indispensable for students of literature. Knowing about the New Criticism will make it a lot easier to understand other, later, modes of reading. More importantly, the New Criticism, like other more traditional approaches to literature, has by no means disappeared. Likewise, an understanding of what is called structuralism makes the complexities of so-called poststructuralist theory a good deal less daunting and has the added value of offering a perspective that is helpful in thinking about culture in general.

This book, then, is an introduction to both literary theory and a history of theory. But it is a history in which what has become historical is simultaneously actual: in the field of literary studies a whole range of approaches and theoretical perspectives, political and apolitical, traditional and radical, old and new, operate next to each other in relatively peaceful coexistence. In its survey of that range of positions *Literary Theory: The Basics* tries to do equal justice to a still actual tradition and to the radicalness of the new departures of the last decades. We still ask 'what does it mean?' when we read a poem or novel or see a play. But we have additional questions. We ask 'what does it mean to whom?' And 'why does it mean what it means?' Or, more specifically, 'who wants it to have this meaning and for what reasons?' As we will see, such questions do not diminish literature. On the contrary, they make it even more important.

# Acknowledgements

Thanks go first of all to Talia Rodgers, the mastermind in the background. I also would like to thank the anonymous readers who reported on my manuscript and who were almost invariably right. The same goes for Liz Brown, and it is one – but only one – of the reasons why she is a wonderful editor.

Chapter 1
_____

# Reading for meaning

*Practical criticism and new criticism*

## English meaning

If we want to understand English and American thinking about literature in the twentieth century we must begin with the nineteenth-century figure of Matthew Arnold (1822–1888), English educator, poet (once famous for his rather depressing but much anthologized 'Dover Beach'), and professor of poetry at Oxford University. Arnold's views, which enormously enhanced the prestige of literature, were not wholly new. In fact, his central idea that, apart from its aesthetic and pleasing qualities, literature also had important things to teach us, was already familiar in antiquity and we see it repeated time and again over the ages. So we find Thomas Jefferson, future president of the future United States of America, observing in a 1771 letter that 'a lively and lasting sense of filial duty is more effectually impressed on the mind of a son or daughter by reading "King Lear" than by all the dry volumes of ethics and divinity that were ever written'. However, Arnold is not interested in

1

the more practical aspects of the idea that literature is a source of instruction – literature as a set of how-to books – but places it in a spiritual context.

Writing in the second half of the nineteenth century, Arnold saw English culture as seriously threatened by a process of secularization that had its origins in the growing persuasiveness of scientific thinking and by a 'Philistinism' that was loosened upon the world by the social rise of a self-important, money-oriented, and utterly conventional middle class. With the spiritual comforts of religion increasingly questionable now that the sciences – in particular Darwin's theory of evolution – had thoroughly undermined the authority of Bible and Church, Arnold foresaw a crucial, semi-religious role for poetry especially:

> More and more mankind will discover that we have to turn to poetry to interpret life for us, to console us, to sustain us. Without poetry, our science will appear incomplete; and most of what now passes with us for religion and philosophy will be replaced by poetry.
>
> (Arnold [1880] 1970: 340)

'The future of poetry', Arnold tells his readers, 'is immense, because in poetry ... our race, as time goes on, will find an ever surer and surer stay'. This radical claim for poetry – made in an 1880 essay called 'The Study of Poetry' – is in fact the culmination of claims that Arnold had for decades been making on behalf of what he called 'culture' and which in a book called *Culture and Anarchy* (1869) he had defined as 'the best that has been thought and said in the world' (Arnold [1869] 1971: 6). As this makes clear, that 'best' is not necessarily confined to poems, but there is no doubt that he saw poetry as its major repository. The special importance that he accords to poetry is not as surprising as it may now seem. It accurately reflects the status of pre-eminent literary genre that it enjoyed in Arnold's time. Moreover, in giving poetry this illustrious, almost sacred, function Arnold builds on ideas that earlier in the nineteenth century had been formulated by Romantic poets like Percy Bysshe

Shelley (1792–1822), who had attributed a special, visionary status to poetry, and on a long tradition, going back to the classics, that likewise gives literature, and especially poetry, special powers. It was only natural, then, for Arnold to put forward poetry as the major embodiment of 'culture'.

What does Arnold have in mind with 'the best that has been thought and said in the world'? Strangely enough, *Culture and Anarchy* is very outspoken, but not very clear on this point. Arnold has no trouble making clear by what forces and in which ways that 'best' is threatened: the evil is summarized by the 'anarchy' of his title, which includes the self-centred unruliness of the working class and 'the hideous and grotesque illusions of middle-class Protestantism' (63). He is, however, not very precise in his definitions of 'the best'. This is partly because he assumes that his readers already know: he does not have to tell them because they share his educational background and his beliefs ('When I insist on this, I am all in the faith and tradition of Oxford' (61)). But it is also due to its elusiveness. Arnold can tell us where to find it, for instance in Hellenism – the Greek culture of antiquity, with its 'aerial ease, clearness, and radiancy' (134) – but can only describe what it expresses: an attitude towards life, a way of being in the world. Included in this attitude we find 'freedom from fanaticism', 'delicacy of perception', the 'disinterested play of consciousness', and an 'inward spiritual activity' that has 'for its characters increased sweetness, increased light, increased life, increased sympathy' (60–64). What culture would seem to amount to is a deeply sympathetic and self-effacing interest in, and contemplation of, the endless variety that the world presents. For Arnold, poetry probes life more deeply, is more sympathetic towards its immensely various manifestations, and is less self-serving than anything else, and so we must turn to poetry 'to interpret life for us'. Because poetry has the power to interpret life, we can also turn to it if we want to be consoled or to seek sustenance. With the persuasiveness of religious explanations seriously damaged, poetry has the now unique power of making sense of life, a sense from which we can draw comfort and strength. Moreover – and here we see the idea of 'instruction' – culture allows us to 'grow', to become more complete and better human beings. As Arnold puts it in *Culture and Anarchy*: 'Religion says, *The kingdom of God is within you*; and culture, in like manner, places human perfection in an *internal* condition, in the growth and predominance of our humanity proper, as distinguished from our animality' (47).

## The problem of time

Let me for a moment turn to one of Arnold's major examples of the culture he extols: 'Hellenism', the complex of intellectual and emotional attitudes expressed in the civilization of ancient Greece. Like all university-educated people of his time, Arnold was thoroughly familiar with classical history and literature. So familiar, in fact, that in some ways he sees Greek epics and plays that are more than 2,000 years old as contemporary texts. The classics and the ideal of culture that they embody are timeless for Arnold. This is a vitally important point: 'the best that has been thought and said in the world', whether to be found in the classics or in later writers, is the best for every age and every place.

From Arnold's perspective, this makes perfect sense. After all, culture and its major means of expression, poetry, must take the place of a religion that equally was for every age and every place. But this introduces what many literary academics, in the fairly recent past, have come to see as a serious problem. Arnold does not consider the possibility that what is 'the best' for one age may not be 'the best' for another, when circumstances have completely changed, or that what within a given period is 'the best' for one party (say, the aristocracy) is not necessarily 'the best' for another (starving peasants, for instance). Arnold's culture and the poetry that embodies it demand an intellectual refinement and sensitivity and a disinterested otherworldliness that under a good many historical circumstances must have been a positive handicap. Arnold would probably not deny this but he would argue that, all things being equal, there is only one cultural ideal – embodied in 'the best' – that we should all strive for.

The way I am presenting this – with starving peasants pitted against the aristocracy – could easily create the impression that

Arnold is an elitist snob. But that is absolutely not the case. Arnold's ideal of culture is certainly exclusive, in the sense that it defines itself against money-grubbing vulgarity, narrow-minded fundamentalism, upper-class arrogance, and so on, but it does not seek to exclude anyone on principle. If we allow ourselves to come under the influence of 'culture', we can all transcend the limitations imposed on us by class, place, and character, and acquire the cultured sensitivity and respectful, even reverent, attitude towards the world that 'culture' holds up for us. In fact, this is what Arnold would like all of us to do: to escape from the place and the time we live in and to transform ourselves into citizens of an ideal world in which time does, in a sense, not pass and in which we are in some ways – the ways that count – all the same. After all, in Arnold's view 'culture' is of all time: it exists in an autonomous sphere where time- and place-bound personal, political, or economic considerations have been left behind. We can only fully enter the realm of culture if we choose, at least temporarily, to disregard the here and now of personal ambition, political manoeuvring, and economic gain.

## Liberal humanism

Although that may not be immediately clear, this view of culture has important implications. Arnold is of course aware that culture will always to some extent reflect its time and place of origin – in the sense that, for instance, medieval and early modern literature will assume that the Sun revolves around a static planet Earth – but with regard to what it *really* has to tell us it stands apart from time and place, that is from history. With regard to its essence, culture *transcends* history. We must assume, then, that its creators – the poet supreme among them – also transcend time and place – at least as long as the act of creation lasts. A timeless culture must be the creation of timeless minds, that is of minds that can at least temporarily disregard the world around them. This brings us to an important question: where does a creative mind that has temporarily soared free of its mundane environment find the insights that will allow it to contribute to 'the best that has been thought and said'? The answer must be that the source of that wisdom can only be the individual creator. Poets find what is valuable and has real meaning in *themselves*; they just *know*.

Arnold was by no means unique in his view of the creative individual. It was shared by the large majority of his contemporaries and by the countless writers and critics who in the course of the twentieth century would more or less consciously follow his lead. More importantly, it is still the prevailing view of the individual – not just the creative ones – in Western society. This view of the individual – or *subject*, to use a term derived from philosophy – is central to what is called *liberalism* or *liberal humanism*, a philosophical/political cluster of ideas in which the ultimate autonomy and self-sufficiency of the subject are taken for granted. Liberal humanism assumes that all of us are essentially free and that we have at least to some extent created ourselves on the basis of our individual experiences. It is easy to see that this view of the subject is pervasively present in our culture and in our social institutions. The legal system, for instance, starts from the assumption that we have a certain autonomy. If your lawyer succeeds in convincing the court that the murder you thought you could get away with was not a conscious act that you could have decided against, you will be declared insane. Likewise, democracies do not set up elections with the expectation that people will wander mindlessly into a voting booth and make a completely arbitrary choice between the candidates. Our social institutions expect us to be reasonable and to be reasonably free. Because of that freedom, we ourselves are supposedly the source of the value and the meaning we attach to things. As liberal subjects we are not the sum of our experiences but can somehow stand outside experience: we are not defined by our circumstances but are what we are because our 'self' has been there all along and has, moreover, remained remarkably inviolate and stable. Not surprisingly, in much of Western literature, and especially in lyric poetry and realistic fiction, individuals present themselves, or are portrayed, along these lines. In the realistic novels of the mid-nineteenth century, characters again and again escape being defined by their social and economic situation because they are essentially free. Since what they are – their 'self' – is largely independent of their situation, the circumstances in which they find themselves can be transcended. Realism suggests that the characters that it presents find the reasons for their actions and decisions inside themselves. Because this liberal humanist view of the individual is as pervasively present in our world as it was in the nineteenth century, it also characterizes much of our contemporary literature.

One might, along another line, even argue that literature as such, and in fact every single artistic object, contributes to the ahistorical perspective that we find in liberal humanism in so far as it makes us forget about our immediate environment. Both the 'eternal' truths that we may find in a work of art, and its aesthetic dimension – its beauty, which, according to the philosopher Immanuel Kant (1724–1804), promotes disinterested contemplation – invite us to disregard the here and now. In so doing, they collude to give us the impression that what is most essential to us – our 'self' – also transcends time and place.

For many present-day critics and theorists this is a deeply problematic view. In the later chapters of this book we will encounter various objections to this liberal humanist perspective. Let me here just point at one possible problem. What if access to Arnold's 'the best' depends for instance on education? If that is the case, Arnold's campaign for a 'culture' that supposedly has universal validity begins to look like arrogance: we would have a person who is convinced of their position as one of the elect implicitly telling the uneducated (or relatively uneducated) that they are barbarians. Arnold might object that ideally all of us should get the same – extended – education. But educational opportunities are not evenly distributed over this world; there are, even within every nation, sharply different levels in education. A sceptic might easily see Arnold's campaign for his idea of culture as a move in a struggle for power and status: for the power to define culture, to decide what the 'best' is, and for membership of the cultural elite. In fact, even if we grant Arnold's claim and accept that his idea of culture does indeed represent the most humane, most tolerant, most morally sensitive perspectives that human civilization has come up with, we would still have a problem. Would we have the right to impose that culture on people who couldn't care less?

In short, there are serious problems with Arnold's humanist conception of culture and poetry. I should, in all fairness to Arnold, say that it has taken almost a hundred years for these problems really to register and that even now his views are still seductive. Isn't it true that many of us, at least at some point in our life, want to see literature as a high-minded enterprise by and for sensitive and fine-tuned intellectuals that is somehow several steps removed from the trivial push and pull of ordinary life? It is an alluring prospect: to have a place to go where in a hushed silence, the sort of silence that we very appropriately find in a library, we meet with the kindred, equally sensitive people who have written the works we read. It is a place where time does not pass and where in some ways – the ways that count – we are all the same. We, the readers, are of course only the passive consumers of what they, the writers, have actively produced, but doesn't that difference tend to fall away? Especially so since the texts we read are in the act of reading lifted out of their historical context and so to a certain extent cut loose from their creators?

It is too good to be completely true, even if it is not necessarily wholly untrue. How can we, apart from everything else, possibly know whether the seemingly kindred spirits that we meet in that timeless place do indeed share our perspectives and concerns? What guarantee is there that we do not only see our concerns in such sharp relief because we ignore what we do not want to see? Perhaps Arnold is right about Hellenism's 'aerial ease, clearness, and radiancy', but where in that phrase are the murder and mayhem of so many of the Greek classics? Can the Greeks, or can Chaucer, Dante, or even Shakespeare, who all lived in worlds dramatically different from our own, really have been in some important way similar to ourselves? Perhaps 'delicacy of perception', the 'disinterested play of consciousness', and the other qualities that Arnold attributes to his ideal culture are indeed of all times, even if in different periods and places they will have been framed by ever-changing historical circumstances. But since we cannot travel back in time we will never know. In the final analysis, Arnold's historical continuum between Hellenism and the high culture of his own time – the poetry that must interpret life for us – is an act of faith.

## Literature as civilization's last stance

Arnold's campaign for poetry as the superior interpreter of life did not immediately lead to the establishment of literature courses in English schools and universities, let alone courses in English literature. Strangely enough, English as a subject only existed outside the United Kingdom, in Scotland, where the University of Edinburgh had already in the eighteenth century taught English literature, in the United States, where Harvard University had created a chair in English in 1876, and in British India, where since the 1830s English literature served to familiarize the 'native' elite with 'Englishness' and to anglicize them as far as they were prepared to have themselves anglicized. In England itself, English literature was not taught as it is today at all. English had first been introduced as an academic subject by University College London in 1828 (Oxford would only follow in 1893 and Cambridge in 1911), but the study of English literature – later expanded to include American literature – as a serious intellectual discipline dates only from the 1920s.

When Matthew Arnold died, in 1888, English was fairly well established in both England and the United States, but not in a form we would now easily associate with it. Academic English was largely devoted to the history of the English language and to its older forms, such as Middle and Old English (the absolutely unintelligible language of *Beowulf*). The study of English literature was largely the province of well-educated men of letters who preferred high-minded evaluations and discussions of an author's sensibility to critical analysis and attention to the structure – the actual workings – of literary texts.

What really changed things and moved them in a direction we can more readily recognize is the intervention of a young American poet, T.S. Eliot (1888–1965), who had moved to England before the outbreak of the First World War, and the British government's desire to find a place for the study of English literature somewhere in its educational schemes. While

Eliot, with whose views I will deal in a moment, was primarily influential in the universities, the government-controlled Board of Education gave English literature a solid place in secondary education. It is worth noting how closely the so-called 'Newbolt Report' of 1921 that the Board had commissioned follows in Arnold's footsteps, even if its language would have been too sentimentally worshipful for Arnold's more robust taste: 'literature is not just a subject for academic study, but one of the chief temples of the Human spirit, in which all should worship' ('Newbolt Report' 1921). However, the Report also employs more straightforwardly Arnoldian tones. 'Great literature', it tells us, is 'a timeless thing'. It is 'an embodiment of the best thoughts of the best minds, the most direct and lasting communication of experience by man to man'. But this is, interestingly, not all that literature can show to recommend itself to a Board of Education. Literature, the Report suggests, could also serve to 'form a new element of national unity, linking together the mental life of all classes'.

We should see this against its historical background. Why this particular role for literature at this particular time? There is, first of all, the emotional devastation and widespread disillusionment that had resulted from the First World War. More important, however, is surely the extension of the right to vote in the years before and after the First World War to large groups of the population that had up till then been excluded from the franchise. Since labourers and women were now active participants in the new mass democracy they had better be civilized and be made aware of the fact that there was a higher realm of culture that was virtually detached from the practical world with its day-to-day problems and conflicting interests. English, with its focus on a spiritual realm of unselfish harmony where all petty quarrels are forgotten or have become irrelevant, could overcome social conflict and anti-patriotic sentiment. What the Report in fact suggests, although it never says so in so many words, is that social and economic inequality pales next to the equality we can find in the study – or perhaps the mere reading – of great texts.

It is always easy to criticize the ideals of the past and we should not come down too hard on these English educators or on their American counterparts, who somewhat earlier had put forward the study of English – and some American – literature as an important binding principle in a nation trying to assimilate large numbers of immigrants. We must give them the benefit of the doubt and assume that, apart from everything else, they also had the spiritual well-being of British and American students at heart. Still, the idea that literature might be instrumental in forging national unity has some consequences we must look at because it introduces a criterion that is absent from Arnold's poetry as the interpreter of life. If literature is supposed to promote national unity it makes good sense to throw out texts that emphasize disunity – tension between social classes, between religious denominations, between regions – or that are openly unpatriotic. For Arnold such texts, if they were sensitive and intelligent enough, were perfectly admissible. In fact, Arnold's 'disinterested play of consciousness' will inevitably – although of course not exclusively – lead to critical assessments of the outside world. But if literature is used to foster national unity, in other words, if it is used to create or keep alive a national identity, critical assessments of the nation's mercenary politics or its cultural vulgarity are no longer very welcome. We should always be aware that good intentions, too, have their agenda and their politics.

## Arnold's academic heritage: the English scene

As I have just noted, in the more academic sphere the most influential spokesman for Arnold's vision was the young expatriate American poet T.S. Eliot who had settled in London before the First World War. In the early 1920s Eliot did what Arnold had largely avoided: he set out to define the criteria that 'the best that had been thought and said in the world' would have to meet and he undertook the mission actually to identify them in so far as they had been expressed in literary form. In other words, after drawing up the admission requirements he used them to establish which texts met his criteria and which failed to do so. The canon – the list of good and even great literary works – that he set out to construe in the 1920s would dominate virtually all

English and American discussions of literature until the 1970s and is still a powerful influence.

Eliot's early essays immediately discredited the writings of the men of letters who before the First World War had mused about a writer's sensibility and those of the Victorian moralists who had found so much lofty truth and profound sentiment in literary works. For Eliot, poetry – the genre in which he was most interested – was profoundly impersonal. This is not to say that he denied poets the right to express themselves in their poetry, although it would not be too difficult to extract that position from his writings. In 'Tradition and the Individual Talent', for instance, we find him claiming that the poet has 'not "a personality" to express, but a particular medium' (Eliot [1919] 1972: 75). Eliot's main aim, however, is to deflect his readers' attention from everything he considers of at best secondary importance – the poet's personal or social circumstances, and so on – and to get poetry itself centre stage. Eliot, then, objects to highly emotional outpourings and personal confidences because they tend to focus our attention on the poet rather than the poetry. What is more, from Eliot's perspective they also make for bad and superficial poems. This does not mean that he is against the expression of deep feelings in poetry. However, expressions of profound emotion should not have an autobiographical dimension. Even if the emotion is unquestionably the poet's, it should be conveyed in such a way that the poet's private life plays no role in its presentation. What the poet needs to look for, Eliot tells us in 'Hamlet', another essay from 1919, is an 'objective correlative': 'a set of objects, a situation, a chain of events which shall be the formula of that particular emotion' (Eliot [1919] 1969: 145). Emotion must be conveyed indirectly. The poet's emotion should be invested in such an 'objective correlative', which will then evoke the proper response in the reader. Moreover, emotion must always be kept in check by what Eliot called 'wit', a quality that he required of all poetry and by which he means an ironic perception of things, a (sometimes playful) awareness of paradoxes and incongruities that poses an intellectual challenge to the reader. It follows from this that Eliot had

little use for, for instance, the low-keyed soft-focus emotionality
of Alfred Tennyson (1809–1892):

> Tears, idle tears, I know not what they mean,
> Tears from the depth of some divine despair
> Rise in the heart, and gather to the eyes,
> In looking on the happy autumn-fields,
> And thinking of the days that are no more.
>
> ('Tears, Idle Tears', 1847)

In contrast with this sort of poetry, Eliot's own poetry presents
what might – somewhat unkindly – be described as a terse, tight-
lipped, ironic melancholy that signals in its striking use of
images, juxtapositions, inversions, and so on just how intellectually agile and alert it is. It is a poetry that fully demands the
reader's close attention. The complexity of its language and
form forces us to take it seriously in its own right and makes it
difficult to see it in, for instance, autobiographical terms.

The integration of intellect and emotion and, less insistently,
of profundity and playfulness, that Eliot sees as an absolute
condition for good poetry drastically limits his list of worthwhile
poets. In fact, for Eliot, writing in the 1920s, literature had taken
a wrong turn more than two centuries before. In 'The
Metaphysical Poets' he argues that the so-called 'Metaphysical
poets' of the seventeenth century still knew how to fuse thought
and feeling, and seriousness and lightness, in their poetry. After
their heyday, however, a 'dissociation of sensibility' had set in in
which intellect, emotion, and other formerly integrated qualities
had gone their separate ways (Eliot [1921] 1969: 288). For Eliot
this had led to poetry that errs either on the one side – sterile
rationality, for instance – or on the other – excessive emotion or
a levity that turns into irresponsibility – and that because of
such failures is always condemned to superficiality.

With hindsight we can see that Eliot proclaims his own poetic
practice and that of his fellow modernists of the early twentieth
century as the general norm. With hindsight we can also see that
Eliot's nostalgia for a past when people were supposedly still
whole in the sense that they knew how to combine harmoniously

thought and feeling – reason and emotion – was fed by a deep dissatisfaction with the contemporary world in which harmony was sadly lacking.

It may at first sight not be clear what this has to do with Eliot's views of literature. However, Eliot consciously places poetry – and by implication all literature that meets his criteria – in opposition to the modern world. He seeks in poetry the sort of profound experience that the modern world, in which materialistic values and a cheap moralism have come to dominate, cannot offer. For Eliot, the natural, organic unity that is missing from the world and that we ourselves have also lost with the advent of scientific rationalism and the utilitarian thinking of industrialization – the 'dissociation of sensibility' – is embodied in aesthetic form in poetry. So even if poetry has no answers to any questions we might ask, it is still of vital importance and it allows us to recapture temporarily a lost ideal of wholeness in the experience of reading. As Eliot's fellow American (and – briefly – fellow expatriate) Robert Frost (1874–1963) phrased it from a slightly different perspective, poetry provides 'a momentary stay against confusion' (cited in Perkins *et al.* 1985: 979). Because of its integration of thought and feeling and of opposing attitudes in a coherent aesthetic form poetry could, rather paradoxically, even serve that function if the confusion itself was its major theme (as for instance in Eliot's 'The Waste Land' of 1922). Simultaneously, poetry deepens our awareness of the important things in life.

Although Eliot is obviously very much interested in poetic technique and in the *form* of specific poems – an interest that would be worked out by a group of American poets and critics, the so-called *New Critics* – he is ultimately even more interested in a poem's *meaning*. Poetry should convey complex meanings in which attitudes that might easily be seen as contradictory are fused and which allow us to see things that we otherwise would not see. Our job, then, is to interpret poems, after which we can pass judgement on them; that is, establish how well they succeed in creating and conveying the complexity of meaning that we expect from them. 'Here lies Fred, / He is dead' would not pass muster. The idea that we read poems, and literature in general, because they contain *meanings* is obvious. This search for the meaning of poems, novels, plays, and other works of literature has from the 1920s well into the 1970s absolutely dominated English and American literary studies and still constitutes one of their important activities. However, as will become clear in the course of this book, the meaning of a specific literary work cannot have a monopoly on our interest. An interest in the *form* of the poem, novel, or play in question – and, by extension, in the form of literature as a whole – is equally legitimate, as is an interest in a literary work's *politics*. But those complications will have to wait.

## Cambridge, England

Eliot, although trained as a philosopher, was not affiliated with a university. But he was one of the most exciting poets of his generation and also one whose philosophical interests made him think long and hard about the nature and function of literature. Inevitably, his views of literature were immediately picked up by young university teachers. Eliot's most influential following emerged at Cambridge University with the literary academic I.A. Richards (1893–1979) and the group that would somewhat later be led by the critic F.R. Leavis (1895–1979). Although each of them in his own way disagreed with some of Eliot's claims, Richards and Leavis initiated two intimately related 'schools' that would give shape to English and American thinking about literature for almost fifty years.

In Richards's hands Eliot's emphasis on the poem itself became what we call *practical criticism*. In a still fascinating experiment Richards withheld all extra-textual information – no author, period, or explanatory commentary – and asked students (and tutors) to respond to poems that were thus completely stripped of their context. It would be difficult to think up a more text-oriented approach. We are now so familiar with this that it is difficult to imagine how revolutionary Richards's experiment once was.

Since Richards developed his practical criticism – the label was popularized through the title of a book he published in 1924

– generations of students on both sides of the Atlantic have struggled with the assignment to make sense of an unfamiliar and at least initially hostile text. We can therefore now hardly appreciate how his method turned reading into an intellectual challenge. Without the help of the biographical, historical, or linguistic information that readers were used to, interpreting a poem, especially an older one, was a formidable task. This should not obscure the fact that Richards stands firmly in the line of Matthew Arnold and T.S. Eliot regarding the importance of literature and, more in particular, poetry. Like so many young intellectuals of the period, Richards had deep misgivings about a contemporary world which seemed to have lost its bearings. He, too, saw in poetry an antidote to the spiritual malaise that seemed to pave the way for chaos. If the moral order would indeed fall apart because of the loss of traditional values that he saw around him, we would, Richards suggested, 'be thrown back, as Matthew Arnold foresaw, upon poetry. It is capable of saving us; it is a perfectly possible means of overcoming chaos' (Richards 1926: 83). Poetry, and the arts in general, could save us because it is there that we find what is truly, and lastingly valuable – what gives meaning to our lives:

> The arts are our storehouse of recorded values. They spring from and perpetuate hours in the lives of exceptional people, when their control and command of experience is at its highest, hours when the varying possibilities of existence are most clearly seen and the different activities which may arise are most exquisitely reconciled, hours when habitual narrowness of interests or confused bewilderment are replaced by an intricately wrought composure.
>
> (Richards [1924] 1972a: 110)

This statement is not in the last place interesting because it so clearly illustrates Richards's view of the creative subject. The keywords are 'control', 'command', 'reconciled', and 'composure'. For Richards the minds of artists are in control of whatever may befall them; they reconcile contradictions, and transcend our usual self-centredness. This command and transcendence would originate within the artists themselves: we are offered a perfect picture of the liberal humanist individual or subject.

Because the arts are our storehouse of recorded values, they 'supply the best data for deciding what experiences are more valuable than others' (111). Literary art, then, helps us to evaluate our own experience, to assess our personal life. It is all the better equipped for this because its language is not *scientific* but *emotive*. Scientific language is for Richards language that refers to the real world and makes statements that are either true or false. Emotive language, however, wants to produce certain emotional effects and a certain attitude in those to whom it addresses itself: 'many, if not most, of the statements in poetry are there *as a means* to the manipulation and expression of feelings and attitudes, not as contributions to any body of doctrine of any type whatever' (Richards [1929] 1972b: 119). Literature, then, conveys a certain type of knowledge which is not scientific and factual but has to do with values and meaningfulness and which makes use of language that expresses and manipulates emotions.

As I have just noted, practical criticism focuses upon the text and the text alone. Because of this exclusively textual orientation, it was an ideal programme for teasing out all the opposites – thought versus feeling, seriousness versus high spirits, resignation versus anger, and so on – that for Richards (following Eliot) were reconciled and transcended in poetry, often through the use of irony. Practical criticism became a major instrument in spreading the idea that the best poems created a vulnerable harmony – a precarious coherence – out of conflicting perspectives and emotions. As we will see, in the United States this view would develop into the *New Criticism* that in the 1930s and 1940s became the major mode of criticism there.

## The novel as great art

So far, we have been almost exclusively concerned with poetry. F.R. Leavis, the other Cambridge academic who would put a –

17

highly personal – stamp on especially English literary studies, was, at least initially, no exception. Leavis, too, started out with poetry and also took Eliot's views as his guiding light. In the course of the 1930s he accordingly subjected the history of English poetry to an icy scrutiny in order to separate the wheat from the chaff, in the process relegating a good many English poets of up till then fine repute (including John Milton) to minor status. In particular nineteenth-century poets, standing collectively accused of a 'divorce between thought and feeling, intelligence and sensibility' – a condemnation in which we clearly hear Eliot's 'dissociation of sensibility' – did not fare well. As the major driving force behind the important journal *Scrutiny* (founded 1932, folded 1953) Leavis built up a large, and often fanatical, following in virtually all Departments of English in the United Kingdom and in Western Europe.

However, his work of the later 1940s, in which he sets out to revaluate the English novel, is more pertinent here. After all, Eliot himself, Richards, William Empson – one of Richards's students – the American New Critics and a growing number of lesser figures all discussed poetry from a perspective that was similar to that of Leavis. But until Leavis changed the picture, fiction had gone largely unnoticed.

Novels cannot very well be subjected to the same sort of analysis that we use with poems, especially not the substantial, if not actually sprawling, novels that until the end of the nineteenth century were more or less the rule. But Leavis's discussions of fiction would in any case have departed from the course set out by Eliot and Richards. By the 1940s Leavis had already in his discussions of poetry begun to include a moralistic dimension that is almost completely absent from the work of his American contemporaries, the New Critics. Although Leavis, too, puts a premium on oppositions, juxtapositions, inversions, and similar techniques, he increasingly comes to judge poems in terms of the 'life' and the 'concreteness' they succeed in conveying. In other words, he begins to discuss content as relatively independent of form while for the New Critics, as we will see below, form and content were inextricably interwoven. In fact, for the New Critics that interweaving determined to a considerable extent the quality of the text under discussion. While for the New Critics and an ever greater number of affiliated academics a text's form created the ironic maturity of its content, for Leavis form became increasingly of secondary importance. What the literary work should provide was a mature apprehension of authentic life, and certainly not one that was too ironic and therefore emotionally sterile (he was not charmed by the ironies of James Joyce's *Ulysses* [1922], which Eliot had thought a great work of art). For Leavis, authentic representations of life depended on a writer's personal authenticity and moral integrity. As he said in his 1948 *The Great Tradition* of the novelists he considered great: 'they are all distinguished by a vital capacity for experience, a kind of reverent openness before life, and a marked moral intensity' (Leavis [1948] 1962: 17) (Note how these novelists are presented as subjects who once again are fully in command of everything.) One of Leavis's 'great' novelists, the English writer D.H. Lawrence (1885–1930), had already offered a characteristically provoking illustration of such openness:

> If the bank clerk feels really piquant about his hat, if he establishes a lively relation with it, and goes out of the shop with the new straw hat on his head, a changed man, be-aureoled, then that is life.
>
> The same with the prostitute. If a man establishes a living relation to her, if only for a moment, then that is life. But if it *doesn't*: if it is just for the money and function, then it is not life, but sordidness, and a betrayal of living.
>
> If a novel reveals true and vivid relationships, it is a moral work, no matter what the relationships may consist in.
>
> (Lawrence [1925] 1972a: 129)

Because they believe that because of its scope and its attention to authentic detail the novel can represent life in all its fullness, it is for Leavis and Lawrence superior to whatever the other arts or the human sciences (such as psychology or sociology) may have to offer. It can, moreover, make us participate in that fullness. As

Lawrence said: 'To be alive, to be man alive, to be whole man alive: that is the point. And at its best, the novel, and the novel supremely, can help you' (Lawrence [1936] 1972b: 135).

This is an attractive programme for the novel – and for us. Who would not want to live authentically and to defend the forces of life against whatever may happen to threaten it? However, like so many attractive programmes it falls apart upon closer scrutiny. Who is to define a mature apprehension of life, a vital capacity for experience, or a reverent openness before life? What is 'life' for me may very well be so monotonous and boring that it seems like 'death' to you. And what about the morals that are felt so intensely? In any case, given his interest in full representations of life in its totality, Leavis almost inevitably came to focus on the novel, with its endless possibilities for presenting character, setting, theme, social background, and everything imaginable. If you want scope, the novel has more to offer than lyrical poetry. So, somewhat belatedly, Leavis brought the novel into the amazing professionalization of the study of English as it had started in the 1920s (drama, and in particular Shakespeare, many of whose plays lent themselves to an approach in poetic terms, had already been embraced in the 1930s). This is not to say that novels had been completely ignored. But Leavis elevated this interest into a programme. Moreover, he significantly expanded its scope.

## Meaning in the United States

In the 1930s, the work of Eliot, Richards, and Leavis found a warm welcome on the other side of the Atlantic among a group of poets, including John Crowe Ransom, Allen Tate, Robert Penn Warren, and Cleanth Brooks, who in the mid-1930s initiated a professionalization of American literary studies comparable to the developments in England.

These *New Critics*, as they came to be called (the label derives from the title of Ransom's 1941 book *The New Criticism*), shared the misgivings of their English colleagues about the contemporary world. They, too, saw around them a world driven by a desire for profit in which the so-called triumphs of modern science, in combination with capitalistic greed, threatened to destroy tradition and everything that was not immediately useful – including poetry. Like their English mentors, they turned to the past, in their case a past of the Southern states, in which organic unity and social harmony had not yet been destroyed by the industrialization and commercialization of the contemporary world. That such a past had never existed, or only for a happy few, was as little to the point as the fact that Eliot's unified sensibility had never existed. On both sides of the Atlantic writers and critics created a mythical past to counterbalance the utilitarian, mercenary present.

The New Critics, then, saw poetry as a means of resisting commodification and superficiality. Because of its internal organization – its formal structure – a poem created harmony out of opposites and tension and thereby presented a vital alternative. In creating coherent wholes out of the full variety and contradictory complexity of life, poetry halted and transcended the chaotic flux of actual experience. As John Crowe Ransom (1888–1974) put it in a 1937 essay called 'Criticism, Inc.': 'The poet perpetuates in his poem an order of existence which in actual life is constantly crumbling beneath his touch. His poem celebrates the object which is real, individual, and qualitatively infinite' (Ransom [1937] 1972: 238). In so doing, one of the poet's main strategies was the use of paradox with, as Cleanth Brooks (1906–1994) said, 'its twin concomitants of irony and wonder'. By means of paradoxes 'the creative imagination' achieves 'union'. That 'fusion is not logical,' Brooks continues,

it apparently violates science and common sense; it welds together the discordant and the contradictory. Coleridge has of course given us the classic description of its nature and power. It 'reveals itself in the balance or reconcilement of opposite or discordant qualities: of sameness, with difference; of the general, with the concrete; the idea, with the image; the individual, with the representative; the sense of novelty and freshness, with old and familiar objects; a more than usual state of emotion, with more than usual order'.

(Brooks [1942] 1972: 300–301)

In this emphasis on paradox – a statement containing contradictory aspects – and irony the New Critics clearly follow Eliot and Richards. They, too, see poems as storehouses of authentic values and as expressing important truths about the complexities of life that no other medium can convey nearly as effectively. (This is so, Brooks suggests, because 'apparently the truth which the poet utters can be approached only in terms of paradox' (292).) In some ways, however, they diverge from their examples. Richards had been seriously interested in the effects of poetry upon its readers. In fact, as we have seen, he argues that the 'emotive' language of poetry seeks to manipulate the reader's feelings and attitudes. The New Critics exclude both the poet – as Richards had also done – and the reader from their approach to poetry. As a result, they focus more on the actual *form* of literary works than their English counterparts. In fact, within the context of English and American criticism their approach to literature might well be considered *formalist* and it does indeed often go by that label. However, compared to the European formalists that I will discuss in the next chapters, their interest in form is rather limited. They are not interested in form for its own sake, but in form as contributing to a text's meaning.

The New Critics' lack of interest in the effects of poems does not mean that they denied the special character of poetic language. As Brooks tells us, 'the poet's language ... is a language in which the connotations play as great a part as the denotations' (295). Moreover, for the New Critics, too, a poem had to be fully experienced in order to be effective. 'A poem should not mean, but be', as they said, meaning that the 'message' that we can extract from a poem cannot possibly do justice to its complexity. Anything but the entirety of its paradoxes, opposites, and reconciling ironies is reductive and damaging. The habit that we all have of summarizing a poem – and other works of literature – in one or two phrases was for the New Critics a deadly sin against the poem and against our own experience of the poem. Turning a poem into a thematic statement – the speaker of this Christian poem regrets that life is so short while realizing simultaneously that its very brevity will all the sooner take us to heaven – was for them the 'heresy of paraphrase'. They were, more in general, rather severe on approaches to poetry that to them did not do full justice to the poem itself. W.K. Wimsatt (1907–1975) and another somewhat younger New Critic, Monroe Beardsley, caught two of their sharpest objections in two famous essays, 'The Intentional Fallacy' (1946) and 'The Affective Fallacy' (1949). The 'intentional fallacy' is to confuse what the author intended in the writing of a poem (or other work of literature) with what is actually there on the page. The actual *text* should be our guideline, not what the author has perhaps wanted to say. As the English novelist D.H. Lawrence had said earlier: 'Never trust the artist. Trust the tale' (Lawrence [1924] 1972c: 123). In other words, when we interpret a literary text, the author's commentary, or what we know of the author's intentions, is of secondary importance. It is not only that the author does not have full control over the text's meaning because in the actual writing process things may slip in of which the author is wholly unaware (which is what Lawrence had in mind), but that the author has in a sense officially relinquished control over the text: it has, after all, been made public and been distributed. The text has become a freestanding object and the rest is up to us.

While the 'intentional fallacy' has to do with the author, the 'affective fallacy' has to do with the reader. Readers who are prone to this fallacy confuse their own emotional response to the poem with what the poem really tells them. The way the poem affects them blinds them to its reality. Tears blur the picture, both literally and figuratively. 'Close reading', that is the focus on the text that Richards and Leavis had promoted so vigorously in England, in the hands of the New Critics became closer than ever. With the author's intentions and the reader's response removed from the scene, the study of literature restricted itself to analysing the techniques and strategies that poems used to deliver their paradoxical effects: the system of checks and balances that creates the diversity in unity that we experience. Although it probably seems counterintuitive, from this perspective it is not the poet – about whose intentions we usually know next to nothing – but indeed the poem itself that does the delivering. What organizes the poem – brings its diverse elements together – is not so much authorial intention as an abstract principle, the principle of *coherence*, which the New Critics assumed present and active in any 'good' poem. In good poetry, and, by extension, all good literature, the principle of coherence keeps the text's paradoxes and possible contradictions in check. Some may object that this does not make much sense because literary texts do not spring up overnight and all by themselves in remote and mysterious areas, so that it might seem a bit perverse to exclude the author from the discussion of a text. But it makes a good deal of practical sense. In some cases we do not even know who the author is and in many cases we can only guess at the author's intentions because we have no information and when we have that information it does not necessarily illuminate the poem, at least not from the perspective that I am discussing here. As we have seen, these critics assume that good literature is not bound by time and place. It transcends the limitations of its place of origin (including the author) and addresses the complexities of an essentially unchanging human condition. The concrete intentions of the author, or the circumstances that triggered the poem, are therefore mostly or even wholly irrelevant. What does it matter if we know that poet X wrote this particular poem because he was hopelessly in love with the undeserving Lady Y? The poem in question will only be worthwhile if it does *not* give us all the details but focuses on scorned love in general. In this sense, information about authorial intention or the direct occasion for a work of literature may be damaging rather than helpful. For humanist critics such as Eliot, Richards, Leavis, and the New Critics, human nature and the human condition have not changed over time and are essentially the same the world all over. Human nature is not black, or white, or brown; it does not speak English or Tagalog; it is not prehistoric, medieval, or postmodern; it does not lean towards deep-sea fishing, pig farming, or business administration. Such details will inevitably feature in a literary work, but they are secondary to what a good poem, novel, or play has to offer.

## The reign of the critics and its limitations

In his 1937 essay 'Criticism, Inc.' the New Critic John Crowe Ransom tells us that criticism 'might be seriously taken in hand by professionals' (Ransom [1937] 1972: 229). Aware that he is perhaps using 'a distasteful figure', he nonetheless has 'the idea that what we need is Criticism, Inc., or Criticism, Ltd.' The essay catches the new professionalism that literary academics on both sides of the Atlantic were not unreasonably proud of and invites us to look at the role that Ransom had in mind for himself and his fellow professionals. One part of their self-appointed task stands out. As we have seen, for the New Critics and their English colleagues literature, and in particular poetry, constituted a defensive line against the world of vulgar commerce and amoral capitalist entrepreneurialism that they held responsible for the moral decline of Western culture. But who was to decide which works of literature among the plenitude that the past has left us (and to which the present keeps on adding) actually contain 'the best that has been thought and said in the world', to use Arnold's words again? Who was to expose the at first sight attractive poems that because of their limited view and superficial emotions ultimately, even if unwittingly, undermined Arnold's 'culture'?

If literature takes the place of religion, as Arnold had prophesied, then poets and critics, in their mutual dependency, are the priests who spread the new gospel. This is indeed the impression one more than occasionally gets (not least in the writings of F.R. Leavis). For a period of fifty years the large majority of literary academics on both sides of the Atlantic saw themselves as the elect, as an intellectual and moral elite that had as its central task to safeguard 'life', the fullness of human experience. In the minds of the New Critics, the Leavisites, and others who partly or wholly shared their views, criticism and social critique were so intimately interwoven that they could not be separated from each other. As we will see later in this book, the interrelatedness of criticism – even if it now usually goes under other names – and social critique is still a hallmark of English and American literary studies.

But let me return to the specific view of literature that we find among the first generations of literary academics. With hindsight, we can easily see the intimate relationship between their discussions of structure, irony, and so on, and a good many indis-

**25**

putably important literary works of the period: Eliot's 'The Waste Land' (1922), Ezra Pound's *Cantos* (1925–1960), Virginia Woolf's *To the Lighthouse* (1927), James Joyce's *Ulysses* (1922), William Faulkner's *The Sound and the Fury* (1929), and countless other poems, novels, and plays. What was essentially an early twentieth-century view of literature, formed under the influence of specific historical circumstances, became a prescription for all ages. Predictably, the large numbers of writers who for one reason or another had operated in a different mode (Walt Whitman, for instance, with his long descriptive passages) fell from grace. Literary history was reshaped in the image of the early twentieth century. Whereas we can see the 'irony' that the writers and the critics of the period valued so highly as a defensive strategy in a confusing world of rapid social and technological change, they themselves genuinely believed it to be an infallible sign of 'maturity' and proceeded to demote all texts (and writers) that did not meet the required standard. (As I have noted, the later Leavis abandoned irony for other signs of maturity.)

We can also see now that the required standard is heavily *gendered*. (This anticipates a much fuller discussion of 'gender' in a later chapter, but it must be mentioned here.) Eliot's 'wit', the 'irony' of Richards and the New Critics, and the 'maturity' of Leavis all serve to underline a shared masculinist perspective. This is not to say that they have no place for female writers – in its first instalment Leavis's 'great tradition' of English novelists includes two male and two female writers. But in a period in which self-discipline (the self-discipline of the poet who refuses to personalize the poem), wit, a controlling irony, and related qualities are all seen as typically male, whereas overt emotions and a refusal to intellectualize experience are seen as typically female, the female writers elected for inclusion in the literary pantheon were admitted because they met a male standard.

Practical criticism and New Criticism have had a lasting influence. Their preoccupation with the text and nothing but the text would live on after its demise. Even now their textual orientation is still a force to reckon with, although always tempered by other considerations and usually – but not necessarily – stripped of its prejudices. It is of course only natural that texts, and not for instance landscaping, should play a central role in literary studies. It is less obvious, however – counterintuitive as it may seem – that *meaning* should be so prominent. In the next two chapters we will look at approaches to literature in which the meaning of individual texts, which in England and the United States provided the major drive for literary studies, is of at best secondary importance.

## Summary

English and American literary studies traditionally focus on the *meaning* of literary texts. Practical criticism (the United Kingdom) and New Criticism (the United States) first of all provide *interpretations*, with the New Critics paying particular attention to the formal aspects of literature, which for them contribute directly to its meaning. Within this Anglo-American tradition, literature is thought to be of great importance because in poems, novels, and plays we find 'the best that has been thought and said'. Literature offers the most profound insights into human nature and the human condition that are available to us. Because of its profundity and its authenticity it offers us a vantage point from which to criticize the superficial, rationalized, and commercialized world we live in. Literary criticism, which seeks out and preserves the very best of what millennia of writing have to offer, functions simultaneously as social critique. Finally, in this traditional form literary studies takes *liberal humanism* and its assumptions for granted. It sees the individual – the *subject*, in technical terms – as not determined and defined by social and economic circumstances, but as fundamentally free. We create ourselves, and our destiny, through the choices we make.

## Suggestions for further reading

There is no shortage of books on the English and American literary–critical heritage. Two very accessible and even-handed studies are Chris Baldick's *The Social Mission of English Criticism, 1848–1932* (1983), which has chapters on Arnold, Eliot, Richards, and Leavis, and his more recent *Criticism and Literary Theory 1890 to the Present* (1996), which covers some of the same ground, but also discusses the New Criticism and later developments. Francis Mulhern's *The Moment of 'Scrutiny'* (1979) is a detailed study of Leavis and the group around *Scrutiny* from a leftist perspective. Michael Bell's *F. R. Leavis* (1988) is a fairly recent defence of Leavis's views.

Gerald Graff's *Professing Literature: An Institutional History* (1987) is a very readable study of the institutionalization of literary studies in the United States. *Masks of Conquest: Literary Study and British Rule in India* (1989) by Gauri Viswanathan is a fascinating history of 'English' in colonial India.

Eliot's early essays – 'Tradition and the Individual Talent', 'Hamlet', 'The Metaphysical Poets' – are still worthwhile reading. The same goes for Wimsatt and Beardsley's 'The Intentional Fallacy' and 'The Affective Fallacy'. Those who would like to see practical criticism or New Criticism in action can also still go directly to the source. Cleanth Brooks's *The Well-Wrought Urn: Studies in the Structure of Poetry* ([1947] 1968) contains a number of now classic essays while his collaboration with Robert Penn Warren in *Understanding Poetry* ([1939] 1976) led to an enormously influential textbook on the New Critical method of interpretation. Leavis's approach to poetry and the poetic tradition comes through vividly in his *New Bearings in English Poetry* (1932) and *Revaluation* (1936); *The Great Tradition* ([1948] 1962) is a good example of his equally uncompromising criticism of the novel.

Finally, English studies feature prominently in a number of recent novels. For those who want to have a look behind the scenes I can recommend David Lodge's three novels dealing with 'English' in both England and the United States (*Changing Places:*

*A Tale of Two Campuses* (1975), *Small World: An Academic Romance* (1984), and *Nice Work* (1989)) and A.S. Byatt's *Possession: A Romance* (1990).

Chapter 2

# Reading for form I
*Formalism and early structuralism, 1914–1960*

In spite of the enormous influence of Eliot, Leavis, and the New Critics, our current perspectives on the study of literature owe perhaps more to continental Europe than to England and the United States. The continental European tradition of literary studies that is responsible for this begins in Russia, in the second decade of the twentieth century, in Moscow and St Petersburg. It finds a new home in Prague in the late 1920s, when the political climate in the Soviet Union has become too repressive, and travels to France (by way of New York City) after the Second World War, where it comes into full bloom in the 1960s and begins to draw widespread international attention. It is in France, too, that it provokes a countermovement that achieved its full force in the 1970s and 1980s and that is still the dominant presence in literary – and in cultural – studies.

Like its Anglo-American counterpart, this originally Russian approach to literature initially concentrated on poetry. But that is about all the two had in common. The English, later Anglo-American, line of development and the Russian one had nothing whatsoever to do with each other. The Russians who developed the so-called *formal method* – which gave them the name *Formalists* – were totally unaware of what happened in England, while the English and the Americans were completely ignorant of the debates that took place in Russia (and later in Prague). It is only when a prominent Formalist, the Russian linguist Roman Jakobson (1896–1982) moved to New York City, just before the outbreak of the Second World War, and when his fellow Formalists began to be translated into English in the late 1950s and 1960s, that the English-speaking world began to take notice of their wholly different approach to literary art. But even then the response was slow, no doubt because the Formalist approach was so foreign to what Eliot, Leavis, the New Critics, and their ubiquitous heirs saw as the mission of literature and of writing about literature. Significantly, the Formalist perspective had to be picked up, assimilated, and further developed by the French before it really made an impact on English and American literary thought. The French had something of an advantage, because the prominent French anthropologist and all-round intellectual Claude Lévi-Strauss (1908), who also had left Europe because of the Second World War, in 1941 became one of Jakobson's colleagues at the New School of Social Research in New York and after the war took what by then had come to be called the structuralist method, or *structuralism*, back home to France. In what follows I will concentrate on the work of the Russians and only look briefly at their Prague colleagues. What is relevant here is not historical comprehensiveness but a certain *way* of looking at literature that would much later have great impact in the English-speaking world.

## Early Formalism

As the phrase 'formal method' will have suggested, the Formalists were primarily oriented towards the *form* of literature. That focus on formal aspects does not mean that they could not imagine a possible moral or social mission for literature. As one of them, Viktor Shklovsky (1893–1984), put it in 1917, literature has the ability to make us see the world anew – to make that which has become familiar, because we have been overexposed to it, strange again. Instead of merely registering things in an almost subconscious process of recognition because we think we know them, we once again look at them: 'art exists that one may recover the sensation of life .... The purpose of art is to impart the sensation of things as they are perceived and not as they are known' (Shklovsky [1917] 1998: 18). The result of this process of defamiliarization is that it enables us once again to see the world in its full splendour or, as the case may be, true awfulness. But although the Formalists were prepared to recognize this as a not unimportant effect of literature, they initially relegated it to the far background. The social function of literature, either as the repository of the best that had been thought and said, or as one of the great revitalizers (with the other arts) of our perception of the world around us, largely left them cold in the first phase of their explorations. What they wanted to know is how literature works, how it achieves its defamiliarizing effects. For the New Critics the formal aspects of literary works were not unimportant because from their perspective meaning was always bound up with form. Still, they were first of all interested in the form in which a poem presented itself because a close scrutiny of its formal aspects would reveal the complex of oppositions and tensions that constituted the poem's real meaning. But the Formalists were after what they considered bigger game and in order to do so ignored literature's referential function, the way it reflects the world we live in, and gave it an autonomous status – or gave at least the aesthetic dimension of literature an autonomous status, as Jakobson qualified their position in 1933.

From their earliest meetings, around 1914, the Formalists are focused on what Jakobson in 1921 started to call 'literariness' – that which makes a literary text different from, say, a piece in *The Economist* or *Time*. In other words, although they always work with individual texts, what they are interested in is what all literary texts have in common, in a literary common denominator. Seeing the study of literature as a science, they concentrated like true scientists on general rules. Whereas practical criticism and the New Criticism focused on the individual meaning of individual texts, Formalism wanted to discover general laws – the more general the better.

The secret of 'literariness', the Formalists decided, was that in poetry – the initial focus of their interest – ordinary language becomes 'defamiliarized'. While an article in *Time* is satisfied to use fairly ordinary language, poetry subjects language to a process of defamiliarization. It is this linguistic defamiliarization that then leads to a perceptual defamiliarization on the part of the reader, to a renewed and fresh way of looking at the world. How does poetry defamiliarize what I have just called 'ordinary' language? It employs an impressive range of so-called 'devices'. It uses, for instance, forms of repetition that one does not find in ordinary language such as rhyme, a regular meter, or the subdivision in stanzas that we find in many poems. But poetry also uses 'devices' that one may come across in non-poetic language (although not with the same intensity) like metaphors and symbols. In so doing, it often also exploits the potential for ambiguity that language always has. Whereas a *Time* article tries to avoid ambiguities because it wants to be as transparent as possible, poetry makes use of all the second meanings that its words and phrases have, plus all the associations they evoke. What these devices have in common is that they always draw attention to *themselves*: they constantly remind us that we are dealing with language and not with the real world because they signal their own difference from the non-literary language that we ordinarily use (and which we take to represent the world). Advertising agencies are well aware of this. At one time the Heinz company tried to boost its baked beans sales with the brilliant slogan 'Beanz Meanz Heinz', a phrase that inevitably draws our attention to its own language. Because its ingenious play with language catches the eye and makes it stand out among other ads it probably also effectively served its purpose: to sell more beans. For the Formalists, then, poetry is not poetry because it employs time-honoured and profound themes to explore the human condition, but rather because in the process of defamiliarizing the language it draws attention to its own artificiality, to the *way* it says what it has to say. As

Roman Jakobson said in 1921, poetry is a form of language characterized by an orientation towards its own form. What it first of all allows us to see in a fresh manner is language itself. What that language refers to – what it communicates – is of secondary importance. In fact, if a work of art draws attention to its own form, then that form becomes part of its content: its form is part of what it communicates. (This is obvious in paintings that are completely abstract: since such paintings do not refer us to the outside world they can only 'be' about themselves. They force us to pay attention to their form, because that is all they have to offer.)

Now the idea of defamiliarization works well enough in the case of poetry and the difficult, wilfully innovative and defamiliarizing Modernist poetry of their own period perfectly confirmed the validity of defamiliarization as the ultimate criterion in establishing 'literariness'. (With hindsight we can seen how much the Formalists' idea of literature, too, was influenced by contemporary poetic practice.) But not surprisingly they ran into trouble in their attempts to make the defamiliarizing 'devices' of poetry work for fiction: the most obvious ones – rhyme, for instance – simply do not occur in fiction and the less obvious ones, like imagery, can also be found, even if not to the same degree, in ordinary usage. It is true that there are novels that in spite of this achieve an impressive degree of defamiliarization. This, for instance, is how Russell Hoban's *Riddley Walker* of 1980 takes off: 'On my naming day when I come 12 I gone front spear and kilt a wyld boar he parbly ben the las wyld pig on the Bundel Downs' (Hoban [1980] 1982: 1). But novels like this are rare. Usually we have to look pretty closely to find real deviations from ordinary language.

## *Fabula* and *syuzhet*

In 1925 Boris Tomashevski, building upon earlier efforts of his colleagues, formulated the fullest Formalist answer to the question of how to distinguish the language of fiction from ordinary language. The difference, he argued, is not so much a difference in language but a difference in *presentation*. In order to clarify this he juxtaposed two concepts: *fabula* (introduced by Shklovsky in 1921) and *syuzhet* (or *suzhet*, depending on how one transcribes the Russian alphabet). The *fabula* is a straightforward account of something, it tells us what actually happened. For instance, John Doe kills his cousin Jack to become the sole heir of a fortune and sits back to wait for the demise of the aged and infirm uncle – old J.J. Doe, his cousin's father and only remaining kin – who controls the money. The police work hard at solving the case but fail to do so. J.J. Doe hires a private eye who naturally succeeds where the police have failed. John Doe is arrested and duly sentenced.

These are the bare bones of the sort of story that one finds in countless private-eye novels. But this is not how the standard private-eye novel, which is usually narrated by the private eye him- (or her)self, would tell it. The novel would begin with the private eye being invited by J.J. Doe to come to his mansion to talk about the case. It would probably describe how the private eye clashes with J.J. Doe over the latter's superior and insulting attitude (our moneyed fellow citizens being an unpleasant lot in private-eye novels) and it would then follow the private eye's investigation. The fact that the murder has been committed by John will not become clear until we have almost reached the end. As in all detective novels, the author manipulates the *fabula* to create maximum suspense. Such a manipulation of the *fabula* creates the *syuzhet* (the story as it is actually told) and it is the *syuzhet* that has the defamiliarizing effect that devices have in poetry: like for instance rhyme, the *syuzhet* calls attention to itself. (I will discuss in a moment why we usually do not experience that attention-calling effect when we read, say, a detective novel.) It will immediately be obvious that one and the same *fabula* can give rise to a good many *syuzhets*. That insight became the basis for a book that much later would enjoy widespread influence, Vladimir Propp's 1928 *The Morphology of the Folktale*, which I will briefly look at because it forms an important link between the Formalists and the French so-called structuralists of the 1960s.

## Folktales

It had struck Propp (1895–1970) that if you looked closer at many Russian folktales and fairytales you actually found one and the same underlying story. In *Folktale* he tries to show how a hundred different tales are in fact variations upon – in other words, *syuzhets* of – what seemed to be one and the same underlying *fabula*. This is a rather free use of the *fabula/syuzhet* opposition and it must be stressed that Propp was not a Formalist. He is not interested in literariness and in any case in many of his tales there is hardly any difference between *fabula* and *syuzhet* as understood in Formalist terms. In a simple, chronologically told fairytale without flashbacks and other narrative tricks the *syuzhet* rather closely follows the *fabula*. Still, Propp's revolutionary idea at the time that a hundred rather widely varying folk- and fairytales might actually tell one and the same underlying story is clearly inspired by the distinction between *fabula* and *syuzhet*.

How is one and the same *fabula* possible if in some fairytales we have characters who play important roles – a prince, a forester, a hunter, a miller, a good fairy, an evil queen – and who are yet wholly absent from others? Or if certain actions, like flaunting an interdiction, lead in some tales to disaster while in others it brings rich rewards? How could all these tales possibly be presentations of the same basic story? Propp very ingeniously solves this problem by thinking in terms of *actors* and *functions*, by which he means acts or events that crucially help the story along. Let me try to give an idea how this works. One of the actors that Propp identifies – and which he sees returning in all his tales – is the 'helper'. Since that is not relevant to the function – all that he or she has to offer is an act of help that keeps the story moving – Propp need not further specify who or what the 'helper' is. The 'helper' can be either male or female, can be a forester (as in 'Little Red Riding Hood', if memory serves me right) or hunter (as in 'Snow White'), can be old or young, rich or poor, and so on – the possibilities are infinite. In one of his examples Propp illustrates the act of helping with examples from four fairytales. In the first one the hero is given an eagle which carries him to another kingdom, in the second one the hero is given a horse that gets him there. In the third tale he is presented with a boat, and in the fourth one he is given a ring that magically produces a number of young men who carry him where he wants to go. The people who help the hero are different, the hero himself has different names, and the means of conveyance (if we can call an eagle a means of conveyance) are different. But the actor – and the function of the event – is in each case exactly the same. We might say that various *syuzhet*-elements correspond to one *fabula*-element (if we take the liberty of seeing all the fairy-tales in terms of one single *fabula*). Theoretically this can also work the other way around, with one and the same *syuzhet*-element representing more than one *fabula*-element. This possibility is what I have in fact smuggled into the discussion with my example of the flaunting of the interdiction and its contradictory results (my embellishment of one of Propp's functions). In this imaginary case we must be dealing with two functions – one leading to disaster and one leading to a happy ending – that are represented by one and the same act.

Propp distinguishes a limited number of actors (or, in his term, 'dramatis personae') – hero, villain, seeker (often the hero), helper, false hero, princess – and thirty-one functions that always appear in the same sequence. I should add that all thirty-one of them do not necessarily make an appearance in every single fairytale. Propp's fairytales get along very well with only a selection, even if the final functions – the punishment of the villain and the wedding that symbolizes the happy ending – are always the same. It is also possible for a fairytale to interrupt itself and start a new, embedded, sequence (and another one) or to put one sequence after another. The individual qualities of the characters, however, are always irrelevant. At Propp's level of abstraction only their acts – which derive from the functions – really count. The villain and the helper are unimportant except for what they *do* and what they do always has the same function in the various tales. This approach in terms of actors – embodied by interchangeable characters – and functions allows Propp to collapse a hundred different *syuzhets* into the skeleton of one single *fabula*. In my example of the detective story, all the different ways in which the story would be told – it could for instance begin with a description of the murder without giving away the identity of the murderer – would still have John Doe as the murderer and his cousin Jack as the victim. At Propp's level of abstraction, however, we ignore the actual characters and concentrate on their function within the story. With the method he uses for his tales, Propp might have proposed one single *fabula* for all detective stories. He might have proposed a basic *fabula* with three acts or functions: that of murdering, that of getting murdered, and that of exposing the killer. If we look at Propp's tales from this abstract vantage point we see similarities between them that otherwise would have escaped our notice.

By presenting things in this way, Propp makes us see his folktales as systems in which the functions that he identifies have a specific place. In my discussion of the New Critics I have suggested that they – a decade after Propp – saw the literary work, and in particular the poetic text they were preoccupied with, as a system of checks and balances, with the checks and balances obviously interrelated. In Propp's book the interrelatedness of the various elements of a text gets more emphasis because his clearly defined functions are part of an equally clearly defined chain (there is, after all, only one underlying *fabula*). The 'helper' is always there to offer help, and not to the 'villain', even if what he or she actually does may vary widely from tale to tale. Each of Propp's folktales, then, contains an underlying *structure* of which the unsuspecting reader will usually not be aware. But if folktales contain such a structure, then maybe other narratives, too, can be made to reveal an underlying structure. That idea would, in an admittedly more sophisticated form, conquer literary academia more than thirty years later.

## Formalism revisited

The Formalists, too, came to see literature in systemic terms so that Jakobson and his colleague Yuri Tynyanov (1879–1943) in the same year that Propp published his work could already speak of the study of literature as a 'systematic science'. In its early phase, Formalism had seen a poem as the totality of its 'devices': as the footing of a column of devices that were not necessarily related in any way. Apart from that, it had assumed that 'literariness' was the product of the inherent qualities of those devices. Those qualities, and the resulting literariness, could be identified, pointed at. And this is where early Formalism went wrong. I have said above that the Formalists were primarily interested in generalities. One general rule could still be upheld: the rule that literariness is created by defamiliarizing devices. But it soon proved impossible to establish rules with regard to those devices. The 'defamiliarizing' potential of certain techniques or ways of presenting things is not an inalienable property. It manifests itself only in the right context. The only rule that can be formulated is that defamiliarization works by way of contrast, of *difference*. Because the early Formalists presupposed a too rigid connection between a fixed set of devices and the principle of literariness, they did not see the devices that they regarded as the building blocks of literary texts in their proper light.

They gradually gave up this position when it became clear that to identify the various ways in which literature differed from ordinary language was only a first step towards explaining how literature works. Why is it, for instance, that we do not ordinarily realize how thoroughly we are being manipulated in a detective novel? Could it be that the suspense keeps us from noticing? Or is it that we have become so familiar with the genre that we no longer see what is happening right under our noses? Could the process of familiarization that is responsible for our relative blindness with regard to our environment, including language, be at work within literature itself? The Formalists decided that that was indeed the case. What is more, familiarization worked at two levels: that of the single literary work and that of literature as a whole. Now where we find familiarization we may also expect defamiliarization, or at least attempts at defamiliarization, and so the Formalists started to look for processes of defamiliarization *within* literary works themselves.

As was the case with Propp, the more abstract level that this way of looking at things brought into the discussion led the

Formalists away from 'devices' in the direction of 'functions'. Let us first look at defamiliarization within one and the same literary text. Imagine a long poem consisting of heroic couplets (iambic pentameters – lines of ten syllables – with the rhyme scheme *aa*, *bb*, *cc*, and so on). Carried along by its rather monotonous cadence we suddenly come across two non-rhyming lines of fourteen syllables each. These two lines function to defamiliarize the reading process because they make us stop and think. But this works also the other way around. Imagine a long poem of unrhymed lines of fourteen syllables each in which you suddenly come across heroic couplets. Now the heroic couplets would have the function of making us stop and think. In other words, whether a certain poetic technique serves as a defamiliarizing device depends on the larger background. To take this a bit further: the ability to defamiliarize our perception is not a quality that certain techniques inherently possess, it is all a matter of how a certain technique *functions* within a given literary work, and that function can change from text to text. What counts is the way and the extent to which it *differs* from its environment. It is of course true that certain techniques, like the use of extreme hyperboles, would defamiliarize most literary texts, but it is equally true that in a text filled from the start with extreme hyperboles another hyperbole would not even be noticed. Every imaginable literary technique, then, can have either a familiarizing or a defamiliarizing effect. Everything depends on the way it functions within a given text. Differentiation is the crucial factor. This led to a view of the literary work as a system that establishes a textual environment that is then again and again made new with the help of defamiliarizing devices. From this perspective it is first of all the system that dictates the actual techniques that will have to be used (long, non-rhyming lines in an environment of heroic couplets; heroic couplets among long non-rhyming lines – hyperbole surrounded by restraint; restraint in the midst of hyperbole). The system will of course offer a wide range of choice, but it will always demand difference.

Extending this insight to literature as such, the Formalists came up with an interesting explanation of literary change. We all know that literature has changed over time. But why? Why do new genres emerge – the novel, for instance – and old ones disappear over the cultural horizon? And why do we find such rather considerable changes within genres themselves? The novel has gone from realism (mid- and late nineteenth century) to modernism (early twentieth century) and postmodernism (1960s and beyond). What is the driving mechanism behind such developments? The Formalist answer will not come as a surprise: defamiliarization. Literature as a whole renews itself through the development of, for instance, new genres, while genres defamiliarize (and thereby change) themselves through, for example, parody – a defamiliarizing strategy because it invariably focuses on peculiarities – and through the incorporation of new materials and techniques taken from other genres or from popular culture. In the postwar period, for instance, writers like Kurt Vonnegut (*Slaughterhouse 5*, 1969), William Burroughs (*Nova Express,* 1964), and Thomas Pynchon (*Gravity's Rainbow*, 1973) have deliberately used science fiction elements in their work. Others, like Angela Carter for instance in *Nights at the Circus* (1985), in which we have the flying woman Fevvers, and in a number of short stories, play with fairytales. Since new elements and new techniques are by definition unfamiliar to the reader they automatically function as defamiliarizing devices. It is not only the individual literary work that can be seen as a system, as a *structure* (a term that in this context dates from the late 1920s) in which everything is interrelated and interdependent, but literature as a whole can and should be seen in those terms. The individual texts that together constitute 'literature' first of all position themselves with reference to other individual texts, to the genre they belong to, and then to that whole corpus of texts that we call literature (which changes, no matter how infinitesimally, with every new addition).

Acts of defamiliarization will only have a temporary effect: even the most innovative devices will with the passage of time lose their capacity to catch our attention. The idea that an everlasting dynamic between an inevitable process of familiarization and acts of defamiliarization is the driving mechanism behind literary change, in other words, the driving mechanism of literary history, is ingenious and interesting. It tries to give answers to questions of historical change that the New Critics, with their focus on the words on the page, could not even begin to address. But the Formalist answers can only be part of a much larger picture. As they themselves realized in the later 1920s, literature is not wholly autonomous; it is not completely divorced from the world it exists in. Far-reaching social changes must have had consequences for the course of literary history. With the disappearance of the medieval world of heroic knights and grave quests, for instance, the long narrative poems that presented knights and quests became obsolete. In Miguel Cervantes' *Don Quixote* (1605–1615) such a knight, although in some ways still admirable, has become the object of gentle ridicule. Moreover, the mechanism of defamiliarization cannot say anything about the nature of the devices that will be deployed. All it tells us is that change is inevitable. It does not tell us which new course that change will take. Surely the individual author plays a significant role in making a selection from the array of devices that are available or, even better, in creating wholly new ones. With their recognition of the interrelatedness of art and world, of literature and the world we live in, the Formalists also developed an interest in the content of literary works. But the political changes that put an end to freedom of speech and academic freedom in Russia made further explorations impossible.

## Prague structuralism

In the later 1920s the cause of Formalism was taken up in Prague, not in the least because Jakobson had moved there to get away from the increasingly repressive regime in what had become the Soviet Union. I will in this brief section focus on what from our vantage point are the most relevant aspects of the way the Prague (or Czech) structuralists contributed to literary theory.

Most importantly – as is illustrated by their name – they further developed the idea that a literary text is a structure in which all the elements are interrelated and interdependent.

There is nothing in a literary work that can be seen and studied in isolation. Each single element has a function through which it is related to the work as a whole. The Formalists tended to focus on the defamiliarizing elements within literary art – either those elements that distinguished literary texts from non-literature or those that served the process of defamiliarization within those texts themselves. As a result, they paid little attention to all the elements that did not directly contribute to the defamiliarizing process. For the structuralists, however, everything played a role in what a text was and did.

One reason for arriving at this position is that, drawing on new insights in contemporary linguistics, they expanded the Formalists' notion of 'function'. In so doing they gave a better theoretical foundation to the idea that literature is concerned with itself while they simultaneously explained how it could also refer to the outside world. As we have seen, for the Formalists 'function' has to do with the way textual elements achieve effects of defamiliarization because of their difference from their environment. For the structuralists, the text as a whole – not just the literary text – has a function too, and it is on the basis of the way a text functions as a whole that we can distinguish between various sorts of texts. A text's function is determined by its orientation. These orientations are basically those of a so-called 'speech act' – they derive from what we do with speech. Let me illustrate some of the possibilities, using speech examples. One of the shortest (and most frequent) texts in the language surely is 'Damn!' Expressing a whole range of emotions – disappointment, anger, surprise, and so on – 'Damn!' is oriented towards the speaker him- or herself. Because everything we say or write may be seen as a message, we could also say that here, perhaps a bit paradoxically, the message is oriented towards its sender. 'Hey, you!', however, is oriented towards the person that is addressed (the addressee). If we tell a friend about the movie we have just seen, or the near-accident we have witnessed, then our 'text' is oriented towards things in the outside world, it refers to the reality we both live in (what one might call the context). From this perspective in terms of orientation, literary texts are oriented towards themselves, but not in the way that 'Damn!' is oriented towards its 'sender'. Literature focuses on its own *form*, its focus is on the *message* rather than on the sender, the addressee, or any other possible target. It is in other words oriented towards the *code* – the code of literature – that it employs.

Of course these orientations almost never occur in a pure form. If I'm all by myself 'Damn!' will probably be wholly oriented towards me, but if there are other people around it will inevitably also function as a message to them, telling them about my disappointment or anger. 'Hey you!' is oriented towards an addressee, but also reveals something about me: I want his or her attention. Literary texts are oriented towards themselves (they are very conscious of their form and the outside world they would seem to refer to is fictional and does not exist), but there are few works of literature that we cannot in one way or another make relevant to the world we live in. In other words, in actual practice texts always have more than one orientation and more than one function simultaneously. What counted for the structuralists is which orientation and accompanying function is *dominant*. This concept of the 'dominant' allowed them a view of literary texts that was a good deal more flexible than that of the Formalists: literature referred primarily to itself, but it could also be taken as referring to the outside world, although the referential element would of course always have to be subservient to its orientation on the literary code, to what the structuralists called the poetic function. (A text would cease to be literature if its dominant orientation shifted from the text itself – its form – to the outside world.) Moreover, as I have just pointed out, from this point of view the whole text functions as a coherent whole, kept together by its 'dominant'. It is a structure in which all elements, whether they defamiliarize or not, are interrelated and interdependent.

In a second move, the Prague group further theorized the idea of defamiliarization and gave it a place in their view of the literary work as a structure. Borrowing from psychological studies of the way our mind processes the infinite number of data that our senses present to it and filters out what seems relevant, the structuralists replaced defamiliarization by *foregrounding* (taken from such perception studies by one of the Russian Formalists who had already described its potential for literary studies). Jan Mukařovský, for instance, tells us that poetic language is an effect of the 'foregrounding of the utterance'. Unlike defamiliarization, which would not seem to affect its immediate textual environment, foregrounding has the effect that it 'automatizes' neighbouring textual elements. It draws the reader's attention to itself and obscures whatever else may be going on right beside it. While defamiliarization points to a contrastive, but static, relationship between the defamiliarizing element and the other elements, foregrounding emphasizes the dynamism of that relationship: what one element gains in terms of being foregrounded is lost by the other elements that constitute its background. In other words, just like the idea of a 'dominant', foregrounding implies a perspective that sees a text as a structure of interrelated elements. As Mukařovský put it:

> The mutual relationship of the components of the work of poetry, both foregrounded and unforegrounded, constitute its *structure*, a dynamic structure including both convergence and divergence, and one that constitutes an indissociable artistic whole, since each of its components has its value in terms of its relation to the totality.
>
> (cited in Jefferson and Robey 1986: 54)

Foregrounding, with its structuralist orientation, has in contemporary literary criticism effectively replaced defamiliarization.

## The axis of combination

In the late 1950s Roman Jakobson formulated what is probably the ultimate attempt to define the aesthetic function in poetry, that is the 'literariness' of poetry. I will briefly discuss Jakobson's definition because it is one of the prime examples of the formal, 'scientific', approach to literature that marks continental European thinking about literature from the 1910s until the 1970s. 'The poetic function' – that is, poetic literariness –

Jakobson said, 'projects the principle of equivalence from the axis of selection into the axis of combination' (Jakobson [1960] 1988: 39). This is not an inviting formula, as uninviting, in fact, as the title of the 1960 article – 'Linguistics and Poetics' – in which he presented this thesis to the English-speaking world. However, it is less impenetrable than it might seem to be.

Jakobson's definition departs from the simple fact that all words can be classified and categorized. Every time we use language what we say or write is a combination of words selected from a large number of classes and categories. Take for instance a bare bones sentence like 'Ma feels cold.' In this sentence we might have used 'Pa' or 'Sis' or 'Bud' or 'John' (and so on) instead of 'Ma' and we might have used 'good', 'bad', 'hot' (and so on) instead of 'cold' without disrupting the sentence's grammar. The alternatives that I have mentioned are grammatically equivalent to 'Ma' or 'cold'. 'Butter feels cold' would definitely be odd, and so would 'Bud feels butter.' The selection process that starts up whenever we are on the point of speaking or writing is governed by invisible rules that make us select words from large classes of grammatically equivalent words: nouns, verbs, adjectives, and so on. However, we also constantly make selections in the field of *meaning*. Here we are on less abstract ground than in the previous example and the starting-point is what we actually want to say. Usually there will be more than one way of saying what is virtually the same thing. The most obvious case is that of a word for which there is a perfect synonym. We will have to choose between two equivalents. Or we can choose from a group of words that are closely related with regard to meaning, for instance: man, guy, fellow, bloke, gent, and so on. Which word we will actually choose may depend on the degree of colloquiality (or dignity) that we want to project or on how precise we want to be: a gent is not only male, but a specific kind of male. In any case, we make a selection from a number of words that have much in common and may even be roughly identical: they are approximately or even wholly equivalent in meaning. Both with regard to its (grammatical) structure and with regard to meaning (its semantic dimension) language knows all sorts of equivalence. It is this principle of (linguistic) equivalence that poetry borrows from what Jakobson calls 'the axis of selection' and then employs in the 'axis of combination'.

This is also less mysterious than it seems. What Jakobson claims is that poetry, like all other language use, not only constantly selects items from long lists of words that are in one way or another equivalent to each other, but also selects to create equivalences *between* the words it chooses. It can do so by way of alliteration, for instance, which is basically an equivalence between the sounds with which two or more words begin: 'The Soul selects her own Society' – to quote an Emily Dickinson poem which uses an initial 's' in three of its six words (one of which also ends with an 's'). Or poetry can create equivalences by way of rhyme, in which almost whole words are equivalent to each other (like 'words' and 'nerds'). But it can also do so by way of meter – iambic pentameters, for instance – which creates metric equivalences unknown or rare in ordinary language, by way of grammatical parallelisms, inversions and juxtapositions (which in order to work presuppose equivalence between the two elements involved) and numerous other ways. This is how Charles Dickens's *A Tale of Two Cities* (1859) opens:

> It was the best of times, it was the worst of times, it was the age of wisdom, it was the age of foolishness, it was the epoch of belief, it was the epoch of incredulity, it was the season of Light, it was the season of Darkness.

Parallelism and juxtaposition go hand in hand to create a 'poetic' effect in a prose text.

This develops Jakobson's early Formalist work in the direction of structuralism, although it also represents a return to the Formalists' hunt for literariness. However, literariness is here not the result of a number of discrete 'devices' that defamiliarize ordinary language, but of the specific organization of poetic language which organizes itself along lines different from the organization of other uses of language. Literariness is the result of a specific structural principle, that of equivalence on the axis of combination. It is that equivalence that contributes to a literary text's coherence. Jakobson even suggests that words that are 'similar in sound' are because of that 'drawn together in meaning', but here he is clearly on extremely speculative and shaky ground and not many commentators have been willing to explore this lead. However, as with the Formalists, the question of meaning hardly arises. And it is obvious that the principle of equivalence has even less to say about the relative *merit*, the *value* of individual works of literature. A text that is absolutely jam-packed with equivalences can still strike us as pretty awful. For instance, how about these lines from a Stephen Sondheim musical:

> What's the muddle
> In the middle?
> That's the puddle
> Where the poodle did the piddle.

Still, Jakobson's formula stands as one of the most serious – and, I should add, successful – attempts to capture that what makes the bulk of Western poetry different from the language we use when we go out shopping.

## Summary

In the first half of the twentieth century, Russian and Czech literary theorists worked to develop a theory of *literariness*: what made literary texts different from, for instance, government reports or newspaper articles? In trying to answer this question they focused on the *formal* aspects of literature, on its specific forms, and on the sort of language that it employs. The so-called Russian Formalists suggested that literature distinguishes itself from non-literary language because it employs a whole range of 'devices' that have a *defamiliarizing* effect. In a later stage, they saw this principle of defamiliarization also as a moving force within literary history:

literature, as an artistic discipline, renews itself by making itself strange again whenever its current forms have become overly familiar and a sort of automatization has set in. Because unfamiliarity is not an inherent quality but depends on contrast – with what is known and has become routine – the emphasis within Formalism soon shifts towards the *function* of devices, rather than on any innate qualities they might possess. Central to that function is the idea of *difference*. The successors to the Formalists, the Prague structuralists, build on this and begin to see the literary text as a structure of differences. After all, the neutral immediate context that a defamiliarizing element needs in order really to stand out is as necessary as that element itself. *Foregrounding* is literally made possible by the existence of a background. Foreground and background – the unfamiliar and the familiar – function within one single structure and together create poetic effects. Finally, the literary text distinguishes itself from other texts because we can see it as a message that is primarily oriented towards itself – its own form – and not towards the outside world or its potential readers. Although a literary text will usually also have other orientations – it generally will refer us in one way or another to the real world – this orientation towards itself, its *poetic function*, is dominant.

## Suggestions for further reading

*Russian Formalism: History-Doctrine*, 3rd edn (1981), by Viktor Erlich is the standard survey of Formalism. Peter Steiner's *Russian Formalism: A Metapoetics* (1984) is a very good introduction; somewhat controversially, but quite helpfully, Steiner includes Jakobson and Propp in his discussion. A bit more recent and also more thorough is Jurij Striedter's *Literary Structure, Evolution and Value: Russian Formalism and Czech Structuralism Reconsidered* (1989). Tony Bennett's *Formalism and Marxism* (1979) looks at Formalism from a Marxist perspective (see Chapter 4).

Boris Eichenbaum's 'Introduction to the Formal Method' and Viktor Shklovsky's 'Art as Technique', both reprinted in 1998, are excellent introductions to early Formalist thinking. Roman Jakobson's 'Closing Statement: Linguistics and Poetics', the ultimate in attempting to establish 'literariness', appeared originally in Thomas Sebeok's *Style in Language* (1960) and has frequently been reprinted, most recently in Lodge and Wood (2000). The major texts of Czech or Prague structuralism are available in Paul L. Garvin's *A Prague School Reader on Esthetics, Literary Structure, and Style* (1964).

# Chapter 3

# Reading for form II

*French structuralism,
1950–1975*

## The inevitability of form

Why were the Formalists and the Prague stuctural-
ists, the French structuralists that I will discuss in
this chapter, and, to a lesser extent, the New Critics
so preoccupied with the *form* of literary works?
Why not concentrate on the *meaning* of a given
work of literature, on what it has to tell us? Why
waste time on something that would seem of
secondary importance? Moreover, apart from their
questionable relevance, discussions about the form
of literary texts can be positively annoying: here we
have this wonderful, profoundly moving poem and
we are supposed to talk about its *form*.

For many readers educated in the Anglo-
American tradition, form and structure are not
only things that are alien to their interests – they do
not read literature to learn about form and structure – but actually threaten the experience of
reading. Many readers do not want to hear about
things like form and structure because they seem to
undermine the spirituality and freedom of the

novel or poem that they are reading. We are dealing here with an underlying humanistic perspective that is uneasy with form and structure because they ultimately seem to diminish our own spirituality and freedom and represent a severely reductionist approach to human beings and their cultural achievements.

Such readers may have a point, as will become clear later in this chapter. Form, however, is inevitable. Art cannot do without form. No matter how lifelike a novel or a movie may seem, it is the end product of countless decisions that involve form. That is even true if we are not talking about fiction or a Hollywood movie, but about their real-life cousins reportage and documentary film. Imagine that we set up a camera on New York's Times Square or in London's Oxford Street, and let it run from dawn till nightfall. We might argue that here we really have a slice of life, the ultimate realism in movie-making: the camera has only registered what actually happened in that part of Times Square or Oxford Street covered by the lens (we have of course not moved the camera because that would have introduced a new perspective and would have constituted formal interference, no matter how rudimentary). But we would above all have the most boring movie ever made. What we would have is thousands of cars, cabs, buses, and pedestrians passing in front of the lens. We might have picked out one of these people, a man with a promisingly grim expression or a woman with extraordinary haste, and followed them with our camera. But in so doing we would immediately have been forced to make decisions on form. We could film the man or the woman while following them, and we could occasionally overtake them and get in front of them. We could rent a helicopter and film them from above. Whatever we do excludes at that particular moment all the other options that we have. Even documentaries, then, no matter how true to life they seem, are the end product of a long line of decisions on the way their material should be presented.

## Language as a system of signs

Form is clearly inevitable. Whatever we do with images (as in movies) or with language always has a formal dimension. But what about the structure that I have just discussed? After all, structure is not something that we can easily identify. It's all very well to say that all the elements of a text are interconnected and that the various functions of these elements and the relations between them constitute a structure, but that does not really help. However, for the French structuralism that is the main subject of this chapter structure is even more fundamental than form. Form is inevitably bound up with meaning; structure, however, is what makes meaning possible. It is that which enables meaning to emerge. This is an enigmatic claim that clearly needs some explanation. After all, we are not even aware of the structures that supposedly play a role in the creation of meaning. It seems to us that we ourselves create meaning. We create meaning by saying something, by making a gesture, through a work of art, if we happen to have the talent – we create meaning because we want to express something by way of language, music, choreography, painting, film, and so on and so forth. Meaning would seem to be produced by you and me, and not by an invisible and intangible structure.

Structuralism has its origin in the thinking of the Swiss linguist Ferdinand de Saussure (1857–1913) who in the early twentieth century revolutionized the study of language. Nineteenth-century linguistics is mainly interested in the history of language – for instance, in how French and Italian develop out of Latin, or how English, Dutch, and German develop out of the West-Germanic language that the ancestors of the English, the Dutch, and the Germans shared some 1,500 years ago. They studied the origin of individual words (modern English 'way', for instance, derives from Old English 'weg') and they tried to formulate the laws that apparently govern processes of linguistic change. A development such as that from 'weg' to 'way' does not stand on its own. Old English 'g' has often been transformed along this particular line: Old English 'weg' becomes modern English 'way' (in Dutch and in German it is still 'weg' or 'Weg'), 'daeg' becomes 'day' ('dag' in Dutch, 'Tag' in German), 'gerd' becomes 'yard' ('gaard' in modern Dutch), 'gearn' becomes 'yarn' ('garen' in Dutch), and so on and so forth. In comparing new and old forms of a language, and using related languages to support their findings, historical linguists were able to discover the rules that govern such transformations as from 'g' to 'y' and to reconstruct how the various European languages had developed over historical time.

Saussure adopted a completely different angle. Instead of the usual historical, diachronic approach – following language through time – he opted for an ahistorical, and far more abstract, approach. To Saussure questions concerning the way particular languages changed over particular periods were subordinate to a more fundamental question: how does language work? It may be good to know that modern English to 'have' derives from Old English 'habban' but it is far more relevant to know how it is possible that language can apparently change and still keep on functioning. So instead of on actual instances of language use – spoken or written – Saussure focused on the question of how language actually works in order to formulate general insights that would be valid for all language use and for all languages. I should perhaps point out that this is also different from what grammarians – the other type of linguist around in Saussure's time – used to do. Grammarians wanted to describe the underlying grammatical rules that we automatically follow when we talk or write. So they analysed instances of language use – our individual utterances, which Saussure called *paroles* (plural) – to get at those rules. But Saussure is interested in how language as such works – in what he called *langue* – and not in the grammatical matrix of this or that language.

This approach led Saussure, whose work only found wider circulation after it was published in 1915, two years after his death, to the idea that language should first of all be seen as a system of signs (he himself did not use the term 'structure'). Secondly, those signs are in first instance arbitrary – after which they have become conventions – and have not taken their specific form because of what they mean, but to be different from other signs. Let me explain this. The 'signs' are simply the words that we use: 'way', 'yard', 'yarn'. As we have just seen, 'way' is 'weg' (or 'Weg') in Dutch and in German. Some of us will know that it is 'chemin' in French and 'camino' in Spanish. We need only a very superficial knowledge of a foreign language, or even of a dialect form of our own language, to know that the words we use to refer to the objects around us are different in other languages. From that knowledge it is only a small step to the realization that the link between a word and what it refers to must be arbitrary. Since other languages have different words for what we call a 'way' – and for all our other words – and in spite of that would seem to function perfectly well, we can only conclude that calling a way a 'way' is not a necessity. There is clearly nothing in what we call a 'way' that dictates the particular word 'way'. In other words, the relation between the sign 'way' and what it refers to is indeed fundamentally arbitrary – in the sense that 'way' could have been quite different. In fact, since it once was 'weg', it already *has* been different. The arbitrariness of course only applies to the *fundamental* relationship between words and what they refer to. In actual practice, those relationships have become a matter of convention. If we want to refer to an object, a table for instance, we automatically use the word that everybody uses. When Dr Seuss in 1950 first used the word 'nerd' in *If I Ran the Zoo*, the relationship between 'nerd' and what it referred to was arbitrary. As a matter of fact, if he had not provided illustrations with his story we would have had a hard time figuring out what to make of 'nerd'. Now it is still arbitrary but also a matter of convention: there is now a standard relationship between 'nerd' and a certain type of person.

If the form of words is not dictated by their relationship with what they refer to, then that form must have its origin elsewhere. Saussure traces the origin of the form of words – of linguistic signs – to the principle of differentiation. New words like 'nerd' take their place among existing words because they are *different*. The whole system is based on often minimal differences: in ways, days, rays, bays, pays, maze, haze, and so on only the opening consonant is different. Words, then, function in a system that uses difference to create its components. (A more practical way of saying this is that we automatically fall back on difference if we want to coin a word.) As Saussure himself says of all the elements that make up a linguistic system: 'Their most precise characteristic is being what the others are not' ([1915] 1959: 117).

This is fairly self-evident. But then Saussure introduces an argument that seems completely counterintuitive. The principle of difference that gives rise to the signs (words) of which language is made up, he tells us, also gives rise to their *meaning*. The usual assumption might be that the meaning of words derives from what they refer to and that it is the world we live in which gives the words in our language their meaning. However, that cannot be true. After all, if that were the case why would words differ from language to language? Does this mean that Saussure's improbable claim is correct? Are language and the world that we intuitively feel is reflected by that language really so separated from each other as he suggests?

A strong point in Saussure's favour is that form and meaning cannot be separated. If we change 'ways' to 'days' or 'rays' we do have not only a new form but also a new meaning. In other words, the differential principle not only works to distinguish words from each other, it simultaneously distinguishes *meanings* from each other. A linguistic sign – a word – is both form and meaning. Saussure calls the form – the word as it is spoken or written – the *signifier* and the meaning the *signified*. A change in the signifier, no matter how minimal, means a new signified. We must accept that meaning is indeed bound up with differentiation. But is it the full story? Not quite. Here I must introduce another counterintuitive complication. A sign's meaning, its signified, is *not* an object in the real world, as we tend to think. That is again the way it might easily seem to us, and I have so far spoken freely of that what words refer to, but what they refer to is not the real world – at least not directly. Take a seemingly uncomplicated word like 'tree' which my *American Heritage College Dictionary* (3rd edn) defines as 'A perennial woody plant having a main trunk and usu. a distinct crown.' What this definition makes clear is that 'tree' does not refer to any single object in the real world but to a category of objects which may or may not have 'distinct crowns'. The meaning of the sign 'tree' includes oaks, beeches, and chestnuts but also dwarf pines and Douglas firs. Its *signified* is a human category, a concept. A little reflection will tell us that this is also true of other signs: love, table, child, field. They all refer to concepts – not unrelated to the real world, but clearly the product of generalization and abstraction. It is those concepts that we then apply in our actual use of language to the real world, where they then have concrete referents. In a sentence like 'That tree over there' the sign 'tree' has an actual referent.

Our intuition that meaning is bound up with the real world is not completely wrong, even if the relation between meaning and the world is a matter of convention and much less straightforward than we tend to think. But 'bound up with' is a vague phrase. Which of the two is dominant in this relationship? Do the real world and everything that it contains indirectly determine the meanings of our language or does our language determine our world? To put this more concretely: does the fact that there are chestnuts somehow give rise to the admittedly arbitrary sign 'chestnut' or does the fact that the sign 'chestnut' has somehow come into being allow us to see chestnuts as a separate species among trees? If we did have the word 'horse' but did not have the word 'pony' would we still see ponies as ponies or would we see them as horses much like all other horses because our language would not offer us an alternative? If the latter were true, then it might be argued that language precedes thought and constitutes the framework within which thought must necessarily operate. Some theorists, including Saussure, have thought so and have argued that our reality is in fact constituted by our language. If that is indeed the case, then the language that we inherit at birth is for all practical purposes an autonomous system that carves up the world for us and governs the way we see it. (It is never quite autonomous because we can tamper with it and for instance expand it – witness Dr Seuss's nerd.) This position which claims that our reality is determined by language is called *linguistic determinism* and I will have occasion to come back to it later in this book. To many people such a position appears unnecessarily radical and turns an interesting insight with a limited range of application into an iron law. We can perhaps agree on two principles, however. If we forget for a moment about the way we use language (or language uses us) and focus on language itself, we can agree that if we see language as a system of signs, then the meanings that arise – the signifieds

– are first of all arbitrary in their relationship to the real world and secondly the product of difference in the sense that difference has a crucial, enabling function. Without difference there would be no language and meaning at all. The role that difference plays in its turn implies that meaning is impossible without the whole system of differences: the structure within which difference operates. After all, signs must differ from other signs and they need these other signs to be different. Although meaning is in first instance produced by difference, it is at a more fundamental level produced by the structure: by the *relations* between the signs that make up a language, or, to give this a wider application, between the elements that together make up a given structure.

## Anthropological structuralism

These principles are indispensable for an understanding of the various approaches to literature that together constitute the French literary structuralism of the 1960s and 1970s. They are even more indispensable for a proper understanding of the so-called *poststructuralism* that developed after structuralism and that I will introduce in a later chapter. It is, in fact, mainly with an eye on poststructuralism that I have offered such a detailed discussion. Poststructuralism is also the reason why I will begin this overview of French structuralism with a discussion of its first, exclusively anthropological, phase. The anthropological structuralism that was developed in the later 1940s by Claude Lévi-Strauss (see Chapter 2) has never had much direct relevance for literary studies but its indirect influence, through its apprehension and adaptation by poststructuralism and poststructuralism's many offshoots, is still immense. So we will first make a detour through an intellectual landscape that may perhaps be rather unfamiliar.

Like all structuralisms, anthropological structuralism is directly indebted to the Saussurean concept of language as a sign system governed by difference. However, anthropological structuralism gave the idea of a system of signs that function in first instance because they are different from each other a much wider range – already foreseen, incidentally, by Saussure himself – and transposed it from linguistics to anthropology; that is, from the study of language to the study of cultures that from a Western perspective seemed 'primitive.'

The first anthropologist to see the potential of Saussure's analysis of language as a way of approaching the most diverse cultural phenomena was Lévi-Strauss, who, as I have mentioned earlier, met Jakobson in the 1940s in New York (the relevance of that encounter will become clear below). In the early decades of the twentieth century anthropology was still largely descriptive and functionalist: it sought to record the myths, taboos, rituals, customs, manners, in short, everything that was recordable, of the non-Western cultures that it studied and it tried to establish their function. Lévi-Strauss broke with that tradition in two major ways. The first way is indebted to Vladimir Propp's study of Russian fairytales. Transposing Propp's idea to the field of myths, Lévi-Strauss tried to show how the most diverse myths, recorded in cultures that seemingly have no connection with each other, can be seen as variations upon one and the same basic pattern.

More important for our purposes here is that Lévi-Strauss saw the possibilities of Saussure's notion that meaning is ultimately the product of difference for the study of discrete cultural phenomena. For the structuralism that Lévi-Strauss developed in a series of major anthropological publications, the almost countless discrete elements that together make up a culture constitute a sign system. Eating customs, taboos with regard to menstruation, initiation and hunting rites, the preparation of food, the rules underlying so-called kinship relations – in short, everything that has a cultural origin and is not biologically determined – counts as a sign. The discrete bits of culture that we can distinguish are not meaningful in themselves, but draw their meaning from the sign system in which they function and, more in particular, from their difference from other signs. As Lévi-Strauss put it with regard to masks: 'A mask does not exist in isolation; it supposes other real or potential masks always by its side, masks that might have been chosen in its stead and substituted for it' (Lévi-Strauss 1982: 144). What a given element signifies within a culture depends on the system, and not on an intrinsic meaning (which it does not have). Just like the relationship between the linguistic sign and its real-world referent, the relationship between a specific cultural phenomenon and what it expresses – its meaning – is arbitrary in the sense that it is determined by convention.

## Binary oppositions

However, the relationship between a cultural sign and what it expresses is not necessarily completely arbitrary. Lévi-Strauss's anthropological structuralism is interested in the question of how our ancestors once, some time during the evolutionary process that gave us the sort of conscious awareness of ourselves and our environment that animals lack, started to make sense of the world they found themselves in. A very basic mental operation consists in the creation of opposites: some things are edible, others are not; some creatures are dangerous, others are not. Classification in terms of such oppositions, in which the opposites are related to each other because they express either the presence or the absence of one and the same thing (edibility, danger, and so on), seems a natural thing to do, the more so since it would seem to be reinforced by nature itself. Man and woman constitute a binary pair, intimately related yet in a crucial way each other's biological opposite; our right hand and left hand constitute another closely related pair of opposites; and so on and so forth. Lévi-Strauss's basic assumption is that our primitive ancestors deployed this simple model, or structure, to get a grip on a world that slowly began to appear to them as something separate and alien. For Lévi-Strauss, the structure of primitive thinking is binary. Having acquired the rudiments of language, our ancestors must have started to categorize their world in very basic terms that always involved a presence and an absence – light/darkness, human-made/natural, above/below, noise/silence, clothes/naked, sacred/profane, and so on. Prehistoric men and women must have organized their experience around such +/− (that is, binary) oppositions, the idea for which Lévi-Strauss derived from the ubiquitous Jakobson.

According to the latter's so-called distinctive feature theory, which again makes use of the differential principle, the smallest sound units in any language – the so-called phonemes – have developed as binary opposites. Vowels have become contrasted with consonants (Jakobson claimed the vowel/consonant pair as the fundamental phonemic opposition), unvoiced consonants with voiced ones, and so on, until a subtle system of binary oppositions had created all the phonemic differences in the thousands of languages that we know.

For Lévi-Strauss such binary oppositions, the most fundamental of which is that between that which is human-made and that which is part of nature (between culture and nature, in simpler terms), constitute the basis of what we call culture. The basic apprehensions of reality that we find in those oppositions get translated into cultural acts. Once they have found expression in certain rites, taboos, customs, manners, and so on, they get permutated over time until as often as not they will become completely unrecognizable. In fact, they may appear in completely different and even contradictory guises in different cultures. In some cases, the meanings that were attached to the original opposites and that found expression in their cultural materialization were clearly rooted in the real world: it makes sense to attach a positive value to things that are edible and it also makes sense to attach a negative value to things that make you sick or will kill you. In other cases, however, those meanings are as arbitrary as the relationship between a linguistic sign and its real-world referent and are based not on factuality (as in the case of edibility), but on what we would call superstition. The standard positive valuation of light and negative valuation of darkness, for instance, ignores the fact that light and darkness are in themselves neutral natural phenomena and that how we value them depends on the circumstances (it is for instance a lot easier to hide from an enemy in the dark). Meanings attributed to the pair above/below (as in a number of major religions) are even more obviously arbitrary. In any case, rites, taboos, customs, and so on function as signs that refer us usually via a tortuous route to a rather limited number of binary oppositions. Cultural signs position themselves somewhere on a gliding scale between pairs of opposites and in so doing express a relation between two terms, one of which represents a presence while the other represents an absence – a notion that, as we will see, is crucial for the poststructuralism of the 1970s and after.

It should be clear that anthropological structuralism, in spite of its overriding interest in the way the human mind has from the beginning interacted with its natural environment, does not take up a humanist position. Whereas an interest in form is wholly compatible with humanism (as in the New Criticism), structuralism denies that the individuals whose behaviour it studies are autonomous and act and think the way they do out of free will. On the contrary: if I was a member of a 'primitive' tribe, my personal contribution to a ritual would only take its meaning from its function in the whole, from its relation to other parts of the ritual, and not from my personal intention. It is, in fact, questionable whether it would be at all possible for me to have a personal intention in a primitive culture in which every-thing, down to the smallest things, is governed by assumptions, conventions, and rules of unknown origin that cannot be ques-tioned. Structuralism is not only anti-humanist, it is also ahistorical in the sense that in the end it retraces all the cultures that we know and their earlier, historical, versions as combina-tions of ever new (and ever-increasing) permutations of a limited number of basic and unchanging givens. Structuralism does of course not deny that cultures change over time, and that we can distinguish between the different historical phases that a culture has gone through, but it will insist that we are only dealing with variations upon what is essentially an unchanging basic pattern (consisting of binary oppositions) and that it is this pattern that must have our attention.

## Semiology (or semiotics)

From the rituals, taboos, customs, and myths of primitive cultures it is only a short step to contemporary culture. After Lévi-Strauss had shown the way, a whole range of contempo-rary cultural phenomena came under structuralist scrutiny. The French literary critic Roland Barthes (1915–1980) – who later would straightforwardly claim that culture is 'a language' – in 1957 published *Mythologies* in which he applies a very loose and freewheeling structuralist analysis to the differences between boxing and wrestling and between soap powders and detergents, to the drinking of wine versus the drinking of milk, to striptease, to the design of the new Citroën, and so on. The method (although Barthes is highly unmethodical) is familiar: the activities under scrutiny are taken apart so that their constituent elements – the various signs that make up the structure – become visible, after which Barthes analyses how they acquire meaning because of their difference from the other elements in the chain. His boxers, wrestlers, and stripteasers do not make personal statements with the motions they go through, but these motions are signs that take their meaning from the underlying structure of their activities. The central insights of this cultural structuralism – called *semiology* (a term coined by Saussure) or *semiotics* – have been enormously productive and still play a prominent role in the way we think about how cultures (and all sorts of subcultures) work. Especially the idea that we can see the most unlikely things as signs and study them as part of a larger sign system in which the meaning of those signs is not inherent in the signs themselves but the product of difference has paved the way for in-depth analyses of virtually everything imaginable.

Fashion has for instance has been a prominent target – in particular of Barthes – because its semiotic character is fairly obvious. In classrooms, where I always wear a jacket, I usually face T-shirts, sweaters, and so on. My jacket is in itself meaningless, just like the T-shirts and sweaters. However, an outside observer could easily draw the conclusion that a jacket clearly 'means' the right to come in late, to forget your book, to hold long monologues, to sit apart from the others, and to tell them what to read and write – in short, that it means authority or power. And, indeed, it does. But in a good many English schools it is the students who wear the jackets. If I taught at one of those schools and wore a sweater in the classroom then my sweater would spell authority and the sign 'jacket' would mean lack of power. What we see illustrated here is first of all that jackets and sweaters have no inherent meaning, but that meaning is enabled by difference – in a situation where everybody wears a jacket, jackets are meaningless (in which case it could be their colour, or their cut, that might enable meaning to emerge). Secondly, the relationship between sign and meaning is arbitrary: exactly the same meaning can attach itself to either jacket or sweater, depending on the circumstances. Thirdly – and here I return to anthropological structuralism – my jacket functions here within the relationship between the poles of one of structuralism's basic binary oppositions: that of dominance/submission. It situates itself somewhere between +power (dominance) and −power (submission) – right at the +power end of the scale, in fact.

As I have just said, my jacket has no inherent meaning. Even in the first case, with me firmly and self-confidently in that jacket, this particular meaning of 'jacket' is limited to the institutional context. If I meet a couple of my students in a local café my jacket does not give me the right to expose them to a long monologue or to tell them what to drink. The sign 'jacket' only acquires meaning on the basis of difference within a certain context. That meaning here finds a very real basis in the institution's rules, in an underlying relation of dominance/submission. But often enough the meaning that attaches itself to difference is not at all based on anything substantial. Fashion as a whole is a system in which mere difference, not backed up by rules or institutional power, often suffices to create meaning. Food, too, functions as a sign system – don't we all prepare special meals for guests? And so do the presents we give each other. In fact, consumer culture as such, which sells us a good many things that we absolutely do not need and usually throw out after we get tired of them, might be said to sell signs (that we only buy because we attach meanings to them on the basis of their difference from other consumer-signs) rather than products. Once we have been alerted to this sign-function of things, we see signs everywhere. Even products that some of us arguably do need – cars, for instance – have on top of their practical value an additional sign value that car commercials expertly exploit. The semiological, or semiotic, approach that I am sketching here, and in which the most diverse things (including many of our actions) are seen as signs that have no meaning in themselves but that take their meaning from their function within a given structure – from their relation with other signs – is still of great importance. Paradoxically, while the literary structuralism that I will discuss in a moment has in the last twenty-odd years received only modest attention, the structuralist view of culture as an assemblage of overlapping sign systems is in a modified form still powerfully present in literary studies. That continued presence has everything to do with the changed nature of literary studies. As we will see later (and as we already have seen in the case of Barthes's *Mythologies*), literary academics have increasingly widened their scope to include culture in general in both their teaching and their writing and have in so doing rather drastically changed the nature of their profession.

## Literary structuralism

In literary studies the term structuralism is fairly generally used for those approaches to literature that are strongly influenced by linguistics. Strictly speaking, however, literary structuralism develops out of linguistics and the structuralist anthropology that I have just discussed (which itself was of course strongly influenced by linguistics). In 1960 Lévi-Strauss, as a logical consequence of his work on myths, proposed a search for the underlying structure of all narratives, not only novels, stories, and other forms of fiction, but also reportage, biography and autobiography, travel literature, and so on. The influence of linguistics is obvious in the work of the (mostly French) theorists who took up the challenge. Tzetvan Todorov (1939), who uses Boccaccio's late medieval *Decameron* (1351–1353) to get at the structure of narrative in general, calls his study *The Grammar of the Decameron* (1969). Roland Barthes tells us that 'a narrative is a long sentence'. But the search for a universal 'grammar' of narrative that would reveal how the human mind arranges experience has never been able to live up to its initial promise. Most of the models that have been proposed are far too abstract to be of much use. A good example of the abstract character of early literary structuralism is provided by an article on 'the logic of possible narratives' that Claude Bremond published in 1966 (later worked out in much greater detail, so that my remarks here do not do justice to his work). Bremond suggests as the basis for a general model of narrative the logical possibilities that any narrative will have. We should distinguish three stages: virtuality, actualization, and realization, which roughly means the possibility of action, the transition to action – widely defined – and the result of action or 'achievement'. Phase 1 is the default position – a narrative sets up a scene that offers the possibility of action. It should be clear that all narratives do this. Even a description of a totally empty landscape has us waiting for what is going to happen next, that is for action. In phase 2 elements are added that set the narrative in motion (+) or they are not added, in which case nothing will happen (−). We will not have much of a narrative if phase 2 chooses for the − option, but logically it is perfectly possible (we will see in a moment that this seemingly silly − option is highly relevant). If the narrative has been set in motion (the + option) phase 3, that of achievement, may either follow or not follow. The transition to action may or may not achieve its objective. The new state of affairs may then function as a new starting-point, that is a new virtuality, in particular if the action has not been successful. In that case a new cycle will start up: the narrative again has the choice between transition to action (+) and inaction (−) and if it opts for action will again have a choice between achievement (+) and failure (−). This cyclical model is typical, for instance, of many action movies. In the James Bond series Bond's mission will usually go through at least two of such cycles. Bond's first encounters with the forces of the enemy will follow a +, +, − pattern: we have potentiality for action, we have the transition to action, but we do not (yet) have achievement because Bond's attempt to get at the master criminal is thwarted. Only the last cycle will be fully positive: Bond achieves his objective and defeats the villain. The villain's end is pretty soon followed by a scene (usually Bond with a young woman) in which we have no transition to action because this is where the movie ends. The − option of phase 2 (transition to action) turns out to be highly relevant: narratives standardly end with a zero transition to action. Bremond's model will perhaps not come as a revelation. We are usually aware that narratives start somewhere, really get going because something happens, end somewhere else, and then may get going again. However, even though the model operates on a high level of abstraction, it allows us to see a pattern – a structure – in for instance the Bond movies that otherwise might have escaped us.

We find a more detailed approach in the model proposed in the same year by A.J. Greimas, whose book *Structural Semantics* stays fairly close to one of his sources, Propp's study of Russian fairytales. A comparison with Propp provides a neat illustration of the structuralist tendency to get away from the actual content of individual literary works and to formulate general rules. Propp, too, offers generalizations on the basis of his fairytales, but his model still works with recognizable actors, or *dramatis personae*, as he calls them: the hero, the villain, the helper, and so on. For Greimas this is still too close to content and not 'structural' enough and so he develops his so-called *actantial* model that, at a high level of abstraction, should be able to describe narrative as such: all the possible elements and combinations of elements that we can find in actual stories, both fictional and non-fictional. In other words, in good structuralist fashion Greimas wants to describe the basic structure that allows meaning to emerge. Let me offer a very brief sketch. Greimas presents as his basic elements six so-called *actants* of which two are more basic than the others: the *subject* and the *object*. The *subject* is the central element in the action of a story – often, but not necessarily, a person – and the *object* is the objective that the *subject* wants to achieve through the action(s) that he or she (or it) initiates. We recognize in this basic structure a relationship of desire – the *subject* 'desires' the *object* and it is this 'desire' that gets the story going. Other 'actants' include a 'helper' and an 'opposer', terms that are self-evident in this context. In actual narratives these 'actants', which could be described as the six different forces that we can encounter in stories, are concretized in what Greimas calls *acteurs* (actors). (I may seem to be stretching things a bit in calling the 'object' – which could be anything at all – a 'force', but since it always is something that the 'subject' *wants* – wants to possess, to see realized, and so on – it always exerts a pull on the 'subject'.) As the *actant* 'object' suggests, these *acteurs* are not necessarily human. Even a seemingly human *acteur* like the 'opposer' need not be human. The 'opposer' might be anything that presents an obstacle to achieving the 'object'. Like all structuralist models, Greimas's model focuses on relations, with the relationship of desire that obtains between 'subject' and 'object' as the most fundamental one. We find the *acteurs* in individual texts by looking at the relations between the various elements – characters, natural forces, institutions, organizations – that we can identify. Since we are dealing with relations we have to be prepared for the possibility that several *acteurs* might represent only one *actant*. And in simple narratives not all *actants* need to play a role. For Greimas, his six *actants* and the unchangeable relations between them constitute the basic matrix of all narratives. But that does not mean that his model is a sort of interpretation machine that you simply feed texts in order to have them analysed. In actual practice the reader will have to decide, for instance, whether a given character functions as a 'helper' or as an 'opposer'. Moreover, since complex novels usually tell more than one story we may have to apply Greimas's model more than once to the same text and may, for instance, find that a character who in one sub-story functions as an 'opposer' operates as a 'helper' in another sub-story. The model focuses the way we look at texts and helps us ask very relevant questions but cannot take over our interpretative role. It is the reader who must finally judge the events and the characters that a story presents. In fact, from the structuralist perspective the meaning of a particular literary work is produced by a collaboration of the reader and the structure that allows meaning to come into existence. Since the author and authorial intention play no role whatsoever in the structuralist view of things, the reader is alone with a particular manifestation of an unchanging structure and must make the best of that confrontation.

## Narratology

After Greimas's *Structural Semantics* (1966, but not translated into English until 1983) and one or two other influential books, the structuralism that was influenced by Propp gradually gave way to another line of development. This other type of literary structuralism, soon to called be *narratology*, focused not on the underlying structure of the content of stories, but on the structure of narration, the way stories – taken in its widest sense – are told. This aspect of literature has of course for a long time had the attention of writers, who after all must take any number of decisions involving the way they are going to tell their story (the English–American writer Henry James, for instance, has said a good many pertinent things about the narratological possibilities that writers have). It has also drawn a good deal of attention on the part of literary critics (*The Rhetoric of Fiction* by the American critic Wayne Booth, published in 1961, is a brilliant exposé of technical strategies). What distinguishes the structuralist approach to the way stories are told is their systematicity and – inevitably – their focus on the underlying structures that make stories (and thus meaning) possible. The ultimate goal of narratology is to discover a general model of narration that will cover all the possible ways in which stories can be told and that might be said to enable the production of meaning.

By general consensus Gérard Genette's *Narrative Discourse* (published in 1972 and translated in 1980) is one of the most important contributions to narratology and I will briefly sketch Genette's project to give an idea of the structuralist approach to narration. Although Genette introduces a number of completely new categories, he more often redefines already existing categories and insights in terms of *relations*. Let me give an idea of how this works by looking at some redefinitions of familiar literary-critical insights. The first concerns the way in which the chronological *order* of the events and actions of, for instance, a novel (the Formalists' *fabula*) is presented in the actual story (the *syuzhet*). We can express the relationship between the chronological order and the narrative order in terms that express the relationship between them at a given point. The narration may temporarily lag behind the chronological order of events (which is what we find in a *flashback* – although Genette does not use the term), it may be synchronic with events, or it may run ahead of them (when the narrator speculates about the future, for instance). Genette offers a detailed analysis of all the possible relations between the order of events and the order of narration and does so in a technical vocabulary that always calls our attention to the fact that we are dealing with a relationship between two givens ('analepis', 'prolepsis', 'achrony', 'proleptic analepsis', 'analeptic prolepsus'). The second relationship that Genette discusses – that of *duration* – concerns the relationship between the time an event has taken up in the reality of the narrated world and the time that it actually takes to narrate that event. In order to avoid disastrous consequences – like our day-long film – narration must speed things up. Equal duration of event and narration may occasionally create unexpected and arresting effects – 'John walked walked walked walked walked walked walked upstairs' – but this is not the way we can usefully describe a marathon. The question that then arises is how we can map the various possibilities of compression. The third relationship is that of *frequency*, which in Genette's scheme of things covers the relation between the number of times that an event occurs in the world that we are told about and the number of times that it is actually narrated. It is quite common for events that occur repeatedly to be described only once (a technique for which Genette uses the term 'iterative'). Such a narration might start off with 'We went for a swim every single day, that whole summer', and might then describe who actually went to the beach, what they talked about, who fell in love with whom, the thunderstorms that gathered on the horizon in the late afternoon, and so on. The reader will understand that this description probably stretches things a bit – not one single rainy day, that whole summer? – but essentially covers a whole series of very similar events. Far more unusual is the reverse situation: an event that occurred only once is narrated repeatedly. But this is also not as strange as it may seem. One single event may be told by different characters from different perspectives, or it may be told by one and the same character at different points in her or his life (in which case we will also expect different perspectives).

Genette's most difficult analyses concern what in traditional literary criticism is called point of view and which he complicates considerably. Let me give an example. We all know that when writers sit down to begin a novel they have a whole range of possibilities at their disposal. There are first-person narratives, in which the story is told by an 'I' who is inside the story, and there are third-person narratives in which the narrator would seem to be absent from the story that is being told. However, as a structuralist, Genette does not take as his starting-point the writer who sits behind a desk and considers the available options, but the variations that are offered by the relations between the various elements that play a role in the way stories are told. This structuralist perspective, in which there is no place for the author, leads him to suggest that, although we usually do not realize it, a third-person narration must have a narrator and that this narrator is always present in the story. This seems an unnecessary manoeuvre – why not simply identify authors as the narrators of their stories? – but it is not so strange as it may seem. Imagine a novel that is told by an invisible third-person narrator and that is set in seventeenth-century New England. That narrator obviously must know the seventeenth-century world that the novel describes. But the reader may not for a second get the impression that the narrator is also very much aware of cellular phones, hard disks, and the Dow Jones index. In other words, the narrator functions as a continuum of the world that is described rather than as a continuum of the author. Even if we have our doubts about Genette's suggestion, we might well have to accept that the invisible, implied, narrator of a third-person narrative is not identical with the author.

In any case, positing an invisible narrator inside a third-person narrative enables Genette to see first- and third-person narration in terms of the relation between narrator and character and allows him to set up a neat binary opposition. In a first-person narrative the narrator is identical with a character; in a third-person narrative the narrator is not identical with one of the characters. In the first case the narrator tells us about him- or herself (a first person); in the second case the narrator tells us about third persons. Genette calls the first type of narration *homodiegetic* and the second type *heterodiegetic* ('self' versus 'other'). The relationship between narrator and character is intimately bound up with the relationship between narrator and the world that is narrated. A 'homodiegetic' narrator is always involved in the world that is narrated. However, that involvement can be rather marginal. If I am a party and tell a story about a weird thing that happened to me six years ago, I will, somewhat paradoxically, not be part of the world that I am narrating. The course of time has made me *external* to that world. First-person stories will often combine 'external' descriptions, in which the narrator presents a former self, with current events in which the narrator participates and in which the relationship between narrator and the world that is narrated is *internal*. Heterodiegetic (third-person) narrators are not part of the world they narrate, not even if their creator – the author – *is* part of it. In Norman Mailer's *The Armies of the Night* (1968) the main character is Norman Mailer, who is participating in a march on the Pentagon. But for Genette the third-person narrator who always refers to Mailer in the third person – as Norman Mailer – is *not* the author and is therefore external to the narrated world.

Any reasonably experienced reader knows that the relationship between narrator and narrated world is a complicated matter. Even if we are well aware of who the general narrator is of the story or novel that we are reading, we may still encounter passages in which the identity of the narrator is far from clear. This is especially the case with what is called free indirect discourse, defined by Dorrit Cohn as 'the technique for rendering a character's thought in their own idiom while maintaining the third-person reference and the basic tense of narration' (Cohn 1978: 100). In free indirect course the narrator's descriptive reportage can so gradually give way to the reflections of one of the characters that at a certain point we honestly can no longer say to whom we are supposed to attribute what is being thought or through whose eyes we see what is being described (with whose 'point of view' we are dealing, in traditional terms). Are we still directly dealing with the narrator or have we slipped into the perspective of one of the characters? ('He realized that they would have to part, but he would always love, adore her, and remember the dimple in her chin.') One of Genette's lasting contributions to the way we talk about literature is his introduction of the term *focalization* for dealing with this complication of the relation between narrator and the world that is being narrated (Genette derived the term from a New Critical source: Cleanth Brooks and Austin Warren's 1943 notion of 'focus of narration'). If the narrator has indeed given way to the perspective of one of the characters – even if that perspective is still described for us by the narrator – the narration takes place through a *focalizer*. 'Focalization' then allows Genette to draw broad distinctions between various types of narrative.

This only scratches the surface of Genette's structuralist narratology. It will be obvious, however, that the relations that I have sketched here and the others that Genette identifies can be further broken down and refined into a highly sophisticated analytical apparatus. Like Greimas's actantial model, Genette's narratology focuses and directs the way we look at texts. It allows us to map how exactly actual stories are embedded in other stories, how focalization shifts during the course of a story, and so on and so forth, and it can, better than Greimas's model, assist us in the interpretation of complex texts. In fact, we know that it can do so, because *Narrative Discourse* is not only a work of structuralist literary theory, but also a brilliant dissection of the narrative strategies of Marcel Proust's *À la Recherche du temps perdu* (*Remembrance of Things Past*, 1913–1927), which functions as Genette's main textual source. But as with Greimas, it is the reader who through a close reading operation must apply the model to the text under consideration and who is in the end, in the absence of authorial control, left alone with the text. Genette exhaustively maps the possibilities, the endless combinations of relational positions, that the narrative form offers; the rest is left to the reader.

## Summary

Taking its clue from linguistics and – in its analyses of culture and its institutions – from structuralist anthropology, structuralism focuses on the conditions that make meaning possible, rather than on meaning itself. It tries to map the structures that are the actual carriers of meaning and the various relations between the elements within those structures. Structuralism in literary studies may for instance examine the underlying structure of a specific genre such as the detective novel; it may try to reduce the at first sight enormous diversity of characters that we meet in stories and in novels to a limited number of roles that always occur in fixed relations to each other; or it may study the narrative aspects of texts (and of film, historical writing, commercials, and other cultural products that make use of narration) in order to systematize the *narratological* possibilities – the narrative strategies – that are available to a writer (or director). David Lodge speaks very appositely of 'the characteristic structuralist pursuit of explanatory models with which masses of literary data may be classified and explained' (Lodge and Wood 2000: 137).

## Suggestions for further reading

Robert Scholes's *Structuralism in Literature: An Introduction* (1974) and Jonathan Culler's *Structuralist Poetics: Structuralism, Linguistics and the Study of Literature* (1975) are despite their age still good introductions to structuralism, with Scholes being satisfyingly accessible. Derek Attridge, 'The Linguistic Model and its Applications' (1995), is much briefer, but to the point. Specifically focused on narratology are two classics: Dorrit Cohn's excellent *Transparent Minds: Narrating Modes for Presenting Consciousness in Fiction* (1978) and

Shlomith Rimmon-Kenan's *Narrative Fiction: Contemporary Poetics* (1983). Wallace Martin's *Recent Theories of Narrative* (1986) offers a highly accessible overview of what in the mid-1980s was the state of the art, and has not lost much of its relevance. Seymour Chatman's *Coming to Terms: The Rhetoric of Narrative in Fiction and Film* (1990) is interesting because of its double focus.

The best, although admittedly not easy, example of narratological criticism is still Gérard Genette's *Narrative Discourse* (1980). Examples of structuralist analyses of specific genres are Tzvetan Todorov's 'The Typology of Detective Fiction' from 1966 (to be found in his *The Poetics of Prose* (1977), and in Lodge and Wood 2000) and his *The Fantastic: A Structural Approach to a Literary Genre* ([1970] 1975), and Will Wright's *Sixguns and Society: A Structural Study of the Western* (1975). Finally, a brief and lucid account of Lévi-Strauss's structuralist anthropology is to be found in Edmund Leach's *Lévi-Strauss* (4th edn, revised and updated by James Laidlaw, 1996).

# Chapter 4

# Political reading
## The 1970s and 1980s

What the major approaches to literature that I have so far discussed have in common is that they focus strongly on literature itself. Richards's practical criticism and the New Criticism limit themselves in their search for a text's meaning to the 'words on the page'. Formalism is primarily interested in what makes literature different from other ways of using language and in the literary reasons for literary-historical change. Structuralism seeks to establish the structures that underlie narratives and that make meaning possible. Conspicuously absent is a serious interest in what many literary academics would now consider very important issues such as the *historical situatedness*, or historical embedment, and the *politics* of literary texts. To what extent are literary texts the product of the historical period in which they were written? The world has gone through enormous socio-economic and political changes in the last millennium. Isn't it reasonable to expect those changes to turn up in our literature? And isn't it at least plausible to assume that those changes have somehow affected the way we experience things? Can the human condition have remained essentially the same? And what sort of view of the prevailing socio-economic and political condition do we find in a given text? Does the text support the status quo or does it take an openly or more implicitly critical stance?

Before the late 1960s – the years that function as a watershed in this book – such questions were by the large majority of English and American literary academics thought to be irrelevant or even detrimental to reading and to interpretation. With only a few exceptions, critics had not much use for historical context and even less for politics. In this chapter on literature and politics I will focus on three major modes of political criticism that became a forceful presence in Anglo-American literary studies in the course of the 1970s: Marxism, feminism, and criticism that concerns itself with racial relations. In Marxist criticism *social class* and *class relations* function as central instruments of analysis, in feminist criticism the concept of *gender* is the crucial critical (and political) instrument, while in criticism concerned with racial relations the fundamental category is of course *race*. I should point out that the 1960s-to-1980s version of these critical approaches, to which I will limit myself in this chapter, are by current standards rather traditional. Literary theory and criticism would go through great changes under the impact of the literary-theoretical upheavals of the later 1970s and the 1980s – of the spectacular rise of *poststructuralism*. Still, the fairly traditional character of the Marxism, the feminism, and the race-oriented criticism that I will look at here in no way diminishes their importance: traditional perspectives still play an important and valuable role within the world of literary studies. It must be kept in mind, however, that there are newer versions of these and other critical approaches which have assimilated the poststructuralist thought that I will discuss in the next chapter and which continue political criticism from somewhat different perspectives. For strategic reasons, which will become clear in my discussion of feminism, I will first discuss Marxist literary criticism.

## The politics of class: Marxism

To discuss Marxism in the early twenty-first century may well seem strangely beside the point. After all, since the fall of the Berlin wall in 1989, one self-proclaimed Marxist regime after the other has been forced to consign itself to oblivion. And the officially Marxist political parties that for a long time were a serious force in Western Europe have either disappeared or have become politically marginal. However, Marxism as an intellectual perspective still provides a wholesome counterbalance to our propensity to see ourselves and the writers that we read as completely divorced from socio-economic circumstances. It also counterbalances the related tendency to read the books and poems we read as originating in an autonomous mental realm, as the free products of free and independent minds.

Marxism's questioning of that freedom is now a good less sensational than it was in the 1840s and 1850s when Karl Marx (1818–1883) began to outline what is now called Marxist philosophy, although it is still controversial enough. When he noted, in the 'Foreword' to his 1859 *Towards a Critique of Political Economy*, that the 'mode of production of material life conditions the general process of social, political, and intellectual life', the Victorian upper class, if aware of this line of thought, would have been horrified, and certainly by the conclusion that followed: 'It is not the consciousness of men that determines their existence, but their social existence that determines their consciousness.'

What does it mean that the 'mode of production' conditions 'the general process of social, political, and intellectual life'? If people have heard about Marxism they usually know rather vaguely that Marxism is about how your social circumstances determine much, if not all, of your life. This seems reasonable enough. If you work the night shift in your local McDonald's, for instance, you are unlikely to fly business class to New York City for a week in the Waldorf Astoria or to bid on the next Rembrandt for sale. But this sort of determinism is perfectly compatible with the idea that we are essentially free. Certain politicians would tell you to get out of the night shift, to get an education, to get rid of your provincial accent, to buy the right outfit, and to start exuding self-confidence. In other words, you have options, like everybody else, and all you have to do is to make the right choices and start moving up that social ladder.

This is not what Marx had in mind. Marxist theory argues that the way we think and the way we experience the world around us are either wholly or largely conditioned by the way the economy is organized. Under a medieval, feudal regime people will have thought and felt different from the way that we think and feel now, in a capitalist economy – that is, an economy in which goods are produced (the 'mode of production') by large concentrations of capital (old-style factories, new-style multinationals) and then sold on a free, competitive, market. The *base* of a society – the way its economy is organized, broadly speaking – determines its *superstructure* – everything that we might classify as belonging to the realm of culture, again in a broad sense: education, law, but also religion, philosophy, political programmes, and the arts. This implies a view of literature that is completely at odds with the Anglo-American view of literature that goes back to Matthew Arnold. If the way we experience reality and the way we think about it (our religious, political, and philosophical views) are determined by the sort of economy we happen to live in, then clearly there is no such thing as an unchanging human condition. On the contrary, with, for instance, the emergence of capitalism some centuries ago we may expect to find a new experience of reality and new views of the world. Since capitalism did not happen overnight we will not find a clean break but we certainly should find a gradual transition to a new, more or less collective perspective. The term 'collective' is important here. If the economic 'base' indeed determines the cultural 'superstructure', then writers will not have all that much freedom in their creative efforts. They will inevitably work within the framework dictated by the economic 'base' and will have much in common with other writers living and writing under the same economic dispensation. Traditional Marxism, then, asserts that thought is subservient to, and follows, the material conditions under which it develops. Its outlook is *materialist*, as opposed to the *idealist* perspective, whose claim that matter is basically subservient to thought is one of the fundamental assumptions of modern Western culture: we tend to assume that our thinking is free, unaffected by material circumstances. In our minds we can always be free. Wrong, says Marxism, minds aren't free at all, they only think they are.

Capitalism, Marxism tells us, thrives on exploiting its labourers. Simply put, capitalists grow rich and shareholders do well because the labourers that work for them and actually produce goods (including services) get less – and often a good deal less – for their efforts than their labour is actually worth. Labourers have known this for a long time and have organized themselves in labour unions to get fairer deals. What they do not know, however, is how capitalism *alienates* them from themselves by seeing them in terms of production – as production units, as objects rather than human beings. Capitalism turns people into things, it *reifies* them. Negotiations about better wages, no matter how successful, do not affect (let alone reverse) that process. Marx saw it clearly at work in his nineteenth-century environment in which men whose grandfathers had still worked as cobblers, cabinetmakers, yeoman farmers, and so on – in other words, as members of self-supporting communities who dealt directly with clients and buyers – performed mechanical tasks in factories where they were merely one link in a long chain. However, this process of reification is not limited to labourers. The capitalist mode of production generates a view of the world – focused on profit – in which ultimately all of us function as objects and become alienated from ourselves. The American Marxist critic Fredric Jameson suggested not too long ago that we now all unknowingly suffer from a 'waning of affect' – the loss of genuine emotion – because of the complete dominance of the capitalist model in our contemporary world (Jameson 1984: 60).

## Ideology

This leads inevitably to the question of how it is possible that we can be so blind to the real state of affairs around us and so terribly delude ourselves. It also leads to the question of how it is possible that apparently some people are not deluded. The answer given to this second question by one important movement within Marxism – so-called 'Western' Marxism – which for this position bases itself upon Marx's earlier, still somewhat humanistically inclined writings of the 1840s (the Paris Manuscripts), is that we always have a certain margin of freedom. To put that in the terms usually employed in the debates over issues such as freedom of action and thought: within Western Marxism there is room for human agency and subjective consciousness; that is, for action and thought that have their origin in human individuals themselves and are not wholly determined by forces over which we have no control. As a consequence, the superstructure – including, of course, literature and culture in general – also enjoys a certain measure of independence (a point that Marx himself also makes). But to return to our (almost) collective delusion, for Marxism we are blind to our own condition because of the effects of what it calls *ideology*. We should not confuse the Marxist use of 'ideology' with the way we often use the term: as referring to a set of beliefs that people *consciously* hold – beliefs of which they are aware and which they can articulate. We can for instance speak of the ideology of the free market – referring to a series of arguments that defends free enterprise against state intervention – and also of the communistic ideology that gave the state total control over production. For Marxists, however, the term is much more encompassing.

In Marxist usage, ideology is what causes us to misrepresent the world to ourselves. As I have just said, for Marxism the basis of any society is its economic organization, which then gives rise to certain social relations – for instance, the class relations between capitalists and workers in nineteenth-century capitalist economies. This socio-economic base then conditions the cultural superstructure. However, there are forces at work that prevent us from seeing this: for instance, the liberal humanist idea that we are essentially free and can remain free as long as we can think. For Marxists, ideology is not so much a set of beliefs or assumptions that we are aware of, but it is that which makes us experience our life in a certain way and makes us believe that that way of seeing ourselves and the world is *natural*. In so doing, ideology distorts reality in one way or another and falsely presents as natural and harmonious what is artificial and contradictory – the class differences that we find under capitalism, for instance. If we succumb to ideology we live in an illusory world, in what in Marxism has often been described as a state of *false consciousness*. As we will see later, the idea that we are blind to our own condition is in more than one way still vitally important for literary studies.

How is ideology able to hide authentic reality from us? One very influential answer was given in the 1960s by the French Marxist philosopher Louis Althusser (1918–1990). Althusser's first thesis regarding ideology is that 'Ideology represents the imaginary relationship of individuals to their real conditions of existence' (Althusser 1971: 18), which roughly corresponds with what I have just said: ideology distorts our view of our true 'conditions of existence'. His second thesis connects ideology with its social sources. For Althusser ideology works through so-called 'ideological State apparatuses', which, although they may have their own sub-ideology, are all subject to the ruling ideology. Althusser's ideological state apparatuses include organized religion, the law, the political system, the educational system – in short, all the institutions through which we are socialized. Ideology, then, has a *material* existence in the sense that it is embodied in all sorts of material practices. Althusser mentions some of the practices that are part of

the *material existence of an ideological apparatus*, be it only a small part of that apparatus: a small mass in a small church, a funeral, a minor match at a sports club, a school day, a political party meeting, etc.

(20)

The list of material ideological practices could be almost infinitely expanded. What is clear is that ideology is waiting for us wherever we go and that practically everything we do and everything we engage in is pervaded by ideology. Althusser puts it this way:

> Ideas have disappeared as such (insofar as they are endowed with an ideal or spiritual existence), to the precise extent that it has emerged that their existence is inscribed in the actions of practices governed by rituals defined in the last instance by an ideological apparatus. It therefore appears that the subject acts insofar as he is acted by the following system ... : ideology existing in a material ideological apparatus, prescribing material practices governed by a material ritual, which practices exist in the material actions of a subject acting in all consciousness according to his belief.
>
> (21)

While we believe that we are acting out of free will, we are in reality 'acted by the ... system'. We recognize in this formulation the anti-humanist structuralist anthropology of Lévi-Strauss. Because within such a perspective there is no room for freedom, Althusser does not attribute the unequal distribution of wealth that we find within capitalist societies to the manipulations of 'a small number of cynical men who base their domination and exploitation of the "people" on a falsified representation of the world which they have imagined to enslave other minds' (18). The driving mechanism behind ideology is not the self-interest of those who profit from the way a given society has economically organized itself and who work hard to hide the exploitative nature of that organization from the lower classes. Those who profit are as blind as everybody else.

But if that is the case where does ideology come from and how has it acquired its immense influence? To answer these questions Althusser draws on the writings of the French psychoanalyst Jacques Lacan (1901–1981), whose work I will discuss in more detail in the next chapter. For Lacan, the processes that we go through when we grow up leave us forever incomplete. Aware of that deep lack – although we cannot name it – and yearning for completion we turn to ideology, the more so since it constantly 'hails and interpellates' (addresses) us as 'concrete subjects' – as if we are complete already. In so doing, it may 'interpellate' us in the different social roles that we play, or, as Althusser would say, the different 'subject positions' that we occupy. One and the same woman could be 'interpellated' as a mother, as a member of a particular church, as a doctor, as a voter, and so on. The way ideology addresses us creates that subject position for us, yet simultaneously that position is already familiar to us because it is part of what we know. Ideology convinces us that we are whole and real, that we are the 'concrete subjects' we want to be. No wonder, then, that we see whatever ideology makes us see as natural, as belonging to the natural, harmonious order of things.

Althusser's analysis showed the way for explorations of the way ideology works in literature. Colin McCabe and other British critics showed how, for instance, the objective realism of the mid-nineteenth-century English novel is not so objective at all. They argued that novels like Charlotte Brontë's *Jane Eyre* (1847) and George Eliot's *Middlemarch* (1871–1872), which present their characters as essentially free, even if not all of them make use of that freedom, 'hail' us just like ideology hails us. As Roger Webster put it with reference to Leo Tolstoy's *Anna Karenina* (1873–1876):

> The reader is drawn towards Levin [one of the novel's main characters] and becomes through him the experiencing centre of the novel's organic vision: unless we resist such positioning by reading against the grain, it is hard to avoid the process.
>
> (Webster 1990: 82–83)

Such novels invite their readers to become part of a world that is essentially free and to look over the shoulders of people who make autonomous decisions. In so doing, they create a specific subject position for their readers and give them the illusion that they, too, are free. Just like ideology, such novels give their readers the idea that they are complete: they make them believe

**87**

that they are free agents and in that way make them complicit in their own delusion.

## Hegemony

Although Althusser's analysis led to valuable insights in the various ways in which literature can conspire with, and simultaneously deceive, its readers, a good many Marxist critics felt uneasy with the deterministic character of his view of ideology. As we have seen, Althusser would seem to leave no room at all for autonomous, non-ideological thought or action. With the publication of the writings of the Italian Marxist Antonio Gramsci (1891–1937) in the early 1970s, a modified concept of ideology became available. Gramsci, writing in the 1930s, is fully aware of the power of ideology, which leads to '[t]he "spontaneous" consent given by the great masses of the population to the general direction imposed on social life by the dominant fundamental group' (Gramsci [1971] 1998: 277). This consent is ' "historically" caused by the prestige (and the consequent confidence) which the dominant group enjoys because of its position and function in the world of production' (277). Although Gramsci's explanation of the power of ideology is perhaps less forceful than Althusser's, it has the merit of allowing us to resist what he calls the *hegemony* – the domination of a set of ruling beliefs and values through 'consent' rather than through 'coercive power'. Gramsci's 'hegemony' is far less inescapable than Althusser's ideology, even if it, too, establishes and maintains itself through 'civil society' and employs cultural means and institutions. Under hegemonic conditions the majority – usually a large majority – of a nation's citizens has so effectively internalized what the rulers want them to believe that they genuinely think that they are voicing their own opinion, but there is always room for dissent. Gramsci's hegemony, although it saturates society to the same extent as Althusser's ideology, is not airtight and waterproof. We can catch on to it and resist its workings with counterhegemonic actions even if we can never completely escape its all-pervasive influence.

In the United Kingdom, the important Marxist critic

Raymond Williams (1921–1988) emphasized this aspect of Gramsci's thought. Although 'hegemony ... is a whole body of practices and expectations; our assignments of energy, our ordinary understanding of the nature of man and of his world' (Williams [1980] 1996: 23), it is by no means homogeneous and omnipotent: 'hegemony is not singular ... its own internal structures are highly complex, and have continually to be renewed, recreated and defended ... they can be continually challenged and in certain respects modified' (22). Although for Williams the economic 'base' and its 'mode of production' are still important factors, the idea that the 'base' completely determines the cultural 'superstructure' is too simple: 'no mode of production, and therefore no dominant society or order of society, and therefore no dominant culture, in reality exhausts the full range of human practice, human energy, human intention' (26). From Williams's perspective, with its far more flexible notion of ideology, hegemony and counterhegemonic tendencies struggle with each other in a literature and culture that are constantly in motion. Marxist critics who follow Williams's example – such as the cultural materialists who I will discuss in Chapter 7 – see literature as an important vehicle for ideology, but are very attentive to the dissenting voices and views that literature may also present.

## Marxist literary studies

This discussion of ideology and hegemony will have made clear that a Marxist perspective leads to an approach to literature that is significantly different from the approaches I have discussed so far. As we have just seen, Marxists may differ on the extent to which the cultural superstructure is determined by the socio-economic base. Marx himself, for instance, is on record as leaving the arts a good deal of leeway – the development of the arts for him did not necessarily immediately reflect changes in the economic arrangement and the relations between classes – while the so-called 'vulgar Marxists' of the prewar period saw a direct cause–effect relationship between the socio-economic base and literature and saw the writer as directly conditioned by his or her social class. Marxists also differ on a question that is intimately related to this: to what extent can we liberate ourselves from ideology? All Marxist critics agree, however, that in the study of literature the social dimension is absolutely indispensable. Writers can never completely escape ideology and their social background so that the social reality of the writer will always be part of the text.

A central question in Marxist approaches to literature concerns the reliability of literary texts as social 'evidence'. If Charles Dickens's *Great Expectations* (1860–1861) and George Eliot's *Middlemarch* (1871–1872) are conditioned by the capitalist society of Victorian England what then are we going to find in these novels: a true picture of Victorian England, or an ideologically distorted reflection? In short, is it possible for writers, or for literary texts – this is a crucial distinction, as we will see – to offer objective insights (as Marxists see them): to present history as a never-ending struggle between antagonistic classes for economic and social gains and to present contemporary reality as only the latest instance of that struggle?

Over time, Marxist critics have given different answers to this question, although most have been inspired by the notion – first formulated by Friedrich Engels in 1888 – that the meaning of a literary work must be seen as independent of the political (and ideologically coloured) views of its author. This by now familiar strategy of separating text and author does, however, not separate the text from social reality (as the Formalists and the literary structuralists did). On the contrary, the idea is that if we remove the author from the picture – or at least the author's political views – we might get an even better picture of the real world of class conflicts and political tension. This idea has the great merit that it allows Marxist critics to read the work of even the most reactionary authors against the grain of their political views so that the 'bourgeois' writers that are part of the general literary canon can also be appreciated from a Marxist perspective. The Hungarian critic George Lukács, the most prominent Marxist critic of the prewar period, holds for instance the work of the French novelist Honoré de Balzac (1799–1850) and the Russian Leo Tolstoy (1828–1910), neither of them known for progressive views, in high regard. In fact, Lukács vastly prefers the panoramic novels of such conservative writers to the fragmentary avant-garde products of the sometimes fiercely leftist artists of the 1920s because it is only in the wide-ranging panorama, and in the merging of individual life stories with the larger movements of history, that the reader is confronted with the historical truth. As Lukács puts it:

> Achilles and Werther, Oedipus and Tom Jones, Antigone and Anna Karenina: their individual existence ... cannot be distinguished from their social and historical environment. Their human significance, their specific individuality cannot be separated from the context in which they were created.
>
> (Lukács [1957] 1972: 476)

The narratives in which these characters appear are to some extent independent of their authors' political convictions and accurately reflect historical reality. They effectively overcome their authors' ideological limitations and they do so because they offer a total overview of all the social forces involved. (For Marxists, such an approach, which takes all parties and positions and their dynamic relationships into account and thereby allows a fuller understanding of the whole, is *dialectical*. In the words of Lukács: 'The literature of realism ... displays the contradictions within society and within the individual in the context of a dialectical unity' [476].)

For the British and American Marxist critics of the 1970 and 1980s, usually influenced by Althusser and his grim view of an enormously powerful ideology, texts do not so easily allow us a view of an undistorted reality. I have already mentioned that, following Althusser, critics sought to demonstrate that the great realistic novels of the nineteenth century, just like ideology, address ('hail') their readers and make them complicit in their own ideological delusion. Ideology is seen as such a strong presence in the text that we more or less have to break down its resistance to get at a truer picture of the reality the text pretends to present. An important influence on especially British critics of the period is the French critic Pierre Macherey's *A Theory of Literary Production* (1966; translated in 1978), whose views of literature also influenced Althusser. For Macherey literary works are pervaded by ideology. So in order to get beyond a text's ideological dimension we will have to begin with the cracks in its façade, with those sites where the text is not fully in control of itself (a lack of control summarized in the title of one of Macherey's later essays, 'The Text Says What It Does Not Say'). In order expose a text's ideology, interpretation must paradoxically focus on what the text does *not* say, on what the text *represses* rather than *expresses*. We find what the text does *not* say in gaps, in silences where what might have been said remains unarticulated. Literature, as Macherey puts it, *reveals* the gaps in ideology (see Macherey [1966] 1978: 59–60). The text might almost be said to have an unconscious to which it has consigned what it cannot say because of ideological repression. (From this perspective, the title of an important literary study by the American Marxist critic Fredric Jameson, *The Political Unconscious* (1981), is less enigmatic than it might otherwise seem.) Macherey finds the cracks in the text's façade not in its major themes, which are fully controlled by ideology, but in textual elements that are only tangentially related to the main theme (or themes). Here is where we see ideology, with its suppression of contradiction and exclusion of what is undesirable, actually at work. And since in a literary text the work of ideology is never completely successful, we also see a void at the heart of the text.

This leads to a way of reading literature that is completely different from that of the English and American critics of the 1920s and beyond whom I discussed in the first chapter. Macherey and like-minded critics in the United Kingdom like Terry Eagleton (*Criticism and Ideology*, 1976b) and Terence Hawkes (*Structuralism and Semiotics*, 1977) are not interested in what makes a text coherent but in what makes it incoherent, in what does not fit or is absent for obscure reasons (see for instance Eagleton's analyses of a number of canonical texts in *Criticism and Ideology*). In so doing, they make the text turn against itself. As we will see, this practice anticipates the poststructuralist approach that I will discuss in the next chapter, with the proviso that for Macherey his approach is 'scientific' (just as Althusser saw his Marxism as a 'science') and leads to objectively true interpretations, while for the poststructuralists there is no such thing as objective truth.

Let me have a brief look at the British critic Catherine Belsey's Macherey-inspired reading of a number of Sherlock Holmes stories in her *Critical Practice* of 1980. Their author, Arthur Conan Doyle (1859–1930), presents his detective hero as unerringly penetrating, a man gifted with a brain that can solve any riddle. The 'project' of these stories – to make everything subject to scientific analysis, as Belsey puts it – would seem to promise a true and unflinching picture of reality. However, if we look closely at the reality that the stories actually present, we see that their presentation of the real world is strangely deficient. As Belsey demonstrates, the women in these stories and their social position are not subjected to analysis at all. They remain mysterious and opaque. The silence of these stories with regard to their female characters reveals the working of a patriarchal ideology in which the males take centre stage and the women are taken for granted. They may at best provide an occasion for Holmes's intellect to dazzle us.

This may well raise a question: do we need a theoretical concept like ideology to find what other readers might have discovered without its help? In fact, Macherey's own analyses of the fiction of Jules Verne raise the same question. However, we should not underrate the added value of this approach. Whereas a more traditional critic might suppose that in the Holmes example we are dealing with a personal blindness or an unwillingness on the part of the author to present a truer picture of late nineteenth-century or early twentieth-century reality, for Marxist critics the omission is not personal at all, but points directly to an impersonal cluster of beliefs and values with an immense social influence. It is this ideology that is the real target of literary investigation, and the aim in this particular case is not to show up Doyle's personal shortcomings, but the differences between ideology and the real world. Through the politics of the text – its ideological dimension – Marxist criticism addresses the politics of the world outside the text.

## The politics of gender: feminism

It is now obvious that it does not make much sense to consider the literature that over the ages has been produced by female writers without taking into account the social realities that female authors have had to face. For one thing, for a very long period women were not really supposed to get an education. It is of course possible to become a writer without a formal education – a fortunate circumstance to which we owe a number of great women writers – but clearly the odds are against members of any group that is discriminated against in this way. The work of female writers has so obviously been under a number of serious historical constraints that it is now hard to understand why the odds they faced were virtually ignored in literary discussions (except by some of these writers themselves: Virginia Woolf, for instance). The answer surely has to do with the general blindness of (male-dominated) Western culture to its treatment of women as second-rate citizens. Moreover, as long as within literary studies interest was virtually limited to the 'words on the page' (Richards, Leavis, the New Criticism), to the underlying structures that enabled literary texts to come into being (the French structuralists), or to ideology and the class struggle as mediated through literary texts (traditional Marxist criticism), the plight of women writers drew little attention. Especially for English and American literary studies the issue of historical constraints would have been a sociological matter, wholly extrinsic to literature itself.

Most critics now believe that it is impossible to cordon off neatly a given field of interest or study from the rest of the world. For better or for worse, everything seems somehow related to everything else. With regard to the social position of women, and therefore also with regard to the field of female writing, that view is to a large extent due to the feminist movement that began to gain momentum in the course of the 1960s. Paradoxically, even Marxism, with its wide-ranging historical theorizing, had largely ignored the position of women. With hindsight, this oversight is all the more incomprehensible since some of its key concepts – the struggle between social classes, the blinding effects of ideology – might have been employed to analyse the social situation of women.

The feminist movement, then, put socio-historical circumstances as a determining factor in the production of literature firmly on the map. Feminism was involved right from the beginning in literary studies, and for good reasons. Kate Millett's trailblazing *Sexual Politics* of 1970, for instance, devotes long chapters to the attitudes towards women that pervade the work of prominent twentieth-century authors like D.H. Lawrence (1885–1930) and Henry Miller (1891–1980). Both were held in high regard by many critics for their daring and liberating depictions of erotic relations. Millett, however, showed that the attitude of their male characters towards women was not so emancipated at all: most of the male characters that she examined – and especially those of Miller – were denigrating, exploitative, and repressive in their relations with women. Feminism saw very clearly that the widespread negative stereotyping of women in literature and film (we can now add rock videos) constituted a formidable obstacle on the road to true equality. At least as important is that in the work of the male writers she discusses Millett finds a relationship between sex and power in which the distribution of power over the male and female partners mirrors the distribution of power over males and females in society at large. In other words, in terms of power, acts that we usually think of as completely private turn out to be an extension of the public sphere. The private and the public cannot be seen as wholly separate – on the contrary, they are intimately linked. Since this is the case, Millett argues, the private sphere is, just like the public realm, thoroughly political: it is a political arena where the same power-based relations exist as in the public world. Feminism and feminist criticism are profoundly political in claiming that the personal and the political cannot be separated. They are also political in the more traditional sense of trying to intervene in the social order with a programme that aims to change actually existing social conditions.

Feminism seeks to change the power relations between men and women that prevail under what in the late 1960s and the 1970s usually was called *patriarchy*, a term that referred to the (almost) complete domination of men in Western society (and beyond).

I will limit the discussion at this point to what one might call the more traditional forms of feminism, such as liberal humanist feminism and socialist feminism, of the earlier feminist period. Around the mid-1970s French feminism began to incorporate the poststructuralism that had emerged in France in the second half of the 1960s, a development that would eventually strongly affect feminism in general. Given this influence, I will delay discussion of French feminism until we have looked at poststructuralism.

## Feminist literary studies

In its first phase, feminist literary studies focused on 'the woman as reader' and on 'the woman as writer'. The American feminist critic Elaine Showalter, from whom I am borrowing these formulations, put it as follows in her 1979 essay 'Towards a Feminist Poetics':

> The first type is concerned with … woman as the consumer of male-produced literature, and with the way in which the hypothesis of a female reader changes our apprehension of a given text, awakening us to the significance of its textual codes …. Its subjects include images and stereotypes of women in literature, the omissions of and misconceptions about women in criticism, and the fissures in male-constructed literary history.
>
> (Showalter [1979] 1985: 128)

When feminist criticism focuses on 'the woman as writer' it concerns itself with

woman as the producer of textual meaning, with the history,

genres and structures of literatures by women. Its subjects include the psychodynamics of female creativity; linguistics and the problem of female language; the trajectory of the individual or collective literary career; literary history; and, of course, studies of particular writers and works.

(128)

The first type of feminist criticism asks questions of the following kind. What sort of roles did female characters play? With what sort of themes were they associated? What are the implicit presuppositions of a given text with regard to its readers? (Upon closer inspection many texts clearly assume that their readers are male – just like those commercials in which fast cars are presented by seductive young women.) Feminist critics showed how often literary representations of women repeated familiar cultural stereotypes. Such stereotypes included the woman – fast car or not – as an immoral and dangerous seductress, the woman as eternally dissatisfied shrew, the woman as cute but essentially helpless, the woman as unworldly, self-sacrificing angel, and so on. Much of the research involved naturally focused on the work of male authors, but female writers, too, came under close scrutiny and were regularly found to have succumbed to the lure of stereotypical representations. Since the way female characters were standardly portrayed had not much in common with the way feminist critics saw and experienced themselves, these characters clearly were *constructions*, put together – not necessarily by the writers who presented them themselves, but by the culture they belonged to – to serve a not-so-hidden purpose: the continued social and cultural domination of males. If we look at the four examples I have given we see immediately that female independence (in the seductress and the shrew) gets a strongly negative connotation, while helplessness and renouncing all ambition and desire are presented as endearing and admirable. The message is that dependence leads to indulgement and reverence while independence leads to dislike and rejection. The desired effect – of which the writer clearly need not be aware – is a perpetuation of the unequal power relations between men and women.

## Gender

To put what I have just sketched in somewhat different terms: this type of feminist criticism leads to a thorough examination of *gender* roles. Gender has to do not with how females (and males) really are, but with the way that a given culture or subculture sees them, how they are culturally *constructed*. To say that women have two breasts is to say something about their biological nature, to say something about what it is to be a female; to say that women are naturally timid, or sweet, or intuitive, or dependent, or self-pitying, is to construct a role for them. It tells us how the speaker wants to see them. What traditionally has been called 'feminine', then, is a cultural construction, a *gender* role that has been culturally assigned to countless generations of women. The same holds for masculinity, with its connotations of strength, rationality, stoicism, and self-reliance. Like femininity, traditional masculinity is a gender role that has far less to do with actual males than with the wishful thinking projected onto the heroes of Westerns, hard-boiled private eyes, and British secret agents. Masculinity, too, is a cultural construction. We can see this, for instance, in one of the traditional representations of homosexuality, in which maleness and masculinity are uncoupled. Although homosexuals are male, they are often portrayed as feminine, that is as lacking masculinity.

Feminism, then, has been focused right from the beginning on gender because a thorough revision of gender roles seemed the most effective way of changing the power relations between men and women. Since no one in their right mind will want to give serious power to a person who must be timid, dependent, irrational, and self-pitying because she is a woman, the effort to purge the culture of such gendered stereotyping is absolutely crucial. (It is all the more crucial because thinking in terms of gender stereotypes has rather paradoxically brought a good many timid, dependent, irrational, and self-pitying males, whom everybody automatically assumed to be 'masculine', to positions of great and dangerous power.) Feminism has politicized gender – by showing its constructed nature – and put it firmly on the agenda of the later twentieth century. Moreover, after its initial focus on the gendered representation of women (and men) in Western culture, it has very effectively widened the issue and shown how often seemingly neutral references, descriptions, definitions, and so on are in fact gendered, and always according to the same pattern. A masculine gendering is supposed to evoke positive connotations, a feminine gendering is supposed to evoke negative ones. Feminism has shown how this binary opposition – to use the structuralist term for such pairs – is pervasively present in the way we think about nature, emotion, science, action (or non-action), art, and so on.

## The woman as writer

The textual focus that we find in studies of how literary representations of women are gendered also characterizes attempts to establish a specifically female tradition – or specifically female traditions – in writing by women. A famous example with regard to the specificity of nineteenth-century female writing is Sandra Gilbert and Susan Gubar's *The Madwoman in the Attic: The Woman Writer and the Nineteenth-Century Literary Imagination* (1979). For Gilbert and Gubar the limitations – social and otherwise – that a nineteenth-century female writer faced led to 'an obsessive interest in these limited options'. In the work of these writers that interest expressed itself in an 'obsessive imagery of confinement that reveals the ways in which female artists feel trapped and sickened both by suffocating alternatives and by the culture that had created them' (Gilbert and Gubar 1979: 64). An example is the madwoman in the attic of Gilbert and Gubar's title: the supposedly mad wife that Jane's employer and future husband Rochester keeps locked up in the attic in Charlotte Brontë's *Jane Eyre* (1847). Female critics, because of their personal experience of the workings of patriarchy, are arguably better equipped to bring to light and analyse such typically female preoccupations. Not unexpectedly, then, the attempt to establish a female literary tradition fairly soon led to calls for a specifically female form of literary studies, for ways of reading and theorizing that could tell us how typically female experience has over the ages been reflected in literature written by women.

Female literary studies focused on specifically female themes, genres, even styles, but also on the origins and development of larger female traditions. The female focus of this search for a female literary tradition has greatly benefited literary studies in general. It has rediscovered forgotten female authors, has rehabilitated ignored ones, and has in its efforts to let women speak for themselves unearthed much writing of a personal nature, such as letters, travel journals, and diaries, that has contributed to a redefinition and expansion of the literary field. Feminism has expanded the canon, has rehabilitated such forgotten genres as that of the 'sentimental,' domestic novel, and has, within the larger literary tradition, constructed a dynamic canon of writing by women.

The rediscovery and rehabilitation of authors raises the question why they had disappeared from sight in the first place. What had eliminated these women writers from the race to lasting literary fame? At first sight the answer is obvious: reviewers and critics must have found their work lacking in quality, as not up to the standards required for admission to the literary pantheon. But that leads to further questions: what exactly were those standards, who had established them, and who were the people who put the work of these female writers to the test? There is an easy general answer to the last two questions: male critics and male reviewers. And so another issue suggests itself: what to make of the fact that historically both the originators of evaluative norms and those who have applied them have been overwhelmingly male? Could maleness have been a factor in literary judgements in general? Is it possible that the whole issue of literary value is in some way gendered? Couldn't for instance T.S. Eliot's preference for impersonality, for irony, and for a sort of stoic resignation be seen as typically masculine instead of as generally valid? Couldn't it be possible that the odds have been against female writing all along, not only with regard to opportunities for writing but also with regard to that writing's evaluation? And isn't the same anti-female bias present in academic circles? What we see here is that the focus has shifted from literature itself to what could be called the *institutional level*, the secondary – but powerful and influential – level at which reviewers, critics, and literary academics operate. Under the pressure of feminist scrutiny this institutional level has in the last twenty years been forced to recognize its masculinist prejudices and has for instance accepted forms of literary criticism in which the personal experience of the (female) critic is brought to bear upon a text in order to illuminate passages that might otherwise remain obscure.

For the defenders of impersonality in literary matters such practices are downright irresponsible – if not typically feminine, too. Feminism has been hard on the impersonalists. In their use of autobiographical material, female academics have followed a trend set earlier by female writers such as the American poets Sylvia Plath (1932–1963), Anne Sexton (1928–1974), and Adrienne Rich (1929–). Since the mid-1960s women writers, drawing on their personal experiences, have increasingly brought female sexuality, female anguish, childbirth, mothering, rape, and other specifically female themes into their work. Still, the feminist criticism and writing that I have so far discussed is in some ways fairly traditional, for instance in its view of the subject. In this (mostly American) feminist criticism of the 1970s and 1980s the female subject, like its male counterpart, is essentially free and autonomous. Once the social and cultural restraints on women have been lifted, women will be as autonomous and self-determining as men. Moreover, in its earlier stages this feminism assumes that it speaks for all women, regardless of culture, class, and race. This is undeniably more modest than liberal humanism's (male) assumption that it speaks for all of humankind, but it still ignores the often rather different experience of women who, unlike virtually all early feminists, are not white, heterosexual, and middle class. As early as 1977 the African–American critic Barbara Smith argued that black women writers were ignored by academic feminism ('Towards a Black Feminist Criticism'). A few years later we find the black poet and writer Audre Lorde noting that

> By and large within the women's movement today, white women focus upon their oppression as women and ignore differences of race, sexual preference, class, and age. There is a pretense to a homogeneity of experience covered by the words *sisterhood* that does not in fact exist.
>
> (Lorde [1984] 1998: 631)

In the wake of such publications and of bell hooks's acclaimed *Ain't I a Woman? Black Women and Feminism* ([1981] 1982) more and more groups of women – African–American women, Chicana women, lesbian women – began to assert an identity of their own and to create separate feminist literary traditions. Smith had in 1977 already taken that initiative with regard to black female writing, arguing that writers like Zora Neale Hurston, Alice Walker, and Toni Morrison presented black women who with their folk memories, their special skills (midwifery, for instance), and their intimacy with the natural world were clearly distinct from white women. As a result of these developments American feminism and the feminist literary studies that it had produced began to fragment along lines of ethnic and sexual identity, while its liberalist perspective also was submitted to severe critique.

## Marxist feminism

A similar fragmentation would ultimately destabilize a specifically British offshoot of feminism: Marxist feminism. From a Marxist perspective, history is dominated by a struggle between social classes that will only end when a truly classless society has been achieved. Given the fact that throughout history women have been collectively denied important rights, it was almost inevitable that a Marxist feminism would emerge that saw women as constituting a seriously underprivileged class. Moreover, many Marxist concepts, especially as these were redefined by Louis Althusser, seemed greatly relevant. In particular Althusser's definition of ideology and his concept of *interpellation*, which explains how ideology addresses us in a certain role and draws us into a conspiracy that is ultimately aimed at ourselves, proved useful for feminist literary studies and film studies. As we have seen, for Althusser we only experience ourselves as complete individuals ('concrete subjects') through the internalization of ideology. Ideology is inescapable because it is what actually gives us what we experience as our individuality. Althusserian feminism examines how literary texts, films, commercials, and so on 'hail and interpellate' their readers or their audience and 'position' them with regard to gender. Into what position does a text, a film, a rock video, or a commercial try to manoeuvre us through specific strategies of narration, specific shots, images, and other forms of representation? How do they persuade a female audience to accept a liberal humanist ideology that so clearly disadvantages them? However, Althusserian feminism is by no means the whole story. We also find a British Marxist feminism that, in Ruth Robbins's words,

> is interested in the material conditions of real people's lives, how conditions such as poverty and undereducation produce different signifying systems than works produced and read in conditions of privilege and educational plenty. This kind of approach is likely to be most interested in the content of a literary text as symptomatic of the conditions of its production.
>
> (Robbins 2000: 13)

However, after its heyday in the early 1980s, Marxist feminism, too, was increasingly charged with being insensitive to *difference*, and came to be seen as the product of a white academic elite (with its standard middle-class background) and as unacceptably neglectful of the specific social problems – and the way these had been given literary expression – of women who did not belong to the white heterosexual middle class. Black Marxist feminists, for instance, were quick to point out that black female writers had to cope not only with biases based on gender, but also with an equally crippling racial bias and that an approach that failed to take race into account would never be able to do justice to the work of black female writers.

Like virtually everything else in literary and cultural studies, feminism and feminist criticism have undergone the impact of *difference*, of the enormous attention that in the course of the last twenty years has been given to the ways we are different from each other. Paradoxically, this has happened in a world that in the same period has become vastly more homogeneous, especially in the West where the idea of difference has come to play such a prominent role. We have now all been brought within the capitalist orbit, so that politics all over the Western world looks more or less the same – and we have all become part of an international, English-speaking, mass culture. But maybe that is exactly why difference is so appealing.

## The politics of race

The third political instrument of analysis that we must look at is that of race. Until the twentieth century, the literatures written in the various Western languages were overwhelmingly the product of white writers, male and female. That picture begins to change in the period between the two world wars. In the 1920s African–American writing, flowering in the so-called 'Harlem Renaissance', becomes almost overnight a permanent force within the field of American literature, and in 1930s and 1940s writers hailing from France's African and Caribbean colonies become a presence on the French literary scene. With the emergence of a black literary presence race enters the agenda of literary studies. In one sense it also enters literature itself, in that it is now presented from the perspective of non-white writers. Racial discrimination is a recurrent theme in African–American writing, from the fiction and poetry of the Harlem Renaissance, via Ralph Ellison's *Invisible Man* (1952) whose theme is that racial prejudice makes blacks invisible as individuals, to the novels of the Nobel Prize-winning (1993) Toni Morrison. In another sense, however, race was not a new theme at all but had been there all along. As we will see in a later chapter, that on postcolonial studies, race seen through the eyes of Western writers had always been part of Western literature but its presence had gone largely unnoticed, at least by Western readers. It is, for instance, not until the Nigerian novelist Chinua Achebe drew attention to the pervasive racism in the representations of Africans in Joseph Conrad's celebrated *Heart of Darkness* – see his essay 'An Image of Africa' (1977) – that Western critics were alerted to the novel's at the very least questionable attitude towards Africa and its inhabitants.

With the idea of *négritude* – which might be translated as 'negro-ness' – French-speaking black writers like Aimé Césaire (originally from Martinique) and especially Léopold Senghor (from Senegal) in the 1940s and 1950s introduced and developed the idea that literature written by Africans was not merely thematically different from Western literature (in its emphasis on race), but that it was *intrinsically* different because Africans, no matter where they lived, were different from whites. Negritude has been variously defined – at one point Senghor equates it with 'feeling', for instance, and at another he sees it in terms of a reverent attitude towards life and a desire to find harmony in an integration with the cosmos – and has been severely criticized both by African and by African–American writers. But the Harlem Renaissance and the development of negritude mark the beginnings of African–American and African or, as the case may be, Caribbean self-definition in the face of a Western racism and of a Western system of colonial oppression that had denied (and continued to deny) substance and validity to non-white cultures and cultural expressions, all of which were considered far inferior to the great achievements of Western culture. Inevitably, that process of self-definition involves a critique of Western representations of Africans and African–Americans, representations that usually repeat the stereotypes that have for instance legitimized colonization (in the essay I have just mentioned Achebe shows how Conrad, or, to be more precise, Conrad's narrator Marlowe, presents the Congo, where *Heart of Darkness* is mostly situated, as a primitive place that lags almost 2,000 years behind Europe). That self-definition and the critique of Western representations stand at the beginning of the interrogation and contestation of

Europe's colonial enterprise and its legacy that is now called postcolonial studies, a relatively new field of literary, cultural, and political enquiry that will be discussed in a later chapter.

The mordant critique of colonialism that we find in the negritude movement – in his *Discourse on Colonialism* we find Césaire stating that Hitler already spoke through those who defended colonial oppression and exploitation (Césaire [1955] 1997: 79) – found a highly articulate and influential supporter in Frantz Fanon (1925–1961), a psychiatrist from Martinique who became involved in the Algerian resistance to French colonialism. Fanon merits attention here not only because he called attention to the debilitating psychological effects of colonialism upon the colonized, which is a major theme in postcolonial studies, but also because in *The Wretched of the Earth* (originally published in French in 1961) he outlines a theory of what we might call colonial literature – that is, the literature of the colonized. In so doing, he distances himself from negritude. The idea that all blacks would have essential features in common, for him mirrors the homogenization that blacks have always suffered at the hands of white culture: 'The Negroes of Chicago only resemble the Nigerians or the Tanganyikans in so far as they were all defined in relation to the whites' (Fanon [1961] 1965: 97). Instead of a homogeneous negritude, he stresses the importance of national culture for 'the native intellectual'. Fanon distinguishes three phrases in the cultural – including the literary – relations between colonized and colonizer. In the first phase the native intellectual takes pride in demonstrating that 'he has assimilated' – that is, mastered – 'the culture of the occupying power'. In the second phase, 'the native is disturbed; he decides to remember what he is' (101). He goes back to his own people, immerses himself in the native culture, and the 'rhyming poetry' of the first phase gives way to 'the poetic tom-tom's rhythms' (103). In the third phase, the 'fighting phase', the intellectual and the writer will break out of this immersion and turn into 'an awakener of the people' and will produce a 'fighting literature, a revolutionary literature, and a national literature' (102). For Fanon, writing in 1961, that is when much of Africa was still under colonial rule, national cultures and literatures play a crucial role in the process of liberation. The poststructuralist theorizing which emerges in the 1970s and the postcolonial theory which then follows in the 1980s take a rather dim view of the idea of 'nation', of the so-called nation-state, which they primarily see in terms of oppression. In the historical context in which he is writing, however, the sort of revolutionary nation-alism and the corresponding national culture that Fanon has in mind seem almost inevitable, if only for the 'psycho-affective equilibrium' of the colonized.

Fanon's view of the differentiation of African writing – which is united only in its desire to resist colonialism – has set the tone for later theories of African, Caribbean, and African–American writing. Abandoning the idea of a Pan-African cultural identity that we can find among all African peoples and among the African communities in the Americas, critics have emphasized the specific identity of all the various literatures that black writers have created. The Caribbean mixture of languages and populations has for instance led a number of Caribbean writers to try and theorize Caribbean literature in terms of cross-cultural exchanges. Writers such as the Guyanese novelist Wilson Harris and the Barbadian poet Edward Brathwaite have argued that the literature of the region must be seen as the product of interlocking cultural traditions, of 'creolization' as Brathwaite called it in his 1974 *Contradictory Omens: Cultural Diversity and Integration in the Caribbean*, a study in which he argued that various black and white cultures, and, to a lesser extent, Indian and Chinese cultures have in a continuous process of exchange created a Caribbean identity and culture. (This emphasis on exchange and mutual influencing has in the later 1980s and 1990s become a major theme in postcolonial studies.) More recently, Brathwaite has in his concept of a 'nation language' come to emphasize the more exclusively black roots of Caribbean literature in English, tracing it to the languages and the African cultures that the slaves brought with them:

> Nation language is the language which is influenced very strongly by the African model, the African aspect of our New World/Caribbean heritage. English it may be in terms of

some of its lexical features. But in its contours, its rhythms and timbre, its sound explosions, it is not English, even though the words, as you hear them, might be English to a greater or lesser degree.

(Brathwaite [1984] 1995: 311)

## African–American literary studies

The development of African–American criticism, which emerged after the mid-1960s when black studies entered the university curriculum and when the so-called Black Arts movement got underway, runs to some extent parallel to that of feminist literary criticism. A major objective was to rediscover and rehabilitate forgotten African–American writers – that is, to have them recognized as serious contributors to the American literary heritage. A second objective was to establish a specifically African–American literary tradition, a tradition that formally distinguished itself from white American writing. The recovery and promotion of forgotten or neglected writers has been successful: all anthologies of American literature now present a good many African–American writers that were absent from their pre-1980s editions. The search for a specific African–American has led to perhaps less definitive results. Although we do now indeed speak of an African–American literary tradition, the question of how this tradition hangs together is still debated. What many African–American texts have in common is the overriding theme of racial discrimination, but it is less easy to say what they have in common in terms of form rather than theme.

In the 1960s the Black Arts movement, in the spirit of *négritude*, posited a 'Black aesthetic' that expressed a Pan-African, organic and whole sensibility. Led by important writers such as the poet and playwright Amiri Baraka, it focused, however, on creative and political writing and on political intervention through theatrical and other performances. Around the mid-1970s, African–American literary academics began to turn to form, paradoxically in a period when – as we will see in the next chapter – the interest in form, in structuralist form as well as the form-cum-meaning of the New Critics, was fast disappearing. Following the inner, historical logic of black studies rather than the change of the times, they sought the 'Blackness' of African–American literature in its specific strategies and use of language. (The idea that African–American literature could be formally distinct from white American literature is of course not so implausible: if we look at the American music scene we immediately recognize musical forms and genres that are distinctly African–American or that derive from African–American sources.) In the course of the 1980s African–American critics assimilated the poststructuralist views that I will discuss in the next chapter and continued their search for a 'Black aesthetic' from a perspective that assumes that whatever African–American texts have in common, there is no such thing as an essential, innate 'Blackness' in their authors. In other words, if African–American literature is 'different' it is not different because African–Americans are essentially different from other Americans but because it has a different origin and has developed under specific historical and cultural circumstances which might have been otherwise. Working on this assumption, a number of critics, the most prominent of whom is Henry Louis Gates, Jr, have begun, in Gates's words, 'to chart the patterns of repetition and revision among texts by black authors'. Gates continues:

> In *Notes of a Native Son*, Baldwin described his own obsession with 'race' in his fiction: 'I have not written about being a Negro at such length because I expect that to be my only subject, but only because it was the gate I had to unlock before I could hope to write about anything else.' Accordingly, many black authors read and revise one another, address similar themes, and repeat the cultural and linguistic codes of a common symbolic geographic. For these reasons, we can think of them as forming literary traditions.
>
> (Gates 1992: 30)

This approach, which combines thematic and formal interests, has in the hands of Gates led to intriguing results. Central to African–American writing is this practice of repetition and revision that he mentions in the passage that I have just quoted, and that he calls 'signifyin(g)', a term which refers to the trickster figure of the 'signifying monkey' of African–American – and more generally African – folktales. A 'black text echoes, mirrors, repeats, revives, or responds to in various formal ways' a textual world of other black texts. 'Signifiyin(g)' is 'this process of intertextual relation … the troped revision, of repetition and difference' (Gates 1987: 2). In the black vernacular tradition 'signifying' has a whole range of meanings related to the trickster aspect of the signifyin' monkey. In African–American culture in general, Gates tells us, 'black rhetorical tropes, subsumed under signifying, would include marking, loud-talking, testifying, calling out (of one's name), sounding, rapping, playing the dozens, and so on' (Gates [1989] 1998: 904). 'The dozens' – a form of verbal duelling, that is an ultimately affectionate exchange of ingenious insults – illustrates Gates's argument that '[t]he Afro-American rhetorical strategy of signifying is a rhetorical act that is not engaged in the game of information giving' (905). Tracing this particular practice to the oral roots of African and African–American literature – in which verbal skills were of course paramount – Gates sees in the 'dozens' one of the elements that are reworked time and again by black writers, just like black musicians borrow riffs from each other and from earlier generations of musicians and rework them. The example of 'the dozens' and the trickster connotation of signifying should not create the impression that we find the practice of signifying only in contexts that are ultimately not very serious. The poet T. Tenton Fortune's poem 'The Black Man's Burden', which for Gates 'signif[ies] … upon Kipling's "White Man's Burden"' (908) – the white race's 'duty' to bring 'civilization' to other peoples through colonial rule – sufficiently demonstrates the seriousness of signifying: 'What is the Black Man's Burden / Ye Gentile parasites / Who crush and rob your brother / Of his manhood and his rights?' (For a book-length discussion of 'signifyin[g]' practices see Gates 1988).

Linked up with the idea that there is no such thing as an innate 'Blackness', but that the distinctiveness of African–American culture is the product of special historical circumstances, we find another major line of enquiry for African–American criticism: what we might call the *construction* of blackness, the ways in which the dominant white culture and its literary products have over the ages *constructed* black males and females as different from their white counterparts. Just like women had to live up to the feminine gender roles created by a male-dominated society, black males and females were confronted with the cultural demands implied by the constructions of black maleness and black femaleness that white society imposed upon them. By means of these constructions, white society practically forced black males and females to live up to the stereotypes that it had itself created. In order to acquire insight into the nature of these highly discriminatory social constructs, African–American criticism analysed representations of black characters – and of blackness in general – in 'white' literature (or in Jewish–American literature, as in Bernard Malamud's *The Tenants* of 1971, in a which a Jewish and an African–American writer entertain a volatile relationship in a condemned and otherwise deserted New York tenement).

Like the more traditional forms of feminist criticism, until the 1980s African–American criticism worked with a view of the subject that was not really different from that of the white, liberal humanist, majority. Although far more sensitive to social constraints – and particularly those of race and class – than the average white critic, black critics, too, saw the subject – black or white – as essentially free and as an autonomous moral agent, able to transcend the limitations imposed by time, place, and colour. Marxist critics once again were the exception. From a Marxist perspective, the relations between the white majority and the black minority could be rewritten in terms of class relations, with the black minority kept subservient by ideology. In a brief discussion of Alice Walker's *The Color Purple*, bell hooks, whom I have already mentioned above, argues that the novel's heroine, who ends as a successful entrepreneur, stays within an individualist, capitalist framework and is therefore not fully liberated: 'Breaking free from the patriarchal prison that is her "home" when the novel begins, she creates her own household, yet radical politics of collective struggle against racism or sexism do not inform her struggle for self-actualization' (hooks [1992] 1997: 222). Like feminism, African–American criticism was strongly affected by the emphasis on difference that emerged in the course of the 1980s. African–American feminists increasingly saw it as male dominated and focused on specifically male issues. Moreover, with the publication of the Palestinian–American Edward Said's *Orientalism*, in 1978, the study of race in relation to literature and culture widened enormously. Said's book focuses on the way the West has over the past two centuries represented the Orient and Orientals, not only in its literature, but also in countless other texts, including colonial documents, histories, travel books, official reports, and so on. Its breadth had the effect of putting the literary and cultural relations between the African–American minority and the white majority within the much wider framework of the relations between the West in general and the great number of non-Western peoples with which the West has dealt in one way or another. With this general reorientation the representation of African–Americans in American literary texts became an instance of Western representations of what increasingly came to be called the 'other' – a general term for non-Western subjects that will be more precisely examined later in this book. As a result, African–American literary theory began to dovetail with the much wider critical and theoretical project called postcolonial studies, which from a number of angles interrogates the relations between the West and pretty much the rest of the world in the light of the history of Western expansion and military and economic domination. The range and depth of postcolonial studies, however, demands separate treatment, after we have looked at the poststructuralism that set it on its way.

## Summary

Literary texts always have a political dimension in the sense that on closer inspection they can be shown to take specific stances with regard to social issues, either through what they say or through what they do *not* say – through the elision of certain themes or topics. Marxist critics are especially interested in issues of class and social exploitation and are specifically attentive to the cultural mechanisms – and their literary versions – that keep people unaware of their exploited status. Literary feminism has called our attention to the pervasive male bias that we find throughout Western history. It has rediscovered forgotten or marginalized female writers and established a history of writing by women; it has expanded the literary field by including the sort of personal writing that we find in letters, in diaries, and journals in its interests; and it has shown how writing by women is thematically marked by the historically difficult position of female authors. A third important political category, on a par with class and gender, is that of race. African, Caribbean, and African–American authors and critics have demonstrated the pervasive presence of racial prejudice in Western writing. Like feminism, African–American criticism has rediscovered forgotten or marginalized black writing. It has sought to establish a specially black tradition in writing that is not only thematically, but also in its recurring tropes different from writing by white Americans. African–American feminists have shown how writing by black women can again be distinguished from that of their male colleagues.

## Suggestions for further reading

### Marxist criticism

A good starting-point is Moyra Haslett's *Marxist Literary and Cultural Theory* (1999), which offers an overview of the field.

Terry Eagleton's *Marxism and Literary Criticism* (1976a) is a good and brief introduction to the work of major twentieth-century Marxist literary theorists. Raymond Williams's *Marxism and Literature* (1977) shows us a very influential Marxist critic in action. Arguing that we must see literature in 'material' terms, Williams elucidates not only the basic Marxist notions, but also Gramsci's 'hegemony' and his own notion of 'structures of feeling'. In *Marxism and Literary History* (1986) John Frow examines the literary criticism of Pierre Macherey, Terry Eagleton, Fredric Jameson, and others. Eagleton's *Ideology: An Introduction* (1991) takes us through the 'ideology' debate from a Marxist perspective. One of the major contributions to that debate, Louis Althusser's 'Ideology and Ideological State Apparatuses' (originally in *Lenin and Philosophy and Other Essays*, 1971) is in spite of its forbidding title quite accessible and has been widely reprinted, most recently in Rivkin and Ryna (1998). Pierre Macherey's *A Theory of Literary Production* (1978) is a very accessible application of Althusserian theory. An interesting and eminently readable example of the application of the notion of ideology to a specific literary genre is Stephen Knight's *Form and Ideology in Detective Fiction* (1980) which reads classics like Agatha Christie and Raymond Chandler as representatives of liberal humanist ideology.

## Feminist criticism

Ruth Robbins's *Literary Feminisms* (2000) offers a good and lucid overview while Robyn R. Warhol and Diane Price Herndl's *Feminisms: An Anthology of Literary Theory and Criticism* (1991) and Maggie Humm's *Feminisms: A Reader* (1992) between the two of them collect a wealth of theoretical and critical material, with Warhol and Herndl focusing in particular on American contributions. Another stimulating collection is Isobel Armstrong's *New Feminist Discourses: Critical Essays on Theories and Texts* (1992), in which a number of prominent feminist critics discuss theory within the framework of actual readings of specific texts. Elaine Showalter's collection *The New Feminist Criticism* (1985) contains some classic older essays.

*Feminist Readings, Feminists Reading* (1989), edited by Sara Mills *et al.*, offers a number of different feminist approaches to Charlotte Brontë's *Jane Eyre*, Alice Walker's *The Color Purple*, and other popular texts. Sandra Gilbert and Susan Gubar's *The Madwoman in the Attic* (1979) is still provocative in its readings of the nineteenth-century classics it considers. In *Practising Feminist Criticism: An Introduction* (1995) Maggie Humm offers very accessible readings of a wide range of texts combining a feminist perspective with a second one (psychoanalytic, Marxist, poststructuralist, lesbian, and so on). Marleen S. Barr's *Alien to Femininity: Speculative Fiction and Feminist Theory* (1987) looks at science fiction writing from a feminist perspective, while Sally R. Munt's *Murder by the Book? Feminism and the Crime Novel* (1994) offers a leftist/feminist critique of recent female crime writing.

The seminal text of black feminist criticism is Barbara Smith's 'Towards a Black Feminist Criticism' (1977). Barbara Christian's *Black Feminist Criticism: Perspectives on Black Women Writers* (1985), Hazel Carby's *Reconstructing Womanhood: The Emergence of the Afro-American Woman Novelist* (1987), Susan Willis's Marxist *Specifying: Black Women Writing the American Experience* of the same year, and Mary Helen Washington's collection *Invented Lives: Narratives of Black Women (1860–1960)*, again of 1987, illustrate the emergence of a forceful black feminism in the mid-1980s. Cheryl Wall's *Changing Our Own Words* (1989) and Henry Louis Gates's *Reading Black, Reading Feminist* (1990) are good and very useful collections of black feminist criticism. Nobel Prize-winning Toni Morrison's *Playing in the Dark: Whiteness and the Literary Imagination* (1992) is a fierce attack on racism in literature. For a more general black feminism, see the work of bell hooks (*Ain't I a Woman? Black Women and Feminism* (1982), *Black Looks: Race and Representation* (1992)), Audre Lorde's *Sister Outsider: Essays and Speeches* (1984), and Patricia Hill Collins's recently revised *Black Feminist Thought: Knowledge, Consciousness and the Politics of Empowerment*, 2nd edn (2000).

## *African–American criticism*

Houston A. Baker, Jr's *Long Black Song: Essays in Black-American Literature and Culture* (1972) collects early but still worthwhile essays in a then developing field. Robert Stepto's *From Behind the Veil* (1979, revised in 1991) is a classic of African–American criticism, dealing with black literature from slave narratives to Ralph Ellison's *Invisible Man* (1952). *Blues, Ideology, and Afro-American Literature: A Vernacular Theory* (1984) by Houston A. Baker, Jr sees the black literary tradition as shaped by the conditions of slavery and in interaction with the blues. Henry Louis Gates, Jr's *Figures in Black: Words, Signs and the 'Racial' Self* (1987) and his *The Signifying Monkey* (1988) together constitute what is probably the most successful effort to theorize a specific African–American writing tradition. A fascinating discussion of the 'invention of Africa' as a homogeneous cultural entity, of the 'illusion' of race, and of a good many other highly relevant issues, is presented by Kwame Anthony Appiah's *In My Father's House: Africa in the Philosophy of Culture* (1992).

# Chapter 5

# The poststructuralist revolution

*Derrida, deconstruction, and postmodernism*

## Introduction

I have already suggested that the late 1960s and early 1970s can be seen a sort of watershed in English and American criticism, and I have in the previous chapter more than once said that the political criticism that I discussed there is rather 'traditional' in comparison with later develop- ments – not only within the field of politically oriented literary studies, but within literary studies in general. How can the Marxist criticism, the feminist criticism, and the race-oriented criticism that I discussed be 'traditional' when to so many literary academics they seemed dangerously radical? There is no doubt that within the context of the 1970s they were radical. However, they also, each in their own way, continued certain traditions. Non-Marxist feminism and black criticism basi- cally work with a liberal humanist view of the individual: the subject is ultimately free, self-deter- mined rather than other-determined (by social background – class – economic position, and so

**117**

on). This liberal humanist form of feminist and black criticism is of course extremely sensitive to the various ways in which women and blacks – both men and women – have over the ages been limited in their options (to say the least) because of discriminatory social forces. However, it believes that ultimately the subject is a free moral agent. It also believes that the 'best' that these subjects have thought and said over time is of timeless significance. Marxist criticism and the Marxist version of feminist and black criticism deny that such autonomous individuals exist. We have seen how in Althusser's explanation of the workings of ideology 'the subject acts insofar as he is acted by the ... system'. Just as in structuralist anthropology, Althusser's subjects genuinely believe that they perform an action because they choose to do so while in reality a pre-existing structure acts through them. Marxist criticism also has its fundamental assumptions. It assumes, for instance, that the Marxist analysis of history as a struggle of social classes for domination and that Marxist concepts such as alienation and ideology essentially reflect the world as it is and has been. Although their assumptions are completely at odds with each other, both liberal humanism and Marxism are convinced that, intellectually, they have solid ground under their feet. Both think not only that their view of reality is correct, but also, and more fundamentally, that it is possible to *have* an accurate and true view of reality.

Strange as it may seem, the idea that it is possible to have a true view of the world is now 'traditional' within literary studies. Although this does not necessarily mean that it is wrong, it is for many critics and theorists working today an untenable proposition. For them the idea that it is truly possible to *know* the world is theoretically unfounded. That idea, which is called *essentialism* because it claims that we can know the *essence* of things, is the main target of the *poststructuralist* thinkers that I will discuss in this chapter and in the next one. As I have just said, to many critics writing today the poststructuralist arguments against essentialism seem convincing. But certainly not to all of them. On the contemporary critical scene we still find liberal humanist criticism, both in its New Critical or Leavisite form and its feminist or African–American form, and we still find 'traditional' forms of Marxist criticism. We also find a good many critics who are willing to accept that absolutely true knowledge of the world is out of reach, but who in spite of that keep on working with traditional assumptions. Accepting that their assumptions no longer have the status they used to have, they present them as a programme, or even only as a point of departure, as a perspective that will still say useful and illuminating things about literary texts. All the time, they are fully aware that that perspective is questionable and is not the last word. In his 1989 article 'Marxism and Postmodernism', for instance, the American Marxist Fredric Jameson suggests that we should see Marxism's 'base and superstructure' no longer as a model – that is, a true representation of the world – but as 'undogmatic', as 'a starting point and a problem' (Jameson 1989: 41–42). Since the arrival of poststructuralism in the late 1960s and early 1970s, literary studies has become enormously varied. The contemporary literary-critical world is a fascinating mixture of the old, the new, and the old in new guises (which does not imply a negative judgement). But let us now turn to the poststructuralism that had such an enormous impact on the way we study literature.

## Poststructuralism: the Cretan paradox and its Albany solution

Poststructuralism is a continuation and simultaneous rejection of structuralism – not only literary structuralism but even more so the anthropological structuralism of Lévi-Strauss. In fact, in France, where it originates, poststructuralism is generally subsumed under structuralism. Since poststructuralism accepts some of the major claims of structuralism, and since it has its origins in the second half of the 1960s, when literary structuralism is still developing, it does indeed make sense to see them as two forks of one and the same broadly anti-humanist and linguistically oriented river. However, for the purposes of this book I will work with the usual labels. I will first discuss the poststructuralism of the French philosopher Jacques Derrida (1930), or *deconstruction*, as it is often called, because it was the first version of poststructuralism to reach the United States.

Spreading from there, it had an enormous impact on English and American literary studies in general. I will then look at the various poststructuralist positions for which deconstruction paved the way in the English-speaking world, even if they do not always derive directly from Derrida's writings. By the late 1970s other poststructuralist thinkers, notably the French historian Michel Foucault (1926–1984), had caught the attention of literary academics. In the chapters that follow the discussion of poststructuralism I will look at the major approaches to literature that have been made possible by poststructuralism and that currently still dominate literary studies.

Poststructuralism is unthinkable without structuralism. As I have already suggested, it continues structuralism's strongly anti-humanist perspective and it closely follows structuralism in its belief that language is the key to our understanding of ourselves and the world. Still, although it continues its anti-humanism and its focus on language, poststructuralism simultaneously undermines structuralism by thoroughly questioning – 'deconstructing' – some of its major assumptions and the methods that derive from those assumptions.

Poststructuralism continues structuralism's preoccupation with language. But its view of language is wholly different from the structuralist view. In fact, language is at the heart of the differences between structuralism and poststructuralism. As we have seen, structuralism applied originally linguistic insights to culture in general and literary structuralism applied them to literary texts. The idea of an underlying structure and the principle of differentiality could apparently be successfully transferred from the field of language studies to the study of a wide range of human activities – perhaps even all human activities, at least as far as the specific form they take is concerned. We clearly do not need structuralism to explain *why* we eat, but it may be very informative on the various *forms* that eating and everything related to it take in the astonishing number of cultures that have developed over time. If we take a closer look, we usually see the principle that meaning (and thus value) is bound up with difference at work.

Structuralism, then, takes language very seriously. But it also takes language very much for granted. It knows that there is no natural link between a word and that which it refers to – that, in other words, the relationship between language and the world that language describes is always arbitrary. It does, however, not really examine the possible consequences of that gap between language and the world. That is on the one hand not so strange. We all know, to repeat what I have said earlier in the chapter on structuralism, that other languages use other words to refer to, say, a house, a tree, a dog. Rather amazingly, that does not appear to undermine our confidence in our own language. We never ask ourselves if 'chien' or 'Hund' – the French and German words for 'dog' – could possibly be more appropriate to what they refer to than 'dog'. We might ask ourselves whether French wine or German beer is better than what is produced in our own country, or whether their cars are more elegant or solid, but we never consider the possibility that the language of the French or the Germans might fit the world better than ours. Our own language is so natural to us that it almost never occurs to us that maybe our confidence in language is misplaced.

On the other hand, we have for a long time been aware that language can be extremely slippery. Think of famous classical paradoxes such as the paradox of the Cretan who says that all Cretans always lie. If all Cretans always lie, then the Cretan's statement is true – but he himself simultaneously proves it untrue, because although he is a Cretan he has at least for once not lied. It is of course possible to disentangle the various threads that go into the making of paradoxes. Here the problem is that it is a Cretan who makes the statement. With a speaker from Albany, New York, the claim would simply be true or false. The problem only arises because the speaker is a member of the group – the category – that his statement refers to, so that he himself is included in whatever claim he makes. Still, language can apparently lead us into strange impasses. Paradoxes such as the Cretan paradox show us that what we need for at least one kind of statement is an outside perspective, an outside point of reference: a person from Albany, New York, so to speak. So if we want to say something about language we ideally want a perspective outside language to say it. With language, however, there is no outside perspective. We can only speak about language with the use of language. No matter what we say, we are always inside.

This is not only true of language, it is also true of the larger cultural structures the structuralists tried to unravel. If we assume that the structures of language and culture speak through us, rather than the other way around, then we are always inside those structures. But then we run into a potentially serious problem. If, like the structuralists, we want to say things about those structures, we find ourselves in a position that is similar to that of the Cretan who makes a claim about all Cretans, himself included: we are inside the structures that are the subjects of our statements. The structuralists never address this problem, operating as if they themselves are never part of structures, as if there is a position outside language and other structures – in short, as if they are from Albany, New York, rather than from Crete.

## The illusion of presence

The fact that we can never step outside language in order to speak about it is, at least at the theoretical level, a problem. There is, however, another problem with language that is potentially even more serious. As I have just pointed out, whatever language we have learned to speak in our infant years always seems totally natural to us and always seems to fit the world we live in. But what *is* this 'naturalness'? Or rather, how is it possible that we *experience* as completely natural what we *know* to be arbitrary: the link between language and reality? Why doesn't that arbitrariness permanently bother us? The answer is pretty simple: the arbitrariness does not bother us, because we see language as only an instrument, as something that makes it possible for us to do something, to express ourselves. Just as it does not really matter whether we write with a pencil, a felt tip, or an old-fashioned fountain pen, or which colour ink we use, the language we use does not really matter, because we only use it to express something that is *prior* to language: something that exists in our minds before we resort to language to give it shape in words. We know beforehand what we want to say and then choose the words we want to say it with. This is the basis of the confidence we feel in language: the certainty that we know what we know, that we are in direct, immediate touch with ourselves, and can then put into words what we know and feel. We know what is, so to say, *present* to us and therefore undeniably true.

Why this emphasis on being in direct, immediate touch with ourselves? Imagine you are standing at a street corner, waiting for the lights to change, and somebody comes up from behind and knocks you out. You regain consciousness in a totally dark and apparently soundproof room. You have no idea what has happened and where you are. You cannot be sure of anything. The room may not even be dark because for all you know you may have been blinded. So what *do* you know? The only thing you really know for sure is that you are scared to death and angry. You know these things for sure because they are *present* to you. Presence, then, is the basis of the last pieces of true knowledge that you have and language allows you to convey that knowledge to the outside world. This (according to him misguided) trust in the combination of presence and language is what the French philosopher Jacques Derrida has called *logocentrism*.

Our trust in language is based upon what happens – or what we think happens – when we ourselves actually use it. It is manifestly not based on hearing others speak: we know from experience that hearing them does not necessarily bring us in touch with *their* authentic situation – they may be lying, for instance, or may not be able to explain what they really want to say. And our trust is certainly not based on writing: writing may be as unreliable as speech, and as unintelligible, and it does not even offer us the opportunity of finding out the truth if we fail to see it. When people are talking to us, we can interrupt them and ask questions if we don't understand what they are saying and we can watch them closely for tell-tale signs if we suspect that they are lying. Although we can never be finally sure that we have access to what they really think – the authentic truth behind the words they use – we have a better chance than we have with writing to get to the bottom of things.

## In defence of absence

The Western philosophical tradition and more popular Western thought have always put more faith in the spoken than in the written word. But is the spoken word reliable? To get to the heart of the matter: are the words that we ourselves speak reliable? 'No', says Derrida, from whose writings the essence of what I have just said is derived. Let me summarize his main arguments. First of all, Derrida tells us, language is inherently unreliable. As we have seen, language operates on the basis of differentiation. What enables words to refer to whatever they refer to is their difference from other words, not a direct link to their so-called referents. However, those words function within a linguistic system (a language) that never touches the real world. There is no single word that is the way it is because it cannot be another way, because its shape is wholly determined by its referent (not even almost instinctive 'words', such as exclamations of pain; these, too, differ from language to language). If we would have such a word, that word would then be wholly subservient to reality and would constitute an absolute fixed and 'true' element within the linguistic system, so that we might then possibly build more and more words around it and in that way anchor language firmly in the real world. Reality would then determine the shape of our language. As it is, however, we have to work with meanings that are produced with the help of 'difference' and do not directly derive from the world they refer to. In language we find only differences without positive terms, as Saussure put it. As a result, Derrida claims, words are never stable and fixed in time.

First of all, because the meaning we see in words is the product of difference, that meaning is always contaminated. Think of a traffic light: we all know the 'meaning' of red, amber, or green. But it never occurs to us that those meanings are not 'pure'. When we see red we do not consciously think of amber and green, but one might argue that amber and green are in a sense present in red. Together, the three constitute a differential structure and it is the structure – including amber and green – that gives red its meaning. After all, in other contexts, red may have a completely different meaning. The red of red roses has for centuries stood for love, and most certainly not for 'stop'. The red of traffic lights, then, carries the 'traces' of amber and green within it, and is not pure, unadulterated red. Derrida argues that the same holds for words: every single word contains traces of other words – theoretically of all the other words in the language system:

> the signified concept is never present in and of itself, in a sufficient presence that would refer only to itself. Essentially and lawfully, every concept is inscribed in a chain or in a system within which it refers to the other, to other concepts.
>
> (Derrida [1982] 1996: 30)

Moreover, since words are not determined by their relationship with what they refer to, they are always subject to change. You might say, Derrida tells us, that the process that gives them meaning never ends. Words never achieve stability, not only because they are related to, and take part of their meaning from, the words that have just preceded them, but also because their meaning is always modified by whatever follows. The word that is next to the word we are looking at, or a word later in the same sentence, or even paragraph, will subtly change its meaning. Meaning, then, is the product of difference and it is also always subject to a process of deferral. In fact, a word's – or sign's – relations to other words and to words that will follow are a *condition* for meaning – without those relations meaning would not be possible. As Derrida puts it:

> the movement of signification is possible only if each so-called 'present' element, each element appearing on the scene of presence, is related to something other than itself, thereby keeping within itself the mark of the past element, and already letting itself be vitiated by the mark of its relation to the future element, this trace being related no less to what is called the future than to what is called the past, and constituting what is called the present by means of this very relation to what it is not.
>
> (32)

The 'present' of a word we speak is therefore not the *true* present, which forever eludes language: 'spacing' and 'temporization' intervene. Derrida captures this in a self-coined term, *différance*, that contains both the idea of difference and the process of deferral of meaning. In the terms used earlier in the chapter on structuralism, Derrida destabilizes the relationship between *signifier* and *signified*. The *signifier* – the word we hear or read – is of course stable enough, but what it signifies – the *signified* – is according to Derrida subject to an inherent instability. We all know that this instability exists at another level: the meaning of words may change over time, for instance, and phrases that once contained vivid metaphors may now have lost their metaphorical edge – who thinks of an actual crack in the phrase 'at the crack of dawn'? (Deconstructionists love to reactivate older meanings and to resurrect dead metaphors in order to destabilize a text.) From Derrida's perspective, then, language never offers us direct contact with reality; it is not a transparent medium, a window on the world. On the contrary, it always inserts itself between us and the world – like a smudgy screen or a distorting lens.

This sets up a confrontation between the authentic 'truth' we want to express – that what we really feel we know – and the slippery medium that we must use to express it. That is, if that authentic truth is really there. That truth is of course what structuralism had already rejected. To recapitulate its argument briefly: we are always part of a structure; to be more precise, we figure in a number of overlapping structures. We inevitably articulate, through whatever we do or say, the structures we are part of. And since the structures were there before we appeared on the scene, it is more appropriate to say that the structures speak through us than that we say or do things that have their origin within us. Derrida has as little use for that authentic knowledge inside us as the structuralists. Although he rejects the structures that according to the structuralists speak through us (a point I will come back to in a moment), like the structuralists he rejects the idea of 'presence', or 'voice' (the voice of a speaker in touch with his or her authentic being). For Derrida, too, we do not directly express what is authentically present to us, what we genuinely know at the moment of saying it. We must make use of a language that simultaneously uses us: that speaks through us. As he tells us in his *De la Grammatologie* of 1967 (translated as *Of Grammatology*, 1976), we can only make use of language by allowing the system to control us in a certain way and to a certain extent. Derrida does not rule out psychological intentions, as the most radically anti-humanist structuralists do. But in comparison with structuralism we may still be worse off. From a structuralist perspective we may at least know what we are saying. Because we articulate the structures that speak through us what we say does not originate in us, but it is stable and, in principle, also knowable. With poststructuralism we lose that cold comfort. In the absence of presence (a phrase that should now make sense), all that is left is a language that is subject to *différance*. Whatever our intentions, they are never fully transparent to ourselves because there is nothing that can escape language. As Derrida puts it, 'il n'y a de hors-texte' – there is nothing that is 'outside-text' – because for the human species everything is always mediated by language (Derrida [1967] 1976: 158).

Now that its fundamental difference with writing has disappeared (that is, the 'presence' and the 'voice' of the authentic individual that we believe we hear in speaking), speaking turns out to be a form of writing ('writing' in the sense of the Western philosophic tradition: as a basically untrustworthy form of language). In speaking, too, true meaning is always deferred. Even if we did have an authentic self that knows things prior to and outside language, we would become the victims of language's inherent unreliability as soon as we started to speak. We could never fully control the meaning of what we say. If what I say contains meanings that I am not even aware of because they have been generated by *différance* rather than by me, I could not even claim authorship if what I had intended to say was wholly authentic and original. The independent 'play' of language that no one can stop is the origin of a surplus meaning that plays havoc with whatever meaning we intended. We might say, then, that what appears to us as meaning derives not from

the intention of the speaker – or writer – but from the structure
of language itself, from the way it works.

## Binary oppositions revisited

It is clear now why we accept what we say as natural and
truthful: we are misled by the illusion of presence. But how
can the written word mislead us? How can we fail to see that
language generates all that excess meaning that we do not know
how to handle?

Poststructuralism's answer is that texts set up one or more
centres – derived from the language they make use of – that must
give them stability and stop the potentially infinite flow of
meaning that all texts generate. If there is a centre, there is also
that which does not belong to it, which is marginal. Setting up a
centre automatically creates a hierarchical structure: the central
is more important than the marginal. *Deconstruction*, as
Derrida's way of reading texts came to be known, first of all
undertakes to bring to light the tension between the central and
the marginal in a text. As the American critic Barbara Johnson
described it: 'The deconstruction of a text does not proceed by
random doubt or arbitrary subversion, but by the careful teasing
out of warring forces of signification within the text' (Johnson
1980: 5).

Such hierarchies between centre and margin (or periphery)
take the form of binary opposition (one of poststructuralism's
most obvious debts to structuralism). Texts introduce sets of
oppositions that function to structure and stabilize them. Quite
often these oppositions are implicit or almost invisible – they
may be hidden in a text's metaphors, for instance – or else only
one of the terms involved is explicitly mentioned. That explicit
mention, then, evokes the other, absent term. There is a wide
range of such oppositions, with some of them pretty general,
while others are more culture bound. Rather general sets of
oppositional terms include good vs. evil, truth vs. falsehood,
masculinity vs. femininity, rationality vs. irrationality, thought
vs. feeling, mind vs. matter, nature vs. culture, purity vs. impu-
rity, and so on and so forth. A notorious oppositional set within

Western culture is white vs. black. One of these terms always functions as the centre – it is *privileged*, in poststructuralist terms. Some terms have always been privileged – good, truth, masculinity, purity, whiteness – others may be found either in the centre or in the margin. In literary history we find texts that privilege 'thought' and 'rationality' – the writings of Samuel Johnson (1709–1784), for instance – but in the work of Romantic poets such as William Wordsworth (1770–1850) and John Keats (1795–1821) 'feeling' occupies the centre.

As I have just suggested, the privileging of certain terms can easily escape our notice. Take for instance fairly recently coined trademarks like 'walkman' and 'gameboy'. The second, that is non-privileged and inferior, term is even absent here. We may never have realized it, but 'walkman' and 'gameboy' set up an opposition between masculinity and femininity. Why is a 'walkman' not a 'walkwoman' or a 'walkgirl'? Why is a 'gameboy' not a 'gamegirl'? Did the original manufacturers and their public relations people believe that listening to a walkman or sitting hunched over a gameboy are typically male activities that would be of no interest to girls and women? This does not seem likely. It is a lot more reasonable to assume that they used the 'man' in 'walkman' and the 'boy' in 'gameboy' to give their product a positive image that would boost its sales. In both cases we have an implicit binary opposition in which the masculine term is the 'privileged' one.

But why should we worry about language if it turns out to be so easy to stop the flow of excess meaning by setting up structures of binary oppositions? Deconstruction argues that binary oppositions are a good deal less oppositional then they would seem to be. Within binary oppositions we do not only find an oppositional relationship between the two terms involved, we also find a strange complicity. Take for instance 'light' vs. 'darkness'. Arguably, light needs darkness. If there were no darkness, we would not have light either because we would not be able to recognize it for what it is. Without darkness, we would in one sense obviously have light – it would be the only thing around – but we would not be *aware* of light. We would not have the *concept* of light so that what we call light (which implies our awareness that there is also the possibility of non-light) would not exist. One might argue, then, that the existence of darkness (that is, our awareness of non-light) creates the concept of light. Paradoxically, the inferior term in this oppositional set turns out to be a condition for the opposition as such and is therefore as important as the so-called privileged one. The two terms in any oppositional set are defined by each other: light by darkness, truth by falsehood, purity by contamination, the rational by the irrational, the same by the other, nature by culture. Here, too, meaning arises out of difference. If there were no falsehood, we would have no concept of truth; if there were no purity, we would have no concept of contamination. Once difference has given rise to meaning, we privilege certain meanings and condemn others. Some privilegings will strike most of us as wholly reasonable – good vs. evil, or truth vs. falsehood – others have done incalculable damage – white vs. black, the masculine vs. the feminine. But whatever the effect of binary oppositions they always have their origin in difference. To analyse and dismantle them, as I have just done, means to 'decentre' the privileged term, to show that both terms only exist because of difference.

Derrida is fully aware that his own language, whether spoken or written, is subject to *différance*. He also knows that it cannot escape the centring effects that language, because of its countless connotations, always has. Even radical critiques of language have to make use of the medium they criticize in order to communicate. The critique undermines the language that it uses, but that language, because of its centring effects, simultaneously undermines the critique. In his early writings Derrida sometimes signals that symbiosis between critique and object of critique by putting a cancelling cross through some of the terms he uses. Putting those terms *under erasure*, as he calls it, he uses them but also lets us know that he is aware that they set up or suggest the very foundations for language that he radically questions. Derrida, you might say, is caught in the middle: he cannot use language, but he also cannot *not* use language. He finds himself not in an either/or position – we can and do use language because it is reliable or we cannot and do not because it isn't –

but in a both/and position: we cannot trust language but still use it. This parallels, in fact, what we find when we deconstruct binary oppositions. Instead of opposites that could not be further apart, we find two terms that are deeply implicated in each other. In the deconstruction of binary oppositions, too, either/or gives way to both/and.

## Literary deconstruction

Although Derrida developed his attack on the so-called logocentrism of Western thought – its unwarranted trust in language as the vehicle of truth – in the mid-1960s, it was not until the early 1970s that he really began to catch the attention of the English-speaking world. In the next ten years he found a large – and outspoken – following in American Departments of English, beginning at Yale University, where Paul de Man (1919–1983) became an important advocate of Derrida's poststructuralism.

Deconstruction takes its name from Derrida's practice: his strategy of analysing and dismantling texts or, more usually, parts of texts in order to reveal their inconsistencies and inner contradictions. At the heart of deconstruction is the effort to dismantle the cover-ups that texts use to create the semblance of stable meaning: their attempt to create 'privileged' centres – implicit or explicit binary oppositions – with the help of all sorts of rhetorical means.

Because deconstruction's point of departure is that language is by definition uncontrollable, it expects to find unwarranted privilegings in all texts. No matter whether a text is literary or non-literary, it can always be deconstructed and can be shown to rely for its internal stability on rhetorical operations that mask their origin in difference and the surplus meaning that is the result of *différance*. Deconstruction tries to demonstrate that the apparent either/or patterns of texts mask underlying both/and situations and to reveal those texts' fundamental undecidability. In literary terms, a text never achieves *closure* – which quite literally means that its case can never be closed: there is no final meaning, the text remains a field of possibilities. In Jeremy Hawthorn's apt formulation: 'Thus for Derrida the meaning of a text is always unfolding just ahead of the interpreter, unrolling in front of him or her like a never-ending carpet whose final edge never reveals itself' (Hawthorn 1998: 39).

In some ways, deconstructionist reading practice is remarkably like the New Critical reading for juxtapositions, tensions, inversions, and the like. Just like the New Criticism, deconstruction depends on close reading. However, while the New Critics emphasized the ultimate coherence of what they considered successful literary works (coherence being one of their touchstones), deconstructionist criticism seeks to expose the centring operations by means of which a false coherence is brought about. It then goes on to de-centre the centres that it finds and, by implication, the whole text that it has under scrutiny. In so doing, it reveals that the text is far more complex than it initially seemed to be and usually makes that text more interesting. In her reading of Herman Melville's *Billy Budd* (1891, first published in 1924), in which a young sailor (Billy) is hanged because he has inadvertently killed the master-at-arms Claggart, who has falsely accused him, Johnson sees a whole series of binary oppositions:

> the fate of each of the characters is the direct reverse of what one is led to expect from his 'nature.' Billy is sweet, innocent, and harmless, yet he kills. Claggart is evil, perverted, and mendacious, yet he dies a victim. Vere [the captain in charge of the ship] is sagacious and responsible, yet he allows a man whom he feels to be blameless to hang.
>
> (1980: 82)

However, the relations between these opposites, and the characters that embody them, turn out to be complex and paradoxical: 'Claggart, whose accusations of incipient mutiny are apparently false and therefore illustrate the very double-facedness they attribute to Billy, is negated for proclaiming the lie about Billy which Billy's act of negation paradoxically proves to be the truth' (86). It is not only that the opposites shift within the structure, but that they also would seem to collapse into each other.

Either/or turns into both/and. After her ingenious reading of the novel, to which I cannot begin to do justice here, Johnson concludes that in *Billy Budd* we have a 'difference' that effectively prevents closure.

Derrida's own reading of the very short story 'Before the Law' by Franz Kafka (1883–1924) emphasizes the same lack of closure. In Kafka's story a man arrives at the door that gives access to the Law. He is not allowed to enter but hears from the doorkeeper that he may perhaps enter later and had better not use force because there are many more doors, and many more doorkeepers that are even more powerful than this first one. He waits all his life and finally, just before he dies, asks the doorkeeper why he is the only one who has sought admittance. Answering that this particular door was meant for him only, the doorkeeper shuts the door on the dying man. Derrida sees the story as exemplifying *différance*:

> After the first guardian there are incalculably many others, perhaps without limit, and progressively more powerful and therefore prohibitive, endowed with the power of delay. Their potency is *différance*, an interminable *différance*, since it lasts for days and 'years,' indeed, to the end of (the) man. *Différance* till death, and for death, without end because ended, finite. As the doorkeeper represents it, the discourse of the law does not say 'no' but 'not yet,' indefinitely.
>
> (Derrida [1985] 1987: 141)

In a similar way, the discourse of any given text, even if it seems at first sight far more accessible than Kafka's enigmatic story, also forever tells us 'not yet' in our search for definitive meaning.

Deconstruction has come in for a good deal of criticism. It has been argued, for instance, that ultimately all deconstructionist interpretations are similar, because they always lead us to *différance*, to the impossibility of final meanings. Although this is true, it disregards the fact that before a deconstructionist reading arrives at that point, it has first uncovered the structures that operate in a text and shown us how these structures can be dismantled by making use of elements of the text itself. As the Yale deconstructionist J. Hillis Miller once put it, 'Deconstruction is not a dismantling of the structure of a text but a demonstration that it has already dismantled itself' (Miller 1976: 341). In the process, texts are subjected to the closest scrutiny and hidden relations of power – which always exist within binary oppositions – are brought to light.

To other critics of deconstruction, its intellectual underpinnings – Derrida's critique of logocentrism – seemed extremely far fetched. You might for instance grant Derrida's original point of departure and agree that language is based on difference and hovers over the world without ever actually touching solid ground, but reject his conclusions: why would that invariably lead to a surplus of meaning that fatally affects the texts we produce? We all know of misunderstandings and misreadings, but we can also point to countless examples of successful communication. So maybe that surplus of meaning – assuming that it really exists – is a good deal less damaging than the deconstructionists would have us believe. From this so-called pragmatic perspective language would seem to do its work reasonably well. If we pragmatically limit our thinking about language to how it actually works – and ignore for a moment the theoretical considerations that lead Derrida to a worst-case scenario – there is no reason for us to worry. From such a perspective one might even say that the poststructuralist loss of faith in language is the product of expectations of absolute certainty that were highly unreal in the first place. However, even for those critics who prefer a pragmatic position deconstruction has its uses. It is, for instance, perfectly possible to approach the sets of opposites that deconstruction habitually finds from a modified humanistic perspective. Such a modest humanism might argue that although ideally free and rational agents, in actual practice we are to a considerable extent determined by, for instance, our cultural environment. For a humanist the revelation that the sets of opposites that we can discover in texts always serve to repress the 'inferior' term (the 'feminine' and the 'non-white', for instance) can only be a step towards a better world in which the full humanity of every single human being is recognized and respected.

Such adaptations of deconstruction, and of poststructuralism in general, are particularly useful for those critics – feminists, African–American critics, Marxist critics – who want to be politically effective. The endless play of *différance* not only affects the texts that Derrida and his followers deconstruct, but also affects their own deconstructions. And it will affect whatever we say about those deconstructions. There is no getting away from *différance* and infinite uncertainty. But for politically motivated criticism uncertainty is a poor starting-point. If I want to achieve certain political ends there is not much help in the thought that all meanings – including the values that have led to my political stance – are merely the result of difference and have no solid foundation. Deconstruction may even seem positively evasive. It is considerations of this sort that often lead critics to adopt the halfway position that I have described above. Like Fredric Jameson, they will accept the force of poststructuralist argumentation, but will keep reading with a set of particular assumptions in mind – Marxist, liberal humanist, or otherwise. The difference, however, is that they now see those assumptions as a 'starting-point' and, because nothing is safe from deconstruction, as a 'problem'.

## Implications

What are the implications of the poststructuralist deconstruction of our faith in language, of its dismantling of 'presence' and of the privileged centres that language sets up?

First of all, poststructuralism is completely at odds with structuralism in its original, 'scientific', form. While for the structuralists the structures they described were objectively present in the texts they dealt with – to be discovered by anyone who seriously examined them – for Derrida such a structure is an arrangement produced by a reader who has temporarily stopped the infinite flow of meanings that a text generates. For Derrida a text is not a structure, but a chain of signs that generate meaning, with none of these signs occupying a privileged, anchored (and anchoring) position. It goes without saying that the idea – briefly floated by some structuralists – that textual structures might in some basic way reveal the way our minds work is unacceptable to the poststructuralists.

Secondly, because of its deconstruction of language post-structuralism is far more wide ranging than structuralism. Western philosophy, for instance, is based on the idea that we possess a faculty called 'reason' that, with the help of its obedient servant language, can get to know the world. Since the basic claim of poststructuralism is that language is not obedient at all, but fundamentally uncontrollable, it also claims that philosophy's pretensions of being capable of getting to know the world must be false.

Thirdly, poststructuralism has important consequences for the way we see ourselves. I have just mentioned 'reason' and earlier I have discussed 'presence'. We usually assume that 'reason' and the way we are 'present' to ourselves have nothing to do with language. 'Reason' and 'presence' are aspects of a unique 'me' that merely uses language as an instrument. As the beagle Snoopy – from the *Peanuts* cartoons – once put it when he woke up right under an enormous icicle that had formed overnight on the roof of his doghouse: 'I am too *me* to die.' As we have seen, the structuralists already objected to that 'me'. If we want to express ourselves we must always use a linguistic structure that was already in place before we arrived on the scene and we invariably express ourselves within the context of cultural structures that were also already in place. The poststruc-turalists accept that the individual subject is to a large (although never knowable) extent the product of those structures. As Roland Barthes wrote in 1970 with regard to reading: 'This "I" which approaches the text is already itself a plurality of other texts, of codes which are infinite, or more precisely, lost (whose origin is lost)' (Barthes [1970] 1974: 10). Moreover, since for the poststructuralists all structures are inherently unstable, mere temporary arrangements within chains of signification that are literally infinite, the subject, too, is only a temporary arrange-ment – an impermanent interruption of the flow of meaning. If we appear to be stable, that stability is mere appearance. In reality we are inherently unstable and, like language itself, without a centre. Since there is no centre, there is no structure: we are made up of conflicting fragments. This is of course not how we experience ourselves and it is a view of the subject that is certainly not uncontested, but as we will see later it has interesting and compelling cultural consequences. In any case, the liberal humanist subject, with its self-determination, moral autonomy, and coherence, has since the 1970s been a major target for poststructuralist critique.

Fourthly, the interpretation of literary texts will never lead to a final, definitive result. Like structures, interpretations are mere freeze-frames in a flow of signification. What is more, the difference between literature and other forms of writing has arguably disappeared. For Eliot, Richards, Leavis, and the New Critics the literary text had timeless significance because it put us in touch with what I have called the 'human condition'. Literature, unlike other uses of language, referred to vital, unchanging truths and values. For the poststructuralists, literature can do no such thing. Like all other forms of language, it is subject to the effects of *différance*. There is, however, one important difference between literature and other forms of language use: there is a category of literary texts that confess to their own impotence, their inability to establish *closure*. To Derrida and to poststructuralists in general such texts are far more interesting than texts that try to hide their impotence such as philosophical texts or realistic novels that claim to offer a true representation of the world. As Derrida puts in it his discussion of Kafka's 'Before the Law': 'A text of philosophy, science, or history, conveying knowledge or information, would not give up a name to a state of not-knowing, and if it did then only by accident and not in an essential or constitutive way' (1987: 142). Kafka's story is of course a prime example of a text that does not establish closure, but so are texts that give in to the play of language such as James Joyce's *Finnegans Wake* (1939). If deconstruction deals with literary texts that present themselves as realistic, it will show how their seemingly realistic surface is an effect of suppression and of the suggestion they create that their readers are unified (complete) and in control of the text they are reading – either through the superior knowledge that the text allows us to have or through the ironic position that we are supposed to take up. (Such a deconstructionist reading would of course come close to what we find in the literary criticism of Macherey – see Chapter 4.)

Since literary texts, realistic or otherwise, generate an infinite flow of meaning, interpretation is a matter of the reader. We have arrived, as the French critic Roland Barthes put it somewhat dramatically in 1968, at 'the death of the author', which simultaneously is 'the birth of the reader' (Barthes [1968] 2000: 150). For the structuralists, solid and stable meaning lies waiting to be discovered either in or behind the structures they study. For the poststructuralist text and reader interact to produce fleeting and always different moments of meaning.

## Postmodernism

In the 1960s and 1970s the mostly realistic fiction of the 1950s begins to give way to a sort of writing that takes extraordinary liberties with the traditions of fiction. Here for instance is the opening of the American writer Donald Barthelme's short story 'The Glass Mountain':

1    I was trying to climb the glass mountain.
2    The glass mountain stands at the corner of Thirteenth Street and Eighth Avenue.
3    I had attained the lower slope.
4    People were looking up at me.
5    I was new in the neighborhood.
6    Nevertheless I had acquaintances.
7    I had strapped climbing irons to my feet and each hand grasped a sturdy plumber's friend.
8    I was 200 feet up.
9    The wind was bitter.
10   My acquaintances had gathered at the bottom of the mountain to offer encouragement.
11   'Shithead.'

(Barthelme [1970] 1981: 178)

And so on, until the story ends with line 100.

In the same Barthelme's *Snow White* we find the story, a bizarre version of the fairytale, interrupted by a questionnaire:

1    Do you like the story so far? Yes ( ) No ( )
2    Does Snow White resemble the Snow White you remember? Yes ( ) No ( )
3    Have you understood, in reading to this point, that Paul is the prince figure? Yes ( ) No ( )
4    That Jane is the wicked stepmother-figure? Yes ( ) No ( )
5    In the further development of the story, would you like more emotion ( ) or less emotion ( )?

(Barthelme [1967] 1984: 82)

Unexpected and unsettling twists abound in this sort of fiction. In the American Thomas Pynchon's *The Crying of Lot 49* (1966) the novel's main character, California housewife Oedipa Maas, tries to unravel the mystery of a powerful secret organization that may or may not have existed for the last 300 years. Unfortunately, the novel stops right when she is on the point of finding out (or perhaps not finding out) whether the allusions to this so-called Tristero that she keeps on seeing have indeed a factual basis. In the Austrian writer Peter Handke's *The Goalie's Anxiety at the Penalty Kick* (1970) the goalie of the title, a man called Bloch, develops in a conversation with a couple of girls a curious problem with regard to language:

when he talked about an indirect free kick, he not only described what an indirect free kick was but explained, while the girls waited for the story to go on, the general rules about free kicks. When he mentioned a corner kick that had been awarded by a referee, he even felt he owed them the explanation that he was not talking about the corner of a room. The longer he talked, the less natural what he said seemed to Bloch. Gradually it began to seem that every word needed an

explanation. He had to watch himself so that he didn't get
stuck in the middle of a sentence.

(Handke [1970] 1977: 49)


Bloch's sometimes unbearable awareness of the inadequacy of
language is indirectly responsible for the murder that he later
commits.

Taking such curious tactics and themes into the 1980s, the
British writer Peter Ackroyd's *Hawksmoor* (1985) presents chapters that alternately tell an eighteenth-century story featuring a
satanic serial killer and a contemporary story featuring a
policeman who happens to be hunting for a similar criminal.
Strangely, the twentieth-century policeman bears the name of
the historical figure on whom Ackroyd bases his eighteenth-
century killer. We find all sorts of tantalizing parallels between
the stories, but just as with the names of the protagonists,
nothing ultimately fits. In the American writer Paul Auster's
*City of Glass* (1985) a writer, Quinn, gets a couple of telephone
calls from a man who wants to hire the private detective Paul
Auster. Giving in to a whim, he pretends to be Paul Auster, and
accepts a strange assignment in the course of which he meets a
writer called Paul Auster. The novel ends with Quinn alone in a
room, getting his meals from one or more unknown persons,
with the days getting shorter and shorter until he finally appears
to have vanished into thin air. A novel by another American
writer, Richard Powers's *Three Farmers on their Way to a Dance*,
also published in 1985, presents three interweaving stories that
increasingly would appear to hang together somehow. At a
certain point, however, one of these story lines is inexplicably
fractured. We are finally forced to conclude that Powers has
taken everything from a picture – ironically enough, featured on
the novel's cover – by the well-known early twentieth-century
photographer August Sander showing three young men who
may or may not be farmers and who may or may not be on their
way to a dance. Finally, the South African writer J.M. Coetzee's
*Foe* (1987) pretends to tell the real story of Robinson Crusoe.
According to *Foe*, Crusoe and his servant Friday are joined after

a number of years by a shipwrecked woman, Susan Barton. After they have finally been rescued, Crusoe dies during the voyage back home to England. Since Friday cannot speak because his tongue has been cut out, Susan is the only one who can inform the world about Crusoe's island and their years together. She succeeds in interesting the writer Daniel (De)Foe in the story and we know the rest: Defoe proceeds to write Susan out of the story and thus out of history.

This list of rather randomly selected examples could be effortlessly expanded. Central to this sort of writing, which we call *postmodernism*, is that it unsettles and deconstructs traditional notions about language, about identity, about writing itself, and so on. If we look closer at the examples I have given, we see that Barthelme makes fun of traditional ways of presenting a story and transgresses the (at that time) fairly strictly observed dividing line between high and popular culture. Pynchon refuses to give us the comfort of *closure*, which Ackroyd and Auster in their own way also refuse to do. In Ackroyd and Auster, identity is made highly problematic, with especially Quinn's identity fading into nothingness in the course of the story. The identity of Handke's Bloch is also highly problematical because he begins to feel that it is bound up with language, and language, as we have seen, is beginning to be a major problem. Powers's novel forces us to realize that we have all the way been caught up in an illusion; it is *self-reflexive* because it calls our attention to the way it has come into existence and to its own constructed nature. As a consequence, it makes us reflect on writing in general. Coetzee creates through his rewriting of Daniel Defoe's *Robinson Crusoe* (1719) the impression that one of the classics of English literature is built upon a misogynistic, discriminatory, act and in so doing reminds us of the historical oppression of women. The fact that Crusoe's servant Friday, a black man, has been literally made incapable of speaking for himself, similarly reminds us of the way the Western world has enslaved and oppressed countless Africans.

It can hardly be coincidental that the advent of postmodernism roughly coincides with that of poststructuralism. Although it would be stretching things to say that postmodernism is a sort of applied poststructuralism – poststructuralist ideas put into practice by writers – there is a good deal of overlap between the interests of postmodern writers and those of poststructuralist critics. Postmodernism, however, is more than a specific literary mode. Rather confusingly, it is also the name of a form of literary criticism that is broadly poststructuralist in its assumptions. The perspective of postmodern criticism on language, on identity, on 'truth', and so on, is strongly influenced by Derrida's deconstructionist philosophy, but it tends to be less technical than deconstruction – a point to which I will return in a moment – and it focuses primarily on postmodern writing while deconstruction will take on any text. In fact, the points I have just made about the texts that I have very sketchily summarized could be called postmodern criticism. I have paid no attention to these texts' characters as individuals, as liberal humanist criticism would do, but I have also not deconstructed the texts in question. I have focused on the absence of closure, the question of identity (cast into doubt by doublings, parallels, disappearances), the problematic nature of language, the artificiality of representation, the deconstruction of binary oppositions (as in *Foe*), and the *intertextual nature* of texts (with *Snow White* borrowing from a fairytale and *Foe* from an eighteenth-century novel) which not only sets up echoes in literary history, but can effectively show us the blind spots of earlier texts.

Although obviously related to deconstruction, postmodern criticism usually casts its net a good deal wider. Just like the New Criticism, deconstruction tends to focus on the 'words on the page', bringing to light the 'warring forces' that operate within a text. Postmodernist criticism shares that interest – although in considerably less detail – but is also interested in connecting what it finds in the texts it reads with social reality, especially after the publication of Jean-François Lyotard's *The Postmodern Condition* in 1984. Lyotard argues that the 'great narratives' that underpin Western civilization – religion, Marxism, the idea of progress through the application of rational principles, the belief that a completely free market will ultimately benefit us all – have at least theoretically been discredited. All those 'metanarratives' are guilty of having declared themselves universally valid and they have all contributed to the West's oppression, if not actual enslavement, of a good deal of the world. What we need, Lyotard tells us, is 'little narratives' – small-scale, modest systems of belief that are strong enough to guide us, but are always aware of their provisional nature and their local rather than universal validity. Postmodern criticism – as exemplified for instance by Linda Hutcheon's *A Poetics of Postmodernism* (1988) – reads (primarily postmodern) texts for their resistance to Lyotard's metanarratives and for the 'local' alternatives that they offer. As we will see later, we find a related literary-critical practice in other forms of contemporary criticism. Postmodern criticism, however, focuses primarily on the white, and often male, writers that created the postmodern literature of the 1960s, 1970s, and 1980s.

I should perhaps say that there are critics that would disagree with this relatively positive view of postmodern criticism (and postmodern writing). For some critics, postmodern writing is apolitical and evasive: it is too self-absorbed, too preoccupied with form and formal tricks, and too ironic (as in the opening of the Barthelme story that I have just quoted). There is no doubt that postmodern writing is deeply ironic, or that postmodern criticism teases out its ironies. The irony, however, is understandable. Linda Hutcheon tells us that postmodern writing 'asserts and then deliberately undermines such principles as value, order, meaning, control, and identity … that have been the basic premises of bourgeois liberalism' (Hutcheon 1988: 5). The large majority of postmodern writers belongs to the group that has historically benefited most from bourgeois liberalism: that of white, middle-class males. It only makes good sense that sawing off the branch they are sitting on strikes them as ironical. It is always possible, then, to read a postmodern novel in two ways. We can see postmodern fiction as liberating because it destabilizes preconceived notions with regard to language, representation, the subject, and so on. It effectively undermines all metanarratives and all beliefs and values that derive from metanarratives. However, it always also undermines itself: it will make fun of itself (as in Barthelme's questionnaire), expose its own fictionality, expressly thwart all attempts at interpretation, deliberately refuse to answer questions it has posed, and so on. One may argue that in doing so it undermines its own under-mining, so to speak, and leaves us with nothing at all. It puts itself *under erasure*, to use Derrida's phrase. Moreover, since it often intertextually refers to the literary tradition, no matter how ironically, it still indirectly affirms traditional texts and perspectives. It might be said then that postmodern writing, no matter how subversive it seems, still tacitly endorses the political status quo in the world outside the text. Linda Hutcheon has suggested that postmodern writing may be seen as 'politically ambivalent, doubly encoded as both complicity and critique' (Hutcheon 1989: 168). How we read postmodern texts is, in good poststructuralist fashion, up to the reader. The same applies to our view of postmodern criticism. For some critics the political criticism that we find in for instance the *new historicism* or in *postcolonial studies* – modes of criticism that I will discuss later – has strong affinities with postmodern criticism; for others postmodern criticism is fundamentally apolitical because it always sits on the fence, hanging on to a both/and position where radical either/or choices are politically necessary.

## Summary

Poststructuralism is unthinkable without structuralism, but in its radical questioning of the structuralists' faith in language and in objective analysis it seriously undermines structuralism's achievements. In its deconstructionist form, primarily associated with Jacques Derrida, it focuses on language and argues that language, even if we have no alter-native, is a fundamentally unstable and unreliable medium of communication. Because we rely on language in articu-lating our perception of reality and in formulating our knowledge of that reality, human perception and knowledge are fundamentally flawed. In a related move, poststruc-turalism argues that we have no genuine knowledge of our 'self', and that our identity, too, is prey to the indeterminacy of language. The deconstructionist criticism that bases itself upon these and other arguments shows how the instability of language always undoes the apparent coherence of literary texts.

The postmodern stories and novels that begin to appear in the 1960s and continue to be written in the 1970s and 1980s have already dispensed with that coherence. Through the techniques and strategies that they employ they, too, raise issues of language, identity, and so on. The postmodern criticism that responds to this mode of writing accepts its premises and links it to poststructuralist theory.

### Suggestions for further reading

Christopher Norris's *Deconstruction: Theory and Practice* (1982) is a good and accessible introduction to deconstruction. Jonathan Culler's *On Deconstruction* (1982) is more thorough but also more complex. Jacques Derrida's writings are notoriously difficult. However, '*Différance*', in the opening section of Derrida's *Margins of Philosophy*, is a reasonably accessible discussion of this central concept. Another text that might serve as an introduction to Derrida's critique of logocentrism is the much reprinted 'Structure, sign, and play in the discourse of the human sciences' (1970), to be found in Lodge and Wood (2000). Roland Barthes' 'The Death of the Author' and his 'From Work to Text', which are far less technical and focus on literary writing, must also be recommended. Orginally published in *Image-Music-Text* (1977), the essays are also available in *The Rustle of Language* (1986). 'Death' in particular has been widely reprinted, most recently in Lodge and Wood. Finally, 'The Resistance to Theory' (1982) of the leading deconstructionist Paul de Man (1919–1983) (again in Lodge and Wood) is a clear exposition of deconstructionist considerations. For an early critique of deconstruction, and a riposte, see M.H. Abrams's

'The Deconstructive Angel' (1977) and J. Hillis Miller's 'The Critic as Host' (1977; both in Lodge and Wood). Miller's reply illustrates the extravagant side of deconstructionist theory and interpretation.

Deconstructionist readings of text are never easy. Derrida's discussion of Kafka's 'Before the Law' (1987) is fairly accessible and gives a good impression of his interpretative practice. Another good starting-point is Barbara Johnson's discussion of Melville's *Billy Budd*, which I have briefly mentioned and which is to be found in her *The Critical Difference* (1980).

For an excellent and very readable overview of the strategies of postmodern novels, see Brian McHale, *Postmodernist Fiction* (1987). For the more thematic aspects of postmodern writing see Linda Hutcheon's *A Poetics of Postmodernism: History, Theory, Fiction* (1988). Brenda K. Marshall's *Teaching the Postmodern: Fiction and Theory* (1992) lives up to its title: it illuminates postmodern theory through a number of postmodern interpretations. Fredric Jameson's 'Postmodernism, or the Cultural Logic of Late Capitalism' (1984) is an influential Marxist analysis of contemporary culture, including both postmodern literature and criticism. Hans Bertens's *The Idea of the Postmodern* (1995) discusses the rise of 'postmodern' and 'postmodernism' as critical concepts in literature, the arts, architecture, and the social sciences. *International Postmodernism: Theory and Literary Practice*, edited by Bertens and Douwe Fokkema (1997), presents essays on postmodernism in a number of literary genres and subgenres, on postmodern uses of intertextuality and other favourite strategies, and on postmodern writing in a large number of Western and non-Western literatures. Finally, Steven Connor's *Postmodernist Culture* (2nd edn, 1997) is an excellent and wide-ranging discussion of postmodern thought and postmodern cultural practice.

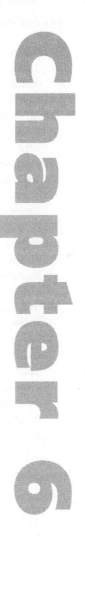

Chapter 6

# Poststructuralism continued

*Foucault, Lacan, and French feminism*

## Foucauldian power

Poststructuralism is deeply subversive. It deconstructs all those binary oppositions that are central to Western culture (and, if we may believe Lévi-Strauss, every other culture) and that give that culture its sense of unique superiority. In deconstructing those oppositions it exposes false hierarchies and artificial borders, unwarranted claims to knowledge, and illegitimate usurpations of power. Its focus is on fragmentation, on difference, and on absence, rather than on the sameness, unity, and presence that are so pervasive in the way we think about ourselves and the culture we are part of. In deconstructionist criticism, however, the dismantling of oppositions and the exposure of hidden hierarchies and relations of power are generally limited to the text at hand. Although the interrogation of power on a wider scale is implicit in Derrida's deconstruction of logocentrism – the belief that language gives us access to truth – the interest in power and its workings that dominates

147

the poststructuralist criticism of the 1980s and 1990s derives mainly from the work of Michel Foucault. During his career as a historian Foucault (1926–1984) wrote books on the history of psychiatry, the origin and rise of clinical medicine, the evolution of biology and economics, the emergence of the modern prison system, and other important social developments that find their origin in the late eighteenth and early nineteenth century – the so-called Enlightenment period. In these books he focuses on what he sees as the Enlightenment desire to establish the procedures by which our societies regulate themselves on a rationalized and orderly basis. In these *genealogies* – he did not describe his books as 'histories' – Foucault seeks to expose the way power was at work in the seemingly 'objective' vocabularies and diagnostic terms developed by the various branches of the budding human sciences as these emerged in the first half of the nineteenth century. For Foucault these new sciences – which included psychiatry, criminology, medicine, and (human) biology – are deeply repressive. They have created general norms and standards that fail to recognize and to do justice to the differences between the characters and experiences of individuals and groups of individuals and between the places where they happen to live. They impose definitions upon us that we might want to reject. The new human sciences have turned out to be straitjackets that, strangely enough, we would seem glad to put on.

## Panopticism

In a section called 'Panopticism' in his book *Discipline and Punish: The Birth of the Prison* (1975, translated in 1977), Foucault gives a succinct account of how in early modern society leprosy and the plague – both highly contagious diseases – were dealt with. Lepers were simply excluded from social intercourse to minimize the risk of infection. However, with regard to the plague, which always affected large numbers of the population, other measures were necessary. And so seventeenth-century society did its utmost to contain the plague through confining people to their houses, once the disease had manifested itself.

But such a drastic measure demands constant surveillance: 'Inspection functions ceaselessly. The gaze [of surveillance] is alert everywhere' (Foucault [1975] 1977: 195). This imprisonment by way of precaution is for Foucault typical of how in the modern world the individual is constantly monitored, inspected:

> This enclosed, segmented space, observed at every point, in which the individuals are inserted in a fixed place, in which the slightest movements are supervised, in which all events are recorded, in which an uninterrupted work of writing links the centre and the periphery, in which power is exercised without division, according to a continuous hierarchical figure, in which the individual is constantly located, examined and distributed among the living beings, the sick and the dead – all this constitutes a compact model of the disciplinary mechanism.
>
> (197)

The 'political dream' of the plague is

> the penetration of regulation into even the smallest details of everyday life through the mediation of the complete hierarchy that assured the capillary functioning of power; not masks that were put on and taken off, but the assignment to each individual of his 'true' name, his 'true' place, his 'true' body, his 'true' disease'.
>
> (198)

It must not be thought that in such attempts to confine the plague one powerful group of citizens controls another, powerless one. There is with regard to power not a 'massive, binary division between one set of people and another', but a distribution of power through many channels and over a large number of individuals.

It is the detailed regulation and constant surveillance that were mobilized against the plague that in the nineteenth century begin to be applied to 'beggars, vagabonds, madmen, and the disorderly' – in short, 'the abnormal individual'. The instrument that the authorities responsible for this use is 'that of binary division' – the binary oppositions we are familiar with: 'mad/sane; dangerous/harmless; normal/abnormal' (199). Foucault's metaphor for this new sort of social regulation is that of the *Panopticon*, a type of prison designed by the English philosopher Jeremy Bentham in the late eighteenth century. This ideal prison consisted of a ring of cells that was built around a central point of observation from which one single guardian could survey all the cells – which were open to inspection – on a given floor. As Foucault puts it:

> By the effect of backlighting, one can observe from the tower, standing out precisely against the light, the small captive shadows in the cells of the periphery. They are like so many cages, so many small theatres, in which each actor is alone, perfectly individualized and constantly visible.
>
> (200)

However, the prisoner cannot see the supervisor. He never knows if he is being watched. This is for Foucault the 'major effect' of the Panopticon:

> to induce in the inmate a state of conscious and permanent visibility that assures the automatic functioning of power. So to arrange things that the surveillance is permanent in its effects, even if it is discontinuous in its action; that the perfection of power should tend to render its actual exercise unnecessary; that this architectural apparatus should be a machine for creating and sustaining a power relation independent of the person who exercises it; in short, that the inmates should be caught up in a power situation of which they themselves are the bearers.
>
> (201)

'A real subjection is born mechanically from a fictitious relation' (202), Foucault concludes in a formulation that strongly resembles Althusser's definition of ideology as a 'representation of the imaginary relationship of individuals to their real conditions of existence' (see the section on Marxist criticism in Chapter 4). For Foucault the Panopticon stands for the modern world in which we, its citizens, are 'the bearers' of our own figurative, mental, imprisonment. As with Althusser, we are complicit in our own confinement.

This may at first sight not seem very plausible. Aren't the various Western democracies supposed to be free and tolerant? Let me therefore offer a simplified account of Foucault's argument with respect to psychiatry and violent crime. Before psychiatry entered the scene, a murder was simply a murder: an act that needed no further explanation beyond the obvious ones – profit, revenge, and so on – and that could be summarily punished. If a murderer somehow escaped punishment and committed another murder, the only thing on the mind of the authorities was to get him or her to the gallows (or guillotine) as soon as possible. But with the advent of psychiatry, the focus began to shift from law enforcement and the meting out of punishment to the underlying reasons for the criminal act. In order words, the focus shifted from the law to the character of the criminal. Before too long, psychiatry had diagnosed one or more specifically criminal personalities. With the introduction of the idea of criminal personalities we have a wholly new situation: it must be possible for an individual to have a criminal personality without actually having committed a violent crime. (We must, after all, assume that people who commit such a crime because they have a criminal personality already had that personality before they committed the crime.) But this must lead to the conclusion that there may be potential murderers among the people we know: one of them could easily have a criminal personality. What began as a psychiatric diagnosis leads to general suspicion and surveillance. We suspect others just like they suspect us: all of us are subject to the 'gaze' of surveillance. Moreover, such diagnoses usually lead to self-surveillance: we become the 'bearers' of our own imprisonment. Another 'personality' that is discovered in the nineteenth century is that of the homosexual. In this case, too, what seemed to be discrete acts are traced back to an underlying, unchanging, homosexual nature. Given the strongly negative connotations surrounding this new 'personality', young males must have started to monitor themselves and, if necessary, to repress undesirable feelings. Foucault argues that over the last two centuries a whole army of psychiatrists, doctors, sociologists, psychotherapists, social workers, and other self-appointed guardians of 'normality' has sprung up that has created a stifling apparatus of social surveillance in which, as we will see in a moment, language plays a major role. But let me first briefly look at a novel that may make this seem more plausible.

Although it predates Foucault's work, Ken Kesey's *One Flew Over the Cuckoo's Nest* (1962) describes a truly Foucauldian world. The novel takes place in a mental institution that is run by a woman ('Big Nurse') whose weapons are surveillance and inspection. The patients regularly take part in group sessions in which they must reveal their problems – ostensibly for therapeutic purposes but in reality because the humiliation of public confession keeps them subservient and in line. One of the major surprises of the novel is that many of the inmates have not been committed at all, but have come to the institution on a wholly voluntary basis. They have had themselves committed because the outside world's insistence on 'normality' and its definition of normality has convinced them that they are abnormal and need treatment. They have, in other words, subjected themselves to the authority of the human sciences. They have, first of all, accepted and completely internalized a *discourse* about normality – a term I will explain below – for which the human sciences are mainly responsible; secondly, they have literally turned their minds and bodies over to one of the human sciences' institutions. The only 'patient' who is sure that he is absolutely sane – and whose sanity is indeed proven by the events of the novel although he, too, is 'abnormal' by society's standards – has escaped this 'discourse' about normality because he has never gone to school or church – two of Althusser's state apparatuses. Ironically, unlike most of the others, he is not free to go.

## Discourses

Why do we accept this 'panoptical' state of affairs – a world in which we are under constant surveillance and, even more importantly, in which we constantly monitor ourselves for signs of abnormality or even mere strangeness? Foucault attributes this to 'power', a term that has provoked much discussion because he may be said to have used it rather loosely. It clearly has much in common with Althusser's 'ideology' and Gramsci's 'hegemony' because it rules by consent. In the example of *One Flew over the Cuckoo's Nest* the 'patients' who have had themselves committed genuinely believe that they are misfits and need treatment. Foucault's power, just like 'ideology' or 'hegemony', derives its strength from the fact that we deeply believe what it tells us. In fact, just like Althusser's ideology, it gives us a sense of belonging and contributes to our well-being:

> If power were never anything but repressive, if it never did anything but to say no, do you really think one would be brought to obey it? What makes power hold good, what makes it accepted, is simply the fact that it doesn't only weigh on us as a force that says no, but that it traverses and produces things, it induces pleasure, forms knowledge, produces discourse. It needs to be considered as a productive network which runs throughout the whole social body.
>
> (Foucault 1980: 119)

We obey power, are loyal to it, even to the point of policing and repressing ourselves, because it makes us feel what we are. What is unclear is the extent to which we can resist power. Although Foucault argues that power always brings about resistance it is by no means clear how we should interpret this. We also find him arguing, for instance, that resistance is the means by which power further strengthens itself. Sometimes Foucault would seem to take up an Althusserian position, which for all practical purposes rules out resistance, at other times he would seem to favour a more Gramscian view, which sees resistance – counterhegemonic views and actions – as a realistic possibility.

In any case, power works through *discourses* and *discursive formations*. In its policing of 'abnormal' behaviour, the power of the human sciences derives from what they claimed to be *knowledge*; it derives from their claims to expertise. Such a cluster of claims to knowledge is what Foucault calls a 'discourse'. To be more precise, a discourse is a loose structure of interconnected assumptions that makes knowledge possible. In his *The Archaeology of Knowledge* (1972) Foucault tells us that a discourse is 'a series of sentences or propositions' and that it 'can be defined as a large group of statements that belong to a single system of formation' – a so-called *discursive formation*. Thus, he continues, 'I shall be able to speak of clinical discourse, economic discourse, the discourse of natural history, psychiatric discourse' (Foucault 1972: 107–108). A given discourse, say that of sexology in the nineteenth century, establishes a field – in this case that of sexual relations and inclinations – within which 'propositions' about sexuality can be formulated that could not be formulated without it: the creation of the field makes it possible to relate phenomena that seemed discrete and unconnected. Such a discourse, then, produces claims to knowledge and it is these claims – which we accept – that give it its power. There is then an intimate relationship between knowledge and power. Knowledge is a way to define and categorize others. Instead of emancipating us from ignorance, it leads to surveillance and discipline. Occasionally, it seems to lead to more positive results. To stay with the field of sexuality, the 'discovery' that there are men who have a 'homosexual personality' has led to disciplining and stigmatizing, but may also be said to have contributed to the creation of homosexual communities, to solidarity at the personal level, and even to collective action at the political level. Foucault is aware of this, but it is not easy to determine whether he sees such a ' "reverse" discourse' (his term) as an instance of successful resistance.

## Power/knowledge

Foucault's view of the relationship between knowledge and power is not uncontested. In a very general way, we are aware that knowledge and power are related. In a number of Western languages we find proverbial expressions that even equate them (*savoir, c'est pouvoir* in French, *Wissen ist Macht* in German, 'knowledge is power' in English). Most people will be aware that in the past false claims to knowledge have served as instruments of power, of social suppression. Take for instance the supposed inferiority of women and coloured people, which endless generations of white males have accepted as factually true, as part of their knowledge of the world. Looking back, we see that we are dealing with binary oppositions that power (the power of white males) turned into factual knowledge. It does not take much effort to show that in many cases so-called knowledge reflects a relation of power between the subject (the knower) and the object (that which the knower knows or studies) rather than what we would call truth.

When I use the term 'false claim', as I have just done, the implication is that there are also correct claims to knowledge. For Foucault, however, that distinction is irrelevant. At this point Foucault's poststructuralism becomes prominently visible: knowledge is for Foucault the product of a certain discourse, which has enabled it to be formulated, and has no validity outside it. The 'truths' of the human sciences are the effect of discourses, of language. Their 'knowledge' does not derive from access to the real world, to authentic reality, but from the rules of their discourses. This view has been the subject of much debate. It implies that the knowledge of the human sciences that Foucault discusses only counts as knowledge because we have somehow been persuaded to accept it as such: it only counts as knowledge because the discourse in question is powerful enough to make us believe that it is knowledge. In first instance knowledge is enabled by the rules of a certain discourse, which decide what qualifies as knowledge and what does not, but ultimately in Foucault's scenario knowledge is produced by power, by the means that a discourse has at its disposal to establish its credibility. Here, too, a look at *One Flew over the Cuckoo's Nest* is instructive. We see that power and knowledge mutually benefit from each other in constant interaction. 'Big Nurse' derives her power from the discourse of psychological normality and abnormality which she commands far more thoroughly than her 'patients' and which they have, moreover, thoroughly internalized. But that power simultaneously makes the discourse more impregnable. It is only when a total outsider, who has remained unaffected by this particular discourse, appears on the scene that her power and 'knowledge' – sometimes indicated by Foucault as power/knowledge – turn out to have no solid foundation.

Foucault, then, is not interested in establishing which discourses, or parts of discourses, are false and which are true – as I have just said, their 'truths' are ultimately produced by power. His focus is on the set of rules, the *discursive formation*, that governs a discourse and holds it together. Here we see that Foucault operates on the dividing line between structuralism and poststructuralism. Just like, for instance, Genette with regard to narrative, he is interested in underlying principles: in the rules and the conditions that make it possible for 'propositions' to acquire the status of knowledge. These rules determine what counts as knowledge with regard to the field in which they operate and thus – as in the case of clinical medicine or psychiatry – establish bodies of 'knowledge' that apply to us all. Because of their claims to expertise such discourses then go on to determine the way we talk and think about the field in question (sexuality, mental illness, and so on) and persuade us to keep ourselves and others under constant surveillance. Like language in general they operate independently of any individual intention and perpetuate themselves through their users. Since we are all extensions of the discourses that we have internalized, we ourselves constantly reproduce their power, even in our intimate relations.

As we will see in the following chapters, the idea of discourses as vehicles for power has been immensely productive in literary studies. Foucault locates power firmly in language, and language is the business of literary studies. I should perhaps emphasize again that Foucault, in discussing the role of discourses, is not thinking of individuals who abuse certain discourses to gain personal power (although that certainly happens) and that he is also not thinking of a central source of power – the state, for instance – that uses discourses cynically to manipulate us and keep us under control. The state's servants believe in such discourses just as much as we do. Discourses work like Gramsci's hegemony and Althusser's ideology: we so completely internalize them that they even 'induce pleasure'. Discourses organize the way we see the world for us. We live and breathe discourses and function unknowingly as links in a good many power chains.

Deconstructionism is certainly not blind to the fact that language is tied up with power – its dismantling of binary oppositions testifies to that. Foucault, however, places language in the centre of *social* power – rather than textual power – and of social practices. The social role of language – including literature – and its hegemonic power is the starting-point for the approaches that I will discuss in the chapters that follow.

## Poststructuralist psychoanalysis

In my discussion of Louis Althusser's explanation of the enormous power of what he calls ideology (see Chapter 4) I have briefly mentioned the French psychoanalyst Jacques Lacan (1901–1981). I might also have brought in Lacan with regard to the power that Foucault ascribes to the discourses that at certain points in his writing so thoroughly control us. In contemporary literary theory and criticism Lacan's work is often evoked to explain how power works, why the individual – the subject – is so extraordinarily susceptible to power. Clearly, we need to look at Lacan. However, a discussion of Lacan's psychoanalytic work cannot take place in a historical vacuum: in order to appreciate fully how it fits into a larger discussion of poststructuralism, we have to see it in relation to the work of the founding father of psychoanalysis, Sigmund Freud (1856–1939), which it both continues and revises. I will first, then, look briefly at some of Freud's most fundamental assumptions – not in the least because they have given rise to a specific mode of literary criticism that deserves attention in a book like this.

In Chapter 4 I have discussed approaches to literature that read texts not primarily for their humanist meaning (as in Chapter 1), or for their form (as in Chapters 2 and 3), but for their *politics*. Seen from that perspective, a literary text is not in the first place the product of an individual author, but rather the product of a much larger culture that speaks through the writer and that conveys political messages that the writer may be completely unaware of. (I have already used the term 'political unconscious' in connection with this.) There is, however, still another mode of criticism in which writers are taken to be largely, or wholly, unaware of their texts' deeper meanings. This criticism takes its inspiration from psychoanalysis, initially the psychoanalysis of Freud, later also from other versions of psychoanalysis, including that of Lacan. For the purposes of this book, Freudian and Lacanian psychoanalytic criticism are the most pertinent.

Freud's psychoanalysis presents a view of the subject that is radically at odds with the liberal humanist view of the subject as an ultimately free, coherent, and autonomous moral agent. For Freud, new-born babies live in an instinctual world dominated by 'oceanic' desires and feelings in which there is no distinction between the baby itself, its mother, or the larger world. Everything radiates from the centre, that is the baby itself, and is geared towards fulfilling its boundless desires (for breastfeeding, for instance). Gradually, however, the awareness breaks through that this supposed physical and emotional continuity between baby, mother, and world is an illusion. As a result, the baby experiences a severe sense of loss which, in its turn, produces *desire* – now used in a more general sense. In a second phase, the baby, now a young child, goes through a further separation from the mother, who for a while has functioned as the primary focus of 'desire'. During this so-called Oedipal stage, which we go through when we are still toddlers, little girls begin to be aware that they lack a penis, as a result of which they develop a sense of inadequacy, and little boys, aware that their mother lacks a penis, begin to suspect that they might lose theirs (which Freud calls a fear of castration). It is this fear that persuades the little boy to give up what Freud takes to be his erotic interest in his mother (in the Greek myth that Freud draws on Oedipus unknowingly marries his mother – hence Freud's use of the term 'Oedipal'). The little boy knows that he is in direct competition with his father and is on his way to a confrontation that he must lose – with the fearsome implication of castration. If you cannot beat them, join them; and so the little boy decides to be like his father – simultaneously accepting social authority – and (with a considerable time lag) directs his erotic interest at other women. The little girl, as disappointed by her mother's lack of a penis as by her own, turns to her father – who possesses one – and will eventually give up her desire for a penis and want a baby instead. The Oedipal stage turns both boy and girl into future hetero-sexual adults.

Freud's account of the little girl's development has infuriated a good many feminists (see for instance Kate Millett's *Sexual Politics*). What concerns me here, however, is the effects of these early developments that we supposedly have all gone through. In our first years, we must again and again give up longings and desires either because we are forced to realize that they are impossible or because their realization would take us into forbidden territory. Those desires, however, do not go away, but take refuge in a part of our mind that is beyond our conscious control: the *unconscious*. In later life, too, we may find that we have to repress desires because they are unacceptable. Although our conscious mind vigorously polices the border with the unconscious – which, among other things, is a source of unful-filled desires and pain – the unconscious has ways of getting past its vigilance. It first of all manifests itself in unguarded moments, in slips of the tongue, for instance, or in unintended puns, or in our dreams. But the unconscious also slips through, according to Freud, in language that we see as figurative – symbols, metaphors, allusions, and so on. The unconscious can for instance hide a repressed desire behind an image that would seem to be harmless – a trick that Freud called *displacement* – or it can project a whole cluster of desires onto an image in a manoeuvre that Freud called *condensation*: a dream figure can for instance combine characteristics of a number of people we know. The language that we use may always have hidden meanings of which we ourselves have no conscious awareness. If we repress our hatred for a person who usually wears red, we may accidentally say 'dead' instead of 'red' in a conversation, or we may dream that a red car is flattened in a traffic accident.

Psychoanalytic criticism focuses on such 'cracks' in the text's façade and seeks to bring to light the unconscious desires of either the author, or the characters that the text presents. It does not ignore what the text ostensibly would seem to be about, but its real interest is in the hidden agenda of the language that the text employs. The proposition that the language of a literary work has both a conscious and an unconscious dimension and that the unconscious elements must find ways to get past the censorship exercised by its conscious dimension has been very attractive to, for instance, Marxist critics. I will return to this point after an equally brief look at Lacan.

## Lacan

In the last twenty-odd years Freudian psychoanalysis has been criticized for its anti-feminism, but even more for its claims to universal validity. Freud's suggestion that the Oedipal model is of all times and all places has become increasingly controversial. As a consequence, many psychoanalytically interested critics have turned to Jacques Lacan, whose work avoids the fixed developmental scheme that Freud proposed and instead proposes a *relational* structure that allows for difference.

Lacan, too, sees the transition from infancy to childhood as absolutely crucial. For Lacan, the pre-Oedipal infant lives in what he calls the *Imaginary*. In this state, in which the child cannot yet speak, it is subject to impressions and fantasies, to all sorts of drives, and has no sense of limitations and boundaries: as in Freud, it simply does not know that its body is not the world. Via the *mirror stage* (to which I will come back in a moment) the child enters the *Symbolic*: it enters the world of *language* in which the *Real* – the real world which we can never know – is symbolized and represented by way of language and other representational systems that operate like language. (We can never know the 'Real' because it can never be fully represented – it is beyond language.) This entrance into the 'Symbolic' necessitates an acceptance of the language and of the social and cultural systems that prevail in the child's environment. Lacan calls this massive configuration of authority that works through language the *nom du père*, the name of the father, in recognition of the patriarchal character of our social arrangements. The same recognition leads him to speak of the *phallus* as the signifier that signifies that patriarchal character. (Note that he avoids the term 'penis' because in Lacan's conception of things male dominance is a cultural construction and not a biological given. The phallus is thus always symbolic.) Hence the term *phallocentric*, which is of feminist origin and denotes the (false) assumption that maleness is the natural, and in fact only, source of authority and power.

But let me return for a moment to the 'mirror stage'. As I have said, real mirrors do not have to come into it, although they may. In the 'mirror stage' we are confronted with the 'mirror' image that the world gives back to us. But that image, just like the image that we see in an actual mirror, is a distortion that leads to a 'misrecognition'. Still, that misrecognition is the basis for what we see as our identity. For Lacan, we need the response and recognition of *others* and of *the Other* to arrive at what we experience as our identity. Our 'subjectivity' is construed in interaction with 'others', that is individuals who resemble us in one way or another but who are also irrevocably different. We become ourselves by way of other perspectives and other views of who we are. We also become ourselves under the 'gaze' of the 'Other' or 'great other' (*'grande autre'*). This 'Other' – 'the locus from which the question of [the subject's] existence may be presented to him' – is not a concrete individual, although it may be embodied in one (father or mother, for instance), but stands for the larger social order. Since our identity is constituted in interaction with what is outside of us and reflects us, it is *relational* – a notion that introduces the idea of difference into the process of identity construction. The relational character of identity suggests that the structure in which we happen to find ourselves more or less situates us as individuals. However, since the social and personal configuration in which we find ourselves at a given point will inevitably change, identity is not something fixed and stable, it is a *process* that will never lead to completion. Identity not only is subject to constant change, it can also never be coherent. First of all, we have been forced to consign many of our pre-verbal fantasies, drives, and so on to our unconscious; secondly, since our identity is construed in interaction and does not originate in ourselves it always depends on 'others'. Finally, since we have left whatever is pre-verbal behind and have entered – and subjected ourselves to – the realm of language, identity can be said to be a linguistic construct: we are constructed in language. That language, however, is not our own and could never express what we would want to say if we had, for instance, access to our unconsciousness.

With the transition from the *Imaginary* to the *Symbolic*, in which we submit to language and reason, we lose a feeling of wholeness, of undifferentiated being, that, again as in Freud, will forever haunt us. Because we do not have access to this pre-verbal self we live ever after with a lack. With Lacan, too, this loss of our original state results in *desire*, in an unspecific but deep-felt longing that can never be fulfilled, but can only (temporarily) satisfy itself with symbolic substitutes. Lacan's view of the conscious and the unconscious is even better suited to feminist and Marxist adaptations than Freud's. Freud sees the repression that leads to the formation of the unconscious in terms of the nuclear family – even if he is of course aware that that family is embedded in a much larger social order. Lacan, however, sees that repression as the direct effect of entry into the social order. For Lacan, there is a direct connection between the repressive character of language and culture and the coming into being of the unconscious. We may expect everything that is ideologically undesirable within a given culture to have found refuge in the unconsciousness of its members. If we see 'ideology' in psychoanalytic terms, that is as the conscious dimension of a given society, then we may posit an unconscious where everything that ideology represses – social inequality, unequal opportunity, the lack of freedom of the subject – is waiting to break to the surface. We may then examine the language that ideology uses for tell-tale cracks in its façade. The social unconsciousness will just like our individual unconsciousness succeed in getting past the censor. This is in fact the presupposition of the literary-critical practice of Pierre Macherey and the British and American critics who followed his example (see Chapter 4).

As I have already suggested in my discussion of Althusser (also in Chapter 4), Lacan's psychoanalytic model has also been invoked to explain the hold ideology has over us. Ideology gives us the illusion that it makes us whole; it would seem to neutralize the desire that results from our entry into the 'Symbolic'. Lacanian criticism sees this repeated on a smaller scale when we read literary texts. In the process of reading, we enter into a complex relationship with a text in which we allow it to master us, to fill our lack. Lacanian critics are interested in the ways in which narrative structures and rhetorical operations take advantage of this rather one-sided relationship between text and reader. However, although Lacanian psychoanalysis has led to classic interpretations such as Shoshana Felman's (1982) reading of Henry James's *The Turn of the Screw* (1898), it has perhaps been more influential on the level of theory. We have already seen how it can be invoked to theorize the power of ideology. Ideology might be seen in Lacanian terms as 'the Other' whose 'misrecognition' of us becomes incorporated in our identity. The misrepresentation that it reflects back leads us to misrepresent what we are to ourselves – a formulation that evokes Althusser's definition of ideology – and this misrepresentation becomes a cornerstone of our identity. We have also seen how psychoanalysis, and Lacanian psychoanalysis in particular, can be used to hypothesize a sort of social, or political, unconscious that manifests itself in literary texts whenever it catches the conscious off-guard, usually in passages that from the point of view of the conscious (that is, ideology) seem trivial or irrelevant. Finally, in one of the following chapters, that on postcolonial studies, we will see how Lacan's thesis that we develop our identity by way of 'others' can be used to analyse the underlying relations between colonizer and colonized.

## French feminism

In the previous chapter, on the politics of literature, I have already suggested that from the mid-1970s onwards we see encounters between feminism and poststructuralist thought. Given the French origin of poststructuralist thinking, it is not surprising that French feminists were the first to see the potential of poststructuralist concepts and arguments for feminist critiques of the patriarchal social order.

An early and influential claim for the relevance of binary oppositions for feminism is 'Sorties', an essay published in 1975 by the French writer and literary critic Hélène Cixous (1938–). 'Sorties' begins with a dramatic question (in a larger type than the rest of the essay) '*Where is she?*' and then presents the following list:

> Activity/passivity,
> Sun/Moon,
> Culture/Nature,
> Day/Night,
> Father/Mother,
> Head/Heart,
> Intelligible/Sensitive,
> Logos/Pathos.

(Cixous 2000 [1975]: 264)

'Thought', Cixous continues,

> has always worked by ... dual, *hierarchized* oppositions. Superior/Inferior. Myths, legends, books. Philosophical systems. Wherever an ordering intervenes, a law organizes the thinkable by (dual, irreconcilable; or mitigable, dialectical) oppositions. And all the couples of oppositions are *couples*. Does this mean something? Is the fact that logocentrism subjects thought – all of the concepts, the codes, the values – to a two-term system, related to 'the' couple man/woman?

Nature/History,
Nature/Art,
Nature/Mind,
Passion/Action.

(264)

For Cixous the answer is that everything *is* related to the man/woman opposition:

> In philosophy woman is always on the side of passivity. Every time the question comes up; when we examine kinship structures; whenever a family model is brought into play; in fact as soon ... as you ask yourself what is meant by the question 'What is it'; as soon as there is a will to say something. A will: desire, authority, you examine that, and you are led right back – to the father. ... And if you examine literary history, it's the same story. It all refers back to man, to *his* torment, his desire to be (at) the origin. Back to the father. There is an intrinsic bond between the philosophical and the literary ... and phallocentrism.

(265)

We see in these passages the influence of structuralism (binary opposites in general and kinship structures more in particular), deconstruction (the reference to logocentrism), and Lacanian psychoanalysis ('phallocentrism'). Cixous integrates these sources in the important argument that the male/female opposition is central to Western culture (if not all cultures) and is pervasively present in all sorts of oppositions that at first sight have nothing to do with either males or females. The inferior term is always associated with the feminine, while the term that occupies the privileged position is associated with masculinity. As we will see in a moment, this opposition, interpreted from a psychoanalytical perspective, plays a prominent role in for instance one form of ecologically inspired criticism. For Cixous, this never-ending privileging of the masculine, which results from what she calls 'the solidarity of logocentrism and phallocentrism', damages us all, females and males alike, because it curbs the imagination and is therefore oppressive in general. '[T]here is no *invention* possible,' Cixous argues, 'whether it be philosophical or poetic, without the presence in the inventing subject of an abundance of the other, of the diverse' (269). But where to start dismantling this repressive male/female opposition?

In her 1974 essay 'The Laugh of the Medusa', Cixous suggests that laughter, sex (if not policed by patriarchal heterosexuality), and writing may have liberating effects. Aware that writing usually serves the consolidation of patriarchal power, Cixous proposes what she calls *écriture féminine*, that is a feminine or female writing that will escape the restrictions imposed by 'the phallocratic system':

> It is impossible to define a feminine practice of writing [*écriture féminine*], and this is an impossibility that will remain, for this practice can never be theorized, enclosed, encoded – which doesn't mean that it doesn't exist. But it will always surpass the discourse that regulates the phallocentric system; it does and will take place in areas other than those subordinated to philosophico-theoretical domination. It will be conceived of only by subjects who are breakers of automatisms, by peripheral figures that no authority can ever subjugate.
>
> (Cixous 1981 [1974]: 253)

Although Cixous does not invoke Lacan, it is tempting to see *écriture féminine* in terms of his concept of the 'Imaginary'. We should not identify her position with that of Lacan, however. In Lacan's universe, the conscious intentionality that is suggested by the phrase 'figures that no authority can ever subjugate' is, in Lacan's own terms, a 'mirage'. We also should not read *écriture féminine* as the exclusive domain of women. It is a sort of writing practice that 'surpasses' what Lacan calls the 'Symbolic' and that we may associate – but not identify – with his 'Imaginary'. However, repression is gender-blind and represses males as much as it does females. Males, too, can escape 'philo-sophico-theoretical domination'. Cixous chooses to call the subversive writing that she has in mind feminine or female because the forces of repression are so clearly male.

Julia Kristeva (1941–), literary critic and psychoanalyst, stays somewhat closer to Lacan with her concepts of the 'Symbolic' and the 'Semiotic' – which is a version of Lacan's 'Imaginary'. For Kristeva, what has been repressed and consigned to the 'Semiotic' finds its way into the not yet fully regulated language of children, into poetry, into the language of mental illness – into all uses of language that for whatever reason are not fully under the control of the speaker or writer. 'Symbolic' and 'semi-otic' language are never to be found in their 'pure' state: all language is a mixture of the two:

> These two modalities are inseparable within the *signifying process* that constitutes language, and the dialectic between them determines the type of discourse (narrative, metalan-guage, theory, poetry, etc.) involved; in other words, so-called 'natural' language allows for different modes of articulation of the semiotic and symbolic.
>
> (Kristeva 1984 [1974]: 24)

Semiotic purity is only possible in 'nonverbal signifying systems' such as music. Whenever we use language, both our conscious (which participates in the 'Symbolic') and our unconscious (Kristeva's 'Semiotic') mark it with their presence. As in Lacanian psychoanalysis, the subject is irrevocably split.

The sort of writing that Cixous and Kristeva have in mind is fairly rare in the history of literature. We might think of James Joyce's *Finnegans Wake* (1939) or of Virginia Woolf's *The Waves* (1931). The attitude that it presupposes is much less rare nowa-days. In *Surfacing* (1972), by the Canadian writer Margaret Atwood, we find a young woman caught in a rational, patriar-chal, and often exploitative world exemplified by her lover, her father, and other male characters. During a trip to the wilder-ness, ostensibly in search for her missing father, she gradually strips herself of the perspective and the accoutrements of the rational modern world. Not accidentally, a dive deep into a pristine lake – into what hides under the surface – is the novel's turning-point. When she figuratively resurfaces at the end of the novel from a brief period of almost complete surrender to instincts, she will always take the experience and the resulting knowledge with her.

A final word on the poststructuralist uses of psychoanalysis: in recent years poststructuralist adaptations of psychoanalysis have proven a useful instrument in for instance criticism that is concerned with ecological issues. In his *Postmodern Wetlands: Culture, History, Ecology* (1996), Rod Giblett examines Western descriptions of, and arguments about, swamps, wetlands, and other places that are neither land nor water, and suggests that '[t]he swamp, and the wetland more generally, is … a smothering place, or perhaps more precisely a (s)mothering place, where various desires and fears about the mother's body are played out' (Giblett 1996: 20). As 'the pre-Oedipal place par excellence' (20) wetlands have over the course of history been structurally maligned and have often even been definitively repressed, through filling or drainage. Giblett offers numerous readings of poems and passages taken from stories and novels to back up his claim. Much more could be said about this and other recent developments, but, given the scope of this book, I must turn to another subject, the Foucauldian-inspired 'new historicism'.

---

## Summary

In the course of the 1970s and the 1980s literary studies begin to incorporate the thought of the poststructuralist historian Michel Foucault and the poststructuralist psychoanalysist Jacques Lacan. Foucault's work calls our attention to the role of language in the exercise and preservation of power. According to Foucault, the modern Western world is in the grip of so-called *discourses* that regulate our behaviour because we have internalized them and for all practical purposes police ourselves. Foucauldian criticism focuses on the role of literary and other texts in the circulation and maintenance of social power. Lacan's psychoanalytic theories serve to explain why we would internalize discourses that effectively imprison us. Lacanian criticism has been especially illuminating with regard to the relationship that readers enter into with the texts they read.

## Suggestions for further reading

*The Foucault Reader*, edited by David Rabinow (1984), is an excellent selection from Foucault's writings, with an emphasis on his later work. The interviews that are included serve as brief and lucid introductions to his thought. Another collection, *Power/Knowledge: Selected Interviews and Other Writings, 1972–1977*, edited by Colin Gordon (1980), also contains helpful characterizations of his work by Foucault himself – see 'Two Lectures' and 'Truth and Power'. Foucault's famous – and quite readable – discussion of 'panopticism' was originally published in Part III of his *Discipline and Punish* (1977). The radically anti-humanist essay 'What Is an Author?' (1969) is reprinted in Lodge and Wood (2000).

Good brief introductions to psychoanalytic criticism are Meredith Skura's 'Psychoanalytic Criticism' (1992) and Peter Brooks's 'The Idea of Psychoanalytic Criticism' (in his *Psychoanalysis and Storytelling*, 1994). A comprehensive and recent overview is offered by Elizabeth Wright in *Psychoanalytic Criticism: A Reappraisal*, 2nd edn (1998). Norman M. Holland's *Holland's Guide to Psychoanalytic Psychology and Literature-and-Psychology* (1991) is a somewhat older comprehensive guide to all types of psychoanalysis and their usefulness for literary criticism. Malcolm Bowie's *Lacan* (1991) is perhaps the best introduction to Lacan.

Lacan's own writings are notoriously difficult. Readers who are not easily discouraged might try 'The Insistence of the Letter in the Unconscious' (in Lodge and Wood), Lacan's discussion of *Hamlet* ('Desire and the Interpretation of Desire in *Hamlet*', 1977), or his reading of Poe's 'The Purloined Letter' (in John P. Muller and William J. Richardson's *The Purloined Poe*, 1988). Bruce Fink provides a very helpful guide to the *Hamlet* discussion in his 'Reading Hamlet with Lacan' (1996). Lacanian criticism, working as it does with highly complex material, is usually not easily accessible either. Shoshana Felman's 'Turning the Screw of Interpretation' (1982a) has become classic. The essays collected by Robert Con Davis in *Lacan and Narration: The Psychoanalytic Difference in Narrative Theory* (1983) illustrate how Lacanian psychoanalysis can be brought to bear upon narrative theory. A good deal more accessible, and highly recommended, are Linda Ruth Williams's Lacanian readings in her *Critical Desire: Psychoanalysis and the Literary Subject* (1995).

*Literary Feminisms* by Ruth Robbins (2000) gives a good and very readable account of French feminism in relation to, in particular, Lacanian psychoanalysis. *Between Feminism and Psychoanalysis* (1990), edited by Teresa Brennan, collects fifteen essays on French feminism by major feminist critics.

Chapter 7

# Literature and culture

*The new historicism and cultural materialism*

## Defining culture

In his *Culture and Anarchy*, first published in 1869, Matthew Arnold, whose formative influence on English and American literary studies I have discussed in the first chapter, sees as one of the sources of the 'anarchy' of his title, which he sees as a threat to the whole fabric of English society, a working class which 'assert[s] an Englishman's heaven-born privilege of doing as he likes' ([1869] 1971: 105). Unfortunately, this personal freedom does not lead the working class towards 'the best that has been thought and said' and towards the 'essentially disinterested' attitude that the appreciation of culture demands. It does, instead, lead to activities and pastimes that in their brashness and thoughtless vulgarity are the antithesis of culture. Another source of anarchy is to be found in the ruthless entrepreneurs who are busy creating an exclusively profit-oriented, dehumanized economy that with its utilitarian mentality has as little genuine interest in what Arnold sees as culture as in

171

the labourers it exploits. As its title already suggests, *Culture and Anarchy* sets up a binary opposition between culture – which for Arnold implies coherence and order – on the one hand and chaos and lawlessness on the other. The term 'culture' is explicitly reserved for what most literary academics would now consider to be a rather narrowly defined 'high' culture – the culture of a specific elite. Arnold never uses the term in the more anthropological or sociological senses in which we now often use it, referring to the way of life and the world view of, for instance, the working class.

The opposition between a superior high culture, whose literary branch preserves the best that has been thought and said, and the debased anthropologically defined 'cultures' that always threaten its existence runs like a red thread through English and American criticism. It is echoed in T.S. Eliot's notion that a once organic and perfectly integrated Renaissance world had suffered a disastrous 'dissociation of sensibility' at the end of the seventeenth century and virtually repeated in F.R. Leavis's conviction that that dissociation was the direct result of industrialization and of the emergence of what he called a 'technologico-Benthamite civilization' (Leavis 1967: 24). It is, in fact, this opposition between high culture and the various – and socially dominant – ways of life or cultures that threaten it that gave English studies its extraordinary self-confidence, determination, and even missionary overtones. The idea that high culture is essentially different from other forms of culture and that it has an inherently oppositional role to play with regard to other cultural expressions explains the missionary zeal and the moral urgency that we so often encounter in classic humanist criticism. It also explains its recurring sense of beleaguerment, the conviction – which is especially prominent in Leavis's later work – that it is surrounded by hostile forces.

However, although it had strong opinions about lower-class and/or mass culture (which we should not conflate or confuse with each other, as we will see in a moment), traditional criticism did not do much to examine and understand it (there are one or two exceptions, but as their influence remained limited I will not discuss them here ). This changed in the late 1950s with the

English critic Richard Hoggart's *The Uses of Literacy: Aspects of Working-Class Life with Special Reference to Publications and Entertainments* ([1957] 1971), which offered a warm, autobiographical account of Yorkshire working-class culture of the 1930s and 1940s combined with a close reading of popular magazines of the period, and with Raymond Williams's *Culture and Society, 1780–1950* ([1958] 1961), which traces the idea of culture as it developed in England from the late eighteenth century to (almost) the time of writing. Both Hoggart and Williams were literary academics, with Hoggart representing the humanist perspective and Williams the Marxist one, and both emphasized the valuable and life-enhancing qualities of cultures, in particular working-class culture, that from the perspective of high culture had generally been condemned and ignored. Here is an example of Hoggart's firm but sympathetic attitude. Admitting that the more genuinely working-class magazines and the fiction that they print for their primarily female readers 'are in some ways crude', Hoggart goes on to stress that 'they still have a felt sense of the texture of life in the group they cater for' ([1957] 1972: 490). (The phrase 'felt sense of the texture of life', to which I will return in a moment, betrays Hoggart's training with Leavis.) 'Most of the material is conventional', Hoggart continues, 'that is, it mirrors the attitudes of the readers; but those attitudes are by no means as ridiculous as one might first be tempted to think' (490). Working-class culture is simple, often even 'childish', but it is genuine and affirmative and it plays a valuable role in the lives of millions of people.

Still, although it does not hesitate to step across the barrier dividing literature from what we might call pulp fiction, Hoggart's book repeats in an important way the traditional, Leavisite, juxtaposition of authenticity and inauthenticity. While for Hoggart the older and more traditional working-class magazines convey authenticity (a 'felt sense of ... life') the newer ones tend to succumb to an inauthentic sensationalism that is a sure sign of the postwar commodification of the genre, a calculated policy aimed at achieving maximum sales – and maximum profit – at the expense of honesty and sincerity. A new, manipulative mass culture is taking the place of an older popular culture in which there was still a bond, a system of shared values, between publisher and writer on the one hand and the audience on the other. Under the new dispensation the audience is just there to be exploited. Just as for Leavis 'serious' literature is more 'true' than the stuff of popular magazines, for Hoggart what he finds in those traditional magazines is more 'true' than what the cheap sensationalism of the new mass publications has to offer. In Williams, who also had studied with Leavis, we find similar echoes of the ideal of an organic and coherent culture. 'We need a common culture,' Williams tells us in the concluding chapter of *Culture and Society*, 'because we shall not survive without it' (Williams 1961: 304). Paradoxically, he is fully aware that in any given society we will find more than one single culture – which in his use of the term signifies 'a whole way of life' that is ultimately characterized by its 'ideas of the nature of social relationship' (311). (In the case of, for instance, working-class culture 'social relationship' is determined by solidarity.) But the coexistence of alternative cultures such as those of the bourgeois middle class and the lower class does not rule out a common culture: 'In our culture as a whole, there is both a constant interaction between these ways of life and an area which can properly be described as common to or underlying both' (313). The further development of that common culture is then described as organic growth monitored by its members: 'The idea of a common culture brings together ... at once the idea of natural growth and that of its tending' (322). Hoggart and especially Williams radically expand the field of study for literary criticism, with Williams introducing a virtually anthropological concept of culture, even if he grants the 'vital importance' of literature:

the ways in which we draw on other experience are more various than literature alone. For experience that is formally recorded we go, not only to the rich source of literature, but also to history, building, painting, music, philosophy, theology and social theory, the physical and natural sciences, anthropology, and indeed the whole body of learning. We go also, if we are wise, to the experience that is otherwise recorded: in institutions, manners, customs, family memories.

(248)

Although in their privileging of authenticity and organic coherence Hoggart and Williams belong to what for many critics writing today is an older intellectual dispensation, with their work what we now call 'cultural studies' becomes a legitimate interest of literary academics, a development reflected in the title of a pamphlet that Hoggart published in 1969: *Contemporary Cultural Studies: An Approach to the Study of Literature and Society*. Since the early 1970s, and starting in the United Kingdom, critics have come to cast their net much wider and have moved far beyond the relations between literature and society that Hoggart's title refers to. The vast influence of Williams has played a crucial role here, but Hoggart, in his capacity as director of the then newly founded Centre for Contemporary Cultural Studies at the University of Birmingham, has also contributed substantially to the explosive expansion of literary studies into other realms that we have witnessed since the mid-1970s and which since then has been strongly boosted by poststructuralism's radical questioning of the supposed difference between literary and non-literary texts. As this already suggests, cultural studies has gone through fundamental changes since the days of Hoggart and Williams. During the 1980s and 1990s most practitioners of cultural studies have accepted the poststructuralist repudiation of origin, presence, and coherence and have turned away from approaches that see culture in authentic and organic terms to embrace views that are strongly influenced by Derrida and, more in particular, Foucault. Culture, no matter whether it is that of the English Renaissance aristocracy or that of contemporary soccer hooligans, is now widely seen as artificial in the sense that it is always manufactured, always the rather arbitrary – and provisional – end product of an endless series of interactions and exchanges. No culture can claim authenticity – although many of them routinely do – and no culture gives access to truths that lie beyond itself, beyond its own discourse, in Foucault's terms.

## The new historicism and cultural materialism

The constructedness of culture and its annexation by literary studies are central in two major modes within contemporary criticism: the new historicism, which was American in origin and has remained largely American, and cultural materialism, which was, and is, mainly British.

Let me, before I discuss them separately, make clear what these critical modes have in common. First of all, both brought to the then still traditional study of Renaissance literature, in particular the work of Shakespeare, a mixture of Marxist and poststructuralist orientations, especially poststructuralist notions of the self, of discourse, and of power, with the new historicism leaning more towards a (Foucauldian) poststructuralism in its focus on power (in Foucault's sense of the term), on the discourses that serve as vehicles for power, on the construction of identity, and so on, and with cultural materialism leaning more towards the Marxism of Raymond Williams (who had coined the term 'cultural materialism' in his 1977 *Marxism and Literature*) and its focus on ideology, on the role of institutions, and on the possibilities for subversion (or dissidence, as some cultural materialists prefer to call it).

Needless to say that with this intellectual background the new historicism and cultural materialism reject both the autonomy and individual genius of the author and the autonomy of the literary work and see literary texts as absolutely inseparable from their historical context. The role of the author is not completely negated, but it is a role that the author is at best only partially in command of. The author's role is to a large extent determined by historical circumstances. As the prominent new historicist critic Stephen Greenblatt has put it: 'the work of art is the product of a negotiation between a creator or class or creators, equipped with a complex, communally shared repertoire of conventions, and the institutions and practices of society' (Greenblatt 1989: 12). The literary text, then, is always part and parcel of a much wider cultural, political, social, and economic dispensation. Far from being untouched by the historical moment of its creation, the literary text is directly involved in history. Instead of transcending its own time and place, as traditional Anglo-American criticism had argued (and was still arguing), the literary text is a time- and place-bound verbal construction that is always in one way or another political. Because it is inevitably involved with a discourse or an ideology it cannot help being a vehicle for power. As a consequence, and just like any other text, literature does not simply reflect relations of power, but actively participates in the consolidation and/or construction of discourses and ideologies, just as it functions as an instrument in the construction of identities, not only at the individual level – that of the subject – but also on the level of the group or even that of the national state. Literature is not simply a product of history, it also actively *makes* history. Because they do not see literature as a special category of transcendent, essentially ahistorical texts – even if it might be formally distinct – new historicists and cultural materialists treat literary texts in the same way that they treat other texts. For their specific purposes – to trace and bring to light relations of power and processes of ideological and cultural construction – there is no longer a difference between literature and other texts, no matter whether these are religious, political, historical, or products of marginal subcultures that so far have been ignored. Finally, in their conviction that culture, including all beliefs and values, is a construction, the new historicists and cultural materialists are willing to grant that their own assumptions must also be constructed and may therefore be deconstructed. But that does not prevent them from taking up political positions that are motivated by a political vision that resists the conservatism of the 1980s (the Reagan years in the United States, the Thatcher era in the United Kingdom). The prominent new historicist critic Catherine Gallagher has argued that new historicist and cultural materialist thought must be seen as a continuation of certain strands within the New Left of the late 1960s (Gallagher 1989). As we will see, with regard to new historicist practice – as opposed to theory – not everybody accepts that claim at face value.

## The new historicism

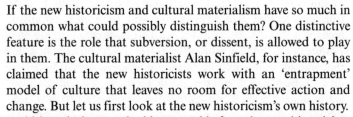

If the new historicism and cultural materialism have so much in common what could possibly distinguish them? One distinctive feature is the role that subversion, or dissent, is allowed to play in them. The cultural materialist Alan Sinfield, for instance, has claimed that the new historicists work with an 'entrapment' model of culture that leaves no room for effective action and change. But let us first look at the new historicism's own history.

Although the term had been used before, the new historicism received its current meaning in 1982, when the prominent new historicist critic Stephen Greenblatt used it to describe recent work of himself and others on the Renaissance period. Most commentators situate its origin in 1980, though, when Greenblatt published his book *Renaissance Self-Fashioning: From More to Shakespeare* and when another prominent new historicist, Louis Montrose, argued for the presence of power in a genre usually not associated with its exercise, that of the pastoral. Following Foucault in his assumption that 'social relations are, intrinsically, relations of power', Montrose examined the role of Elizabethan pastorals in 'the symbolic mediation of social relationships' in his essay ' "Eliza, Queen of Shepeardes", and the Pastoral of Power' (Montrose 1994: 88). *Renaissance Self-Fashioning* (in which Greenblatt described his critical practice as 'a poetics of culture', a label to which he would return in the late 1980s) argues that 'in the sixteenth century there appears to be an increased self-consciousness about the fashioning of human identity as a manipulable, artful process' (Greenblatt 1980: 2). This should not be taken to mean, however, that it was possible for Renaissance individuals to fashion a truly autonomous identity – indeed to fashion themselves fully and authentically. Thomas More finds that his 'condition' or 'project' – a term which does grant a measure of autonomy – is 'to live [his] life as a character thrust into a play, constantly renewing [him]self extemporaneously and forever aware of [his] own unreality' (31), while Wyatt 'cannot fashion himself in opposition to power and the conventions power deploys; on the contrary, those conventions are precisely what constitute Wyatt's self-fashioning' (214). An increased awareness of the ways in which the self can be fashioned leads to an increased awareness of how the self is subject to power relations and how it always functions within larger structures that may even completely control whatever self-fashioning seemed initially possible. *Self-Fashioning* ultimately subscribes to the poststructuralist notion that the self is always a construction, that our identity is never given, but always the product of an interaction between the way we want to represent ourselves – through the stories we tell (or the incidents we suppress) and our actual presentations – and the power relations we are part of. Inspired by Foucault's interest in large-scale historical ruptures, Greenblatt's study also introduced a major theme of the new historicism's earlier years: the way in which the workings of power and practices of regulation change with the advent of a new era, in this case the transition from the premodern to the early modern period, with its notion of the autonomy and freedom of the subject.

There is good reason, then, to accept John Brannigan's definition of the new historicism as 'a mode of critical interpretation which privileges power relations as the most important context for texts of all kinds' and his claim that '[a]s a critical practice it treats literary texts as a space where power relations are made visible' (Brannigan 1998: 6). It is probably not necessary to point out that power in this context does not refer to physical power and not even to coercion through pressure, although it is usually in a position to be backed up by the threat of physical violence. In this Foucauldian context, power works through discourses and, like ideology, gives the subject the impression that to comply with its dictates is the natural thing to do and thus a free, autonomous decision. It does not need to appear repressive because it effectively turns the subject into its own watchdog. George Orwell's Big Brother watches from inside our minds. The new historicists see literature as actively involved in the making of history through its participation in discursive practices. To give another example, Louis Montrose's 1983 essay ' "Shaping

Fantasies": Figurations of Gender and Power in Elizabethan Culture' discusses a wide range of texts – including autobiography, travel writing, and a Shakespeare play – to examine how representations of Queen Elizabeth I – the 'shaping fantasies' of his title – contribute to the creation of the cult of the 'virgin queen'.

This is not literary history, but it is also not cultural history, at least not cultural history as it developed as a subdiscipline within the much larger field of history during the 1970s. The new historicism – and this is another interest that it has in common with cultural materialism – is in the tradition of Foucault focused on thus far hidden and unsuspected sources of, and vehicles for, power and on the question of how power has worked to suppress or marginalize rival stories and discourses. Its methods, in so far as it can be said to be methodical, are anthropological rather than literary critical – although a good deal of close reading is involved – or historical. History, such as the socio-economic circumstances of a specific literary text's creation or biographical data regarding its author, is not read to illuminate literature, nor is literature read to shed a direct light on history. Rather, the historical period in question is seen as a remote culture whose various discursive manifestations – the texts of all kinds that have come down to us and which constitute all that we have to work with – need detailed attention and need to be brought into contact with each other so that the power relations and the forces operating in that culture may be brought to light. This means that it does not much matter from which point we try to access it – the earlier new historicism of the 1980s is famous for opening its enquiries with seemingly anecdotal material that is later on shown to have great relevance. Since under the regime of a specific hegemony (to use Gramsci's term) or dominant ideology everything is interrelated, and since no specific body of texts has a privileged status, we can always go where we want to go in our exploration of past cultures. In its focus on relations of power the new historicism follows the discursive forms that power takes – its figures of speech, its larger rhetorical manoeuvres – wherever they appear. Distinctions that for other approaches to literary studies are of the highest importance, such as that between literature and non-literary texts or that between economic base and cultural superstructure, are from this perspective irrelevant. Everything is culture, and culture can be read and picked apart like a literary text. In its rather loose methodology the new historicism is indebted to the American anthropologist Clifford Geertz, not only because of his insistence that all culture is 'manufactured', and for all practical purposes without origins – which is roughly in line with the poststructuralist view of culture – but also because of his method of 'thick description', that is analysis by way of detailed and minutely observed social and cultural practices. New historicist criticism borrows both from Geertz and from Foucault's large-scale studies of 'discursive practices' and their repressive effects.

It is the pervasive influence of Foucault that has elicited a good deal of criticism. Foucault's views of power and its effectiveness have been widely, and inconclusively, debated, but no matter how we finally judge those views there are passages in his work that suggest a deep pessimism regarding the possibility of resistance. In a seminal new historicist essay, 'Invisible Bullets' of 1981, Stephen Greenblatt echoes Foucault's pessimistic strain and argues that Renaissance subversion inevitably played into the hands of power. In fact, power *needs* subversion and actively produces it: 'subversiveness is the very product of that power and furthers its ends' (Greenblatt 1981: 48). This pessimism, which for a number of commentators has thrown doubt on the new historicism's commitment to a progressive, emancipatory politics, is not necessarily shared by all new historicists and I should in all fairness say that Greenblatt himself has also defended himself against charges such as Alan Sinfield's claim that the new historicism works with an 'entrapment' model. Still, although he argues that '[a]gency is virtually inescapable' (Greenblatt 1990: 74), he immediately goes on to sketch a very limited horizon for agency:

> new historicism, as I understand it, does not posit historical processes as unalterable and inexorable, but it does tend to discover limits or constraints upon individual intervention:

> actions that appear to be single are disclosed as multiple; the apparently isolated power of the individual genius turns out to be bound up with collective, social energy; a gesture of dissent may be an element in a larger legitimation process, while an attempt to stabilize the order of things may turn out to subvert it.
>
> (74–75)

Greenblatt's defence has, in any case, not convinced all his critics. In his recent discussion of the new criticism John Brannigan repeats the claims that, because resistance is always produced by the power it seemingly would seek to subvert, '[n]ew historicism often makes for grim reading with its insistence that there is no effective space of resistance' (Brannigan 1998: 8).

The new historicists are aware that the at best limited freedom of the subject *vis-à-vis* the culture's hegemonic discourse and its inevitable involvement with that discourse did not stop with the Renaissance period. As Louis Montrose has put it: 'I have a complex and substantial stake in sustaining and reproducing the very institutions whose operations I wish to call into question' (Montrose 1989: 30). More generally, new historicists – like the cultural materialists – are very much aware that their understanding of historical texts is to an important extent shaped by the socio-cultural reality that they themselves are part of. If the texts that they study are to a substantial degree co-produced by the social reality of their authors then clearly that must also be the case with their own texts.

New historicist arguments are then always to some degree the product of the author's personal, social, and institutional situation and can therefore only be partial and provisional. We might well ask what the point of new historicist research is if we know beforehand that whatever it comes up with will be flawed and therefore incomplete. One important answer to this question is that new historicist arguments about the past, no matter how flawed, are relevant for our own contemporary situation. Inevitably, we too live within discourses that we have at least partly been shaped by. However, as Montrose suggests, although the 'possibility of political and institutional agency cannot be based upon the illusion of an escape from ideology', an *awareness* of the omnipresence and power of ideology may give us some breathing space:

> the very process of subjectively *living* the confrontations or contradictions within or among ideologies makes it possible to experience facets of our own subjection at shifting internal distances – to read ... one fragment of our ideological inscription by means of another. A reflexive knowledge so partial and unstable may, nevertheless, provide subjects with a means of empowerment as agents.
>
> (30)

The awareness of the role that discourses have played in shaping us, and the possibility of letting opposed and competing discourses collide and thereby implode, may make room for relatively independent thought and action which can then have emancipatory effects in the present. The assumption here is that the resistance that is thus made possible is not a product of power but is genuinely subversive.

Let me conclude this section with a few observations. I have up till this point created the impression that the new historicism is only concerned with the Renaissance. Although it did indeed first emerge within Renaissance studies, where it caused a true revolution, by the mid-1980s new historicist approaches had already spread to the study of other periods – to Victorian studies, for instance – and in the 1990s we find them virtually everywhere. Secondly, and this is also true of cultural materialism, in the later 1980s and early 1990s, the dividing lines between the new historicism (and cultural materialism) on the one hand, and feminism and the newly emerging field of postcolonial studies on the other, begin to fade away.

Greenblatt's *Marvellous Possessions: The Wonder of the New World* of 1991, for instance, operates in a field of enquiry that we would now call postcolonial. It examines the role that 'wonder' plays in the response of European explorers and travellers to the

New World. He characteristically sees that wonder as 'an agent of appropriation' (Greenblatt 1991: 24), in the sense that the representations of wonder that we find in those (written) responses function as an instrument of power. Under Greenblatt's scrutiny, 'European representational practice' turns out to have played a vital role in the process of colonization that followed exploration and travel. Although its focus is on the Europeans and not on the new worlds and new peoples that give rise to European wonder – as is usually the case in the so-called postcolonial studies that I will discuss in the next chapter – *Marvellous Possessions* is as much postcolonial as it is new historicist. The new directions we find in 1990s new historicism can be interpreted as a sign of the times, as testimony to the sudden, and pervasive, influence of the new field of postcolonial studies, but it is also a response to serious critique. Feminist and other critics had begun to object to the steamroller effect of the new historicism's view of power – to how in new historicist criticism structures of power flattened and homogenized all subjects that lived within them so that differences in class, sex, and race completely disappeared from view. Responding to such criticisms, the new historicism had begun to take such differences into account in its analyses of the way subjects are constructed. In the new historicism of the 1990s, subjects are not simply the product of the dominant ideology, but can to various degrees – and at various times – be co-constructed, so to speak, by one or more subcultures. Such a view immediately brings issues of sex and race, for instance, to the foreground. But the contemporary theorizing of sex and race that has emerged from the – ultimately – poststructuralist insistence on difference will have to wait until later.

## Cultural materialism

Cultural materialist criticism established itself permanently within the field of literary studies in the mid-1980s, with the publication of Jonathan Dollimore's *Radical Tragedy: Religion, Ideology and Power in the Drama of Shakespeare and his Contemporaries* (1984), of Catherine Belsey's *The Subject of*

*Tragedy: Identity and Difference in Renaissance Drama* (1985), and of two collections of essays: *Alternative Shakespeares* (1985) edited by John Drakakis, and *Political Shakespeare: Essays in Cultural Materialism* (1985) edited by Jonathan Dollimore and Alan Sinfield.

Let me briefly recapitulate the major assumptions that the new historicism and cultural materialism have in common. First of all, subjects cannot transcend their own time but live and work within the horizon of a culture constructed by ideology, by discourses. The ideological constructions that authors live in, and have internalized, inevitably become part of their work, which is therefore always political and always a vehicle for power. As Dollimore and Sinfield put it in their introduction to *Political Shakespeare*, '[a] play by Shakespeare is related to the context of its production – to the economic and political system of Elizabethan and Jacobean England and to the particular institutions of cultural production (the church, patronage, theatre, education)' (Dollimore and Sinfield 1985: viii). Because it plays an active role in the creation and consolidation of power relations, literature does not merely reflect the culture in which it is produced, but actively contributes to the constitution of culture, and thus of history. Like the new historicism, cultural materialism brings to light how ideology – and thus the existing social (and religious) order – tries to maintain itself or, as the case may be, adjust itself to new circumstances, without losing its grip. Finally, since the status of literature is not essentially different from that of other texts (religious, political, economic, legal, and so on) in the sense that it has no special access to genuine, transcendent truth, it merits no special treatment, but is read alongside a wide variety of non-literary texts.

What sets cultural materialism apart from its slightly older sibling? I have already briefly indicated that cultural materialists object to what they see as the new historicism's downplaying of subversion and dissent or at least of dissent's effectiveness. Cultural materialists agree that literary texts will at first sight seem supportive of contemporary ideology, but see that ideology as less pervasive than their new historicist colleagues. Although Foucault is an obvious influence in their work – especially with regard to their interest in the insane, the criminal, the exploited, and all those who over the course of history have been marginalized – cultural materialism follows Williams in his adaptation of Gramsci's view of hegemony. For Williams, as we have seen, the dominant culture is never more than one player in the cultural field, even if it is by far the most powerful. There are always residual and emergent strains within a culture that offer alternatives to what Gramsci called the hegemony. In Williams's own words: 'no dominant culture ever in reality includes or exhausts all human practice, human energy and human intention' (Williams 1977: 125). In other words, the dominant culture is always under pressure from alternative views and beliefs. So while cultural materialist analyses of literary texts bring to light how these texts are (inevitably conservative) instruments of a dominant socio-cultural order, they also demonstrate how the apparent coherence of that order is threatened from the inside, by inner contradictions and by tensions that it seeks to hide.

Alan Sinfield's discussion of Shakespeare's *Othello* in his *Faultlines: Cultural Materialism and the Politics of Dissident Reading* (1992) is a case in point. In the patriarchal culture that the play presents Desdemona is of course bound to obey her father and the role of obedient daughter should in the normal course of things lead her to follow his wishes in her marital choice. However, in the early modern period we also find an increased emphasis on the idea that marriage should be personally fulfilling. This 'contradiction in the ideology of marriage' – one of Sinfield's 'faultlines' – allows Desdemona to disregard her father's wishes and to marry a man who from the perspective of the social group to which she belongs is totally unsuitable. As a result, the social order comes under immediate pressure. I should hasten to point out that Sinfield does not portray Desdemona in liberal humanist terms: she is not a free, autonomous agent in the dissident choice that she makes. It is the faultline in question that creates what Sinfield calls 'dissident potential'. Dissidence is not so much a matter of individual agency but is first of all produced by the inner contradictions that characterize any social order.

Since such faultlines are to be found in all cultures, it is only natural that they should turn up in literary texts – especially in literary texts, in fact, because literature offers a place where, with ideology still firmly in control, contradictions and tensions can be addressed and worked through. Focusing on the cracks in the ideological façade that texts offer, cultural materialism reads even the most reactionary texts against the grain, offering readings of dissidence that allow us to hear the socially marginalized and expose the ideological machinery that is responsible for their marginalization and exclusion. Cultural materialists are also interested in the way in which the reception of literary texts – by, for instance, traditional Anglo-American criticism – has obscured the presence of such ideological faultlines in those texts. Dollimore's *Radical Tragedy* argues (among many other things) that traditional interpretations of the Jacobean tragedies that he discusses – including Marlowe's *Dr. Faustus* and Tourneur's *The Revenger's Tragedy* – have ignored how the plays undermine humanist assumptions because they focus on what fits the humanist framework. Such a demonstration of complicity between criticism and text obviously legitimizes alternative, subversive readings.

Cultural materialism sees such dissident readings of texts from the past as political interventions in the present, as political challenges to the conservative, humanistically oriented positions and critical practices that are still very much in evidence among literary academics and among those that control educational institutions. Its critical practice, then, not only tries to offer alternative understandings of the past – although it certainly does so – but equally, and overtly, tries to effectuate political change in the present from a broadly socialist and feminist point of view. (Catherine Belsey's discussion, in *The Subject of Tragedy*, of the various literary – and non-literary – representations of the sixteenth-century murderess-by-proxy Alice Arden immediately announces cultural materialism's investment in feminism, even if Belsey's interest in the intrinsic instability of the text as proclaimed by Derridean poststructuralism sets her somewhat apart from the cultural materialist mainstream.) As Dollimore and Sinfield polemically announce in their introduction to *Political Shakespeare*:

Cultural materialism does not, like much established criticism, attempt to mystify its perspective as the natural, obvious or right interpretation of an allegedly given textual fact. On the contrary, it registers its commitment to the transformation of a social order which exploits people on grounds of race, gender and class.

(Dollimore and Sinfield 1985: viii)

Where new historicists would be satisfied to bring to light hidden power relations in a cluster of Renaissance texts, cultural materialists seek to find instances of dissidence, subversion, and transgression that are relevant in contemporary political struggles. Because of this double focus, cultural materialism is deeply interested in the ways in which literature from the past, say the works of Shakespeare, has been made to function in later periods and in our contemporary culture. As Dollimore and Sinfield point out: 'culture is made continuously and Shakespeare's text is reconstructed, reappraised, reassigned all the time through diverse institutions in specific contexts. What the plays signify, how they signify, depends on the cultural field in which they are situated' (viii). Cultural materialism could for instance ask which plays, or parts of plays, feature on secondary school reading lists. And which plays we find within university curricula or which sonnets are standardly anthologized. Which plays are performed, and where, and within what context? How do we read the recent version of *Richard III* – starring Ian McKellen – which lifts the play right out of its historical period and has its protagonist set up a monstrously fascist regime in 1930s Great Britain? In other words, how is 'Shakespeare' constructed, and from what ideological position? In one of the essays collected in *Political Shakespeare* Sinfield concludes that '[i]n education Shakespeare has been made to speak mainly for the right', adding that 'that is the tendency which this book seeks to alter' (Dollimore and Sinfield 1985: 135). As was the case for Raymond Williams, for cultural materialists ideology takes on a tangible, material form in institutions like the university, the museum, the army, the school, the labour union, the church, and so on. And it becomes material in the ways in which images and representations from the past are deployed in the service of contemporary ideology – in for instance the merchandising of the product called 'Shakespeare' (and other big sellers in the heritage industry) and the use of 'Shakespeare' in commercials. In *Faultlines* Sinfield shows how a reference to Shakespeare's Globe Theatre, evoking the continuity of British tradition, is used by a manufacturer of defence equipment to promote itself and its wares. From the perspective of cultural materialism, contemporary culture, both in its institutionalized and in its popular and mass-produced forms, is a battlefield where an omnipresent conservative ideology must constantly be challenged.

The acrimony of the debate that followed cultural materialism's emergence in the mid-1980s testifies to the effectiveness of its intervention, although it also demonstrates the strength and number of those literary academics who prefer a more traditional, and still broadly humanist, approach to, in particular, Shakespeare ('The Bard'), whose work was the focus of a protracted battle. Just like the new historicism, cultural materialism has in the years since its intervention in the field of Renaissance studies become an important critical practice in virtually every period and just like the new historicism it has in the early 1990s expanded its original interests and incorporated issues of empire and sexuality (feminism had from the beginning been on its agenda) – always with the intention of effecting political change in our current arrangements. Jonathan Dollimore's *Sexual Dissidence: Augustine to Wilde, Freud to Foucault* (1991) and Alan Sinfield's *The Wilde Century: Effeminacy, Oscar Wilde and the Queer Moment* (1994b) and his *Cultural Politics – Queer Reading* of the same year exemplify this development, but the so-called 'queer theory' that we see in the making in these texts – and in a whole range of other texts from around the same time – will have to wait until a later chapter. We will turn first to postcolonial theory – the issues of empire – that I have already briefly mentioned and that in the 1990s became another direction in which cultural materialism developed.

## Summary

After the assimilation of poststructuralist theory, literary criticism increasingly begins to see literature as an integral part of a much wider cultural context. Initially in the field of Renaissance studies, but later on in literary studies in general, critics start from the assumption that literary texts are inevitably situated within the sort of discourses that, according to Foucault, carry and maintain social power. The American new historicists and the British cultural materialists read literary texts for their role in the circulation of power, with the British critics having an additional interest in signs of genuine dissidence and in the usually conservative roles that cultural icons such as Shakespeare have been made to play in later times. In order to bring to light the political dimension of literary texts, new historicists and cultural materialists often read them in connection with non-literary texts and with reference to the dominant discourse or discourses of a given period.

## Suggestions for further reading

John Brannigan's *New Historicism and Cultural Materialism* (1998) is an excellent introduction while Kiernan Ryan's *New Historicism and Cultural Materialism: A Reader* (1996) presents important intellectual sources and examples of critical practice. Brief but to the point is Louis Montrose's 'New Historicisms' (1992). H. Aram Veeser's collection *The New Historicism Reader* (1994) brings together a number of important examples of the new historicism in action. Excellent examples of new historicist readings are Stephen Greenblatt's 'Invisible Bullets' and Louis Montrose's ' "Eliza, Queene of Shepeardes", and the Pastoral of Power'. Greenblatt especially is not exactly easy, but certainly rewarding. Christine Gallagher and Greenblatt's recent *Practicing New Historicism* (2000) offers essays on a wide range of topics. Ryan presents an excerpt from Alan Sinfield's *Faultlines* that wonderfully exemplifies cultural materialism's interest in dissidence. The second chapter of Sinfield's *Cultural Politics – Queer Reading* (1994a) is a lively introduction to cultural materialism. Also very readable is the polemical introduction to Jonathan Dollimore and Sinfield's *Political Shakespeare: New Essays in Cultural Materialism* (1985), a book that with its interest in 'Shakespeare' in the twentieth century also illustrates cultural materialism's contemporary focus.

Chapter 8

# Postcolonial criticism
and theory

## Introduction

As we have seen in Chapter 4, in the 1920s and
1930s, with the so-called Harlem Renaissance and
with the introduction of the concept of *négritude*,
'race' began to be a factor of importance in literary
studies. Refusing to be defined, on the basis of
race, by the dominant white culture,
African–American and French-speaking writers
from Africa and the Caribbean began to define
themselves and their culture in their own terms.
After the Second World War, this project of
cultural self-definition developed alongside the
project of political self-determination that we find
in the American Civil Rights movement and in the
African and Caribbean demand for political independence and nationhood. This should not create
the impression that cultural self-definition and
political self-determination moved along two
parallel lines that never met. On the contrary, the
one cannot really be separated from the other, and
not just in the sense that art is inevitably political.

**193**

The African–American Black Arts movement saw itself for instance as the cultural wing of the political Black Power movement of the 1960s and we have seen how Frantz Fanon, a radical critic of colonialism, saw national cultures – including national literatures – as important instruments in the struggle for political independence. Cultural self-definition and political self-determination were two sides of the same coin.

The desire for cultural self-determination, that is for cultural independence, is one of the moving forces behind the literatures that in the 1960s and 1970s spring up in the former colonies. Wilson Harris (Guyana), Yambo Ouologuem (Mali – a former French colony), Chinua Achebe (Nigeria), Wole Soyinka, the winner of the 1986 Nobel Prize for literature (also from Nigeria), Derek Walcott, the 1992 Nobel laureate (Saint Lucia), and a whole range of other writers create novels and poems that respond to, and reflect, their immediate cultural environment. In their response to specific cultural contexts, these texts signal the emergence – and in some cases, where a literary tradition had already developed, the confirmation – of new national literatures. (I have already sketched how, simultaneously, such national or, as the case may be, regional or ethnic literatures were retroactively created: critics in for instance the Caribbean began to establish a pedigree for the writing of the region and thereby asserted a long-standing cultural independence.) The desire to draw directly on one's own culture is defended vigorously in an essay called 'Colonialist Criticism' that Chinua Achebe first presented in 1974 (see Achebe 1995). Arguing that the 'universal' qualities that Western criticism expects from literature are not so much 'universal' as 'European' in a universal disguise, he attacks the idea that literary art should transcend its time and place. (Perhaps paradoxically, his own *Things Fall Apart* from 1958, which describes the effects of colonialism on an Igbo community in moving detail, has spoken to large audiences all over the world, and continues to do so.)

As its title indicates, *Things Fall Apart* is written in English, just as the large majority of literary works written in the former British colonies. That is not self-evident: English is often the second language of these writers, in particular in Africa. The choice for English, then, is a conscious choice, and one that is not uncontroversial. The Kenyan novelist Ngugi wa Thiong'o, for instance, has argued that the continued use of the language of the colonizer is a form of self-inflicted neo-colonization. However, even if African writers use English, they often let the rhythms and idioms of their own language be heard because the defamiliarization that results from such a practice automatically draws our attention to the non-English linguistic and cultural context of their work. But how should we classify that work? We cannot very well claim that *Things Fall Apart*, although written in English and dealing with British colonialism, belongs to English literature, just as we cannot seriously claim that Derek Walcott's epic poem *Omeros* (1990) is English. In recognition of this new situation, in which writing in English from the former colonies – including India, Pakistan, Sri Lanka, and other Asian colonies – has proved itself as vital and as important as the literature written in England itself, we now usually speak of 'literatures in English' rather than of 'English literature' if we want to refer to English-language writing.

## Commonwealth literary studies and Eurocentrism

When in the later 1960s it first became clear that the former colonies were busy producing literatures of their own, the idea that 'English literature' was mutating into 'literatures in English' of which the literary production of England was only one – although important – example, was still unthinkable. Instead, English critics interested in the writings that came out of the former colonies developed the idea of a 'Commonwealth literature': the English-language literature of the dependencies and former colonies that, with Great Britain at its centre, formed the so-called Commonwealth of Nations, or British Commonwealth. With hindsight, we can see that the idea of a Commonwealth literature followed the hierarchy of the political Commonwealth in that it placed the literature of Great Britain at the centre of this otherwise rather loose configuration. Although Commonwealth literary studies will rarely say so explicitly, English literature and English criticism set the norm.

In its early stages, the study of Commonwealth literature was traditionally humanistic. Its critical practice focuses on characters as free moral agents and on character development and mostly ignores the historical and cultural context within with they are placed by their creators. It concentrates on interpretation – that is, on meaning – and sees literature as having a special moral authority. Literature transforms all that is pedestrian and contingent about our problems and dilemmas and elevates them to a timeless aesthetic realm. This liberal humanist approach to English literature believed that it had universal validity because it drew on an unchanging, universal human condition, and was therefore without much further thought applied to the work of writers ranging from Jamaica to Nigeria and from India to New Zealand. Moreover, the perspective of this liberal humanism was specifically English. A writer like Chinua Achebe was not primarily seen as Nigerian, or even African, but as contributing to the English literary tradition and as an outpost of the great, humanistic, European civilization on which that tradition is based. It was in fact this idea that all Commonwealth writers were working within the English tradition that gave the otherwise hopelessly heterogeneous field of Commonwealth studies its unity. No matter how different writers from, say, New Zealand and Trinidad might be, what they were supposed to have in common was the heritage of English literature.

At that time, admission to the ranks of English literature might for writers from former colonies like Australia or Canada still have counted as an official stamp of approval. However, African, Asian, and Caribbean Commonwealth writers were on the whole not happy with the Western or *Eurocentric* perspective of Commonwealth criticism, not in the least because their memories of British colonial rule had not invariably convinced them of European civilization's humanistic superiority. In the course of the 1970s their objections – voiced in Achebe's 'Colonialist Criticism' and other critiques – began to find a serious echo in the writings of a number of British literary academics who had themselves begun to question the supposedly universal validity of humanist values. These critics argued that, first of all, overseas writers must be seen within the specific context of the culture they were part of and which informed their writing and that, secondly, that culture was not necessarily inferior to, but only different from, the culture of the mother country. Some critics even argued that the relationship between the former colonial powers and their colonies could most rewardingly be analysed with the help of Marxist concepts (with the colonized as the oppressed class) and that the role of literature should therefore also be considered from a Marxist perspective, that is as the vehicle of ideology. Looked at from this perspective, not only the literatures of other Commonwealth nations but also English literature itself begin to appear in a new light. As I have mentioned in the first chapter, English literature was in the course of the nineteenth century introduced in colonial India in order to 'civilize' the colonized elite. It is not implausible to suppose that the literature of the colonizers has indeed played a substantial ideological role in the process of colonization. From this perspective the work of Commonwealth writers will be read as either involved in an ideological struggle with (neo-)colonial forces or else ideologically complicit with them (as has happened with the work of the Trinidadian author V.S. Naipaul and, to a lesser extent, with the work of Salman Rushdie).

## From Commonwealth literary studies to postcolonial questions

In the last twenty-odd years, the question of how we should read writers who, like the Commonwealth writers, write in a European language but are geographically and often ethnically not European, has become more and more pressing. We now find African writers writing in English, French, Afrikaans, and Portuguese; Caribbean writers writing in English, French, Dutch, and Spanish; Indian and Pakistani writers writing in English; North African writers writing in French; and so on and so forth. These writers may still live in their home country or they may have moved to the *metropolis*, that is the centre of cultural power in a specific colonial relationship – London, and by extension all of England, for the Commonwealth nations, Paris (or France in general) for the French-speaking colonies.

However, wherever they live, the question of how we should read them remains the same. Is it appropriate – and relevant – to read them in a 'Western' way, for instance from a New Critical, a structuralist, or a cultural materialist perspective? Can such a 'Western' approach do justice to a literary text that is the product of a non-Western culture? And is it at all possible for Westerners to read non-Western literature, even if it is presented in a European language, without any sort of prejudice? There is now, moreover, a new category of writers that confronts us with the same question. All industrialized nations have in the postwar period absorbed substantial numbers of immigrants: people moving in from the former colonies, from labour reservoirs like Turkey and Morocco, and from war zones like Vietnam, Angola, or Iraq. The sons and daughters of these immigrants have by now begun to have an impact on the literatures of the places where they have grown up. In so doing they only rarely completely forsake their cultural heritage. Although German-born and educated, German writers of Turkish descent will usually work on the line where their own culture and the majority culture meet. They may for instance focus on the position of the Turkish minority and the various ways in which Islamic Turkish culture is forced to adjust itself to a wholly new cultural and political environment, or they may take German-born and German-educated Turkish men or women back to their parents' home town in Turkey and show the reader how such second-generation German Turks do not belong to either culture: not to a still largely Christian German culture and no longer to the culture of their parents. In a nation shaped by immigration like the United States such meetings of culture and the cultural displacements that usually follow from them are standard fare, from the encounters (and clashes) of Amerindian and English culture in James Fenimore Cooper's Leatherstocking novels to the uneasy negotiations between traditional Chinese and modern American culture that we find in, for instance, Maxine Hong Kingston's *The Woman Warrior* (1976). For Europe, however, such cultural encounters and the consequent displacements are new. Or perhaps it is more correct to say that the recognition of those encounters is new. After all, most European nations, no matter how small, have cultural and as often as not linguistic minorities within their borders.

The interest in such meetings of culture and in the displacements that they cause is more generally of very recent vintage. The United States, for instance, may have a long tradition of immigration, and may right from its revolutionary start in 1776 have harboured important ethnic minorities, but its attitude towards immigrants and its citizens of non-European descent has for a long time been assimilationist. To be a true American was to subscribe to the liberal humanist value system that pervaded – and still pervades – mainstream American culture. However, to take another culture seriously means to accept it on its own terms, to accept the distinctive ways in which it differs from our own culture. And it entails a genuine interest in the predicament of those who belong to the minority culture – in such encounters the cultures that are involved usually do not meet on equal terms – and who see their culture and their identity threatened by that of the dominant majority. To take another culture seriously means that we cannot take for granted that its literature shares our preconceptions and our systems of value or that it will reflect a universal human condition.

As I have just suggested, Commonwealth literary studies made little difference between English literature and the new literature from overseas. And the same holds true for the Marxist approach that developed in the course of the 1970s. From the perspective of Nigerian or Pakistani writers, Marxism, although fundamentally at odds with liberal humanism, is also alien to their own culture. The emphasis on class in Marxist Commonwealth studies has been a valuable contribution, but in its focus on class Marxism, too, was not much interested in the specific cultural context from which a given literary text emerged. With hindsight it is easy to see to what extent the field of Commonwealth literary studies was still marked by what we now call 'Eurocentrism'.

## Postcolonial studies

In the course of the 1980s Commonwealth literary studies became part of the then emerging and now vast field of literary,

cultural, political, and historical enquiry that we call postcolonial studies. In the process, it was radically transformed.
Whereas Commonwealth studies tacitly assumed common
ground between the cultural products of the former colonies and
the culture of the *metropolis*, postcolonial theory and criticism
emphasizes the tension between the metropolis and the (former)
colonies, between what within the colonial framework were the
metropolitan, imperial centre and its colonial satellites. It
focuses on the cultural displacements – and its consequences for
personal and communal identities – that inevitably followed
colonial conquest and rule and it does so from a non-
Eurocentric perspective. Postcolonial theory and criticism
radically questions the aggressively expansionist imperialism of
the colonizing powers and in particular the system of values that
supported imperialism and that it sees as still dominant within
the Western world. It studies the process and the effects of
cultural displacement and the ways in which the displaced have
culturally defended themselves. Postcolonial theory, in particular, sees such displacements, and the ambivalences and hybrid
cultural forms to which they lead, as vantage points that allow us
to expose the internal doubts and the instances of resistance that
the West has suppressed in its steamrolling globalizing course
and to deconstruct the seamless façade that the combination of
imperialism and capitalism has traditionally striven to present.
Homi Bhabha, one of the most prominent postcolonial theorists, has put it this way:

> Postcolonial perspectives emerge from the colonial testi-
> mony of Third World countries and the discourses of
> 'minorities' within the geopolitical divisions of east and
> west, north and south. ... They formulate their critical revi-
> sions around issues of cultural difference, social authority,
> and political discrimination in order to reveal the antago-
> nistic and ambivalent moments within the 'rationalizations'
> of modernity.

(Bhabha 1992: 438)

The postcolonial perspective, just like that of 'the marginal' in general, is a 'substantial intervention into those justifications of modernity – progress, homogeneity, cultural organicism, the deep nation, the long past – that rationalize the authoritarian, "normalizing" tendencies within cultures in the name of national interest' (Bhabha 1990: 4). For Bhabha, the postcolonial perspective has that disruptive potential because the effects of colonialism have in a curious way foreshadowed current poststructuralist views and concerns:

> the encounters and negotiations of differential meanings and values within 'colonial' textuality, its governmental discourses and cultural practices, have enacted, *avant la lettre*, many of the problematics of signification and judgment that have become current in contemporary theory – aporia, ambivalence, indeterminacy, the question of discursive closure, the threat to agency, the status of intentionality, the challenge to 'totalizing' concepts, to name but a few.
>
> (Bhabha 1992: 439)

Bhabha might have added 'otherness' – which he mentions later in the essay from which I am quoting – and which remains a vexing problem: how to deal with *real* otherness, with the absolute 'incommensurability of cultural values and priorities' (439) that has often characterized colonial encounters?

Not all postcolonial theorists and critics would agree with Bhabha's suggestion that we can already discern poststructuralist themes and perspectives in colonial situations, although they would surely agree with his claim that 'the language of rights and obligations' that operates in the various Western cultures 'must be questioned on the basis of the anomalous and discriminatory legal and cultural status assigned to migrant, diasporic, and refugee populations' (441; I will return to Bhabha's work later in this chapter). They also would not agree on what exactly postcolonial studies may rightfully claim as its historical and geographical scope. Some critics have vigorously defended the inclusion of white settler colonies such as

Australia, New Zealand, and Canada, arguing that their inhabitants, too, have suffered displacement and marginalization at the hands of imperialism and have been forced to develop cultural identities against the odds of imperial relations. Others have argued that white settler colonies cannot be fruitfully put in one and the same scholarly framework as for instance Kenya or India because the question of race does not feature in the relations between white overseas subjects and the metropolis. Those critics claim instead that in settler colonies the postcolonial approach is only relevant for the encounter between (white) settlers and indigenous populations (such as the New Zealand Maori). The range of postcolonial studies is still debated. Should for instance African–American history and culture be included? (African–American critics have of course followed postcolonial studies as it developed with great interest.) And what about its historical range? Does colonization start in the wake of Columbus's voyage to the Americas? Or should we see the medieval Anglo-Norman conquest and consequent occupation of Ireland already within the framework of colonizing imperialism? Although these and other questions are relevant, they do not touch the heart of postcolonial studies. What all postcolonial theorists and critics would agree on is that they are all engaged in a reassessment of the traditional relationship between the metropolis and its colonial subjects and in the radical deconstruction – either along poststructuralist or along more traditional lines – of the imperialist perspective. They agree in their focus on colonial (and neo-colonial) oppression, on resistance to colonization, on the respective identities of colonizer and colonized, on patterns of interaction between those identities, on postcolonial migration to the metropolis, on cultural exchanges between colonizer and colonized, on the ensuing hybridity of both cultures, and so on and so forth. Central to these interests are issues of race and ethnicity, language, gender, identity, class, and, above all, power. Postcolonial theorists and critics would also agree on the relevance of their enterprise for the world of the early twenty-first century, from which colonies may have (largely) disappeared, but in which neo-colonial relations abound – not only between

Western nations and their former colonies, but also between the majorities within those nations and the ethnic minorities that have settled within their borders in the postwar period.

## Orientalism

With all due respect for the pioneering work done by Commonwealth literary studies and by postcolonial writers such as Edward Brathwaite, Wilson Harris, Chinua Achebe, and Wole Soyinka, postcolonial studies in its current theoretically oriented form starts with the publication, in 1978, of the Palestinian–American critic Edward Said's book *Orientalism*. Drawing on Foucault and, to a lesser extent, Gramsci, Said's study completely changed the agenda of the study of non-Western cultures and their literatures and pushed it in the direction of what we now call postcolonial theory.

*Orientalism* is a devastating critique of how through the ages, but particularly in the nineteenth century – the heyday of imperialist expansion – which is the book's focus, Western texts have represented the East, and more specifically the Islamic Middle East (for the sake of convenience I will simply refer to 'the Orient' or 'the East' here). Using British and French 'scholarly works ... works of literature, political tracts, journalistic texts, travel books, religious and philological studies' (Said 1991: 23), Said examines how these texts *construct* the Orient through imaginative representations (in for instance novels), through seemingly factual descriptions (in journalistic reports and travel writing), and through claims to knowledge about Oriental history and culture (histories, anthropological writings, and so on). Together, all these forms of Western writing form a Foucauldian *discourse* – a loose system of statements and claims that constitutes a field of supposed knowledge and through which that 'knowledge' is constructed. Such discourses, although seemingly interested in knowledge, always establish relationships of power. In Foucault's work, power is first of all a force that serves itself. We may think we use it for our own purposes in our capacity as free agents, but in reality it works first of all *through* us and not *for* us. From Foucault's anti-humanistic perspective we are functions within networks of power. For Said, however, the West's representations of the East ultimately work within the framework of a conscious and determined effort at subordination. For Said, Orientalism – this Western discourse about the Orient – has traditionally served *hegemonic* purposes. As we have seen, Antonio Gramsci thought of 'hegemony' as domination by consent – the way the ruling class succeeds in oppressing other classes with their apparent approval. In Gramsci's analysis it does so through culture: the ruling class makes its own values and interests central in what it presents as a common, neutral, culture. Accepting that 'common' culture, the other classes become complicit in their own oppression and the result is a kind of velvet domination. Orientalism, then, has traditionally served two purposes. It has legitimized Western expansionism and imperialism in the eyes of Western governments and their electorates and it has insidiously worked to convince the 'natives' that Western culture represented universal civilization. Accepting that culture could only benefit them – it would, for instance, elevate them from the 'backward' or 'superstitious' conditions in which they still lived – and would make them participants in the most advanced civilization the world had ever seen.

For Said, Western representations of the Orient, no matter how well intentioned, have always been part of this damaging discourse. Wittingly or unwittingly, they have always been complicit with the workings of Western power. Even those Orientalists who are clearly in sympathy with Oriental peoples and their cultures – and Said finds a substantial number of them – cannot overcome their Eurocentric perspective and have unintentionally contributed to Western domination. So instead of the disinterested objectivity in the service of the higher goal of true knowledge that Western scholarship has traditionally claimed for itself, we find invariably false representations that have effectively paved the way for military domination, cultural displacement, and economic exploitation. I should perhaps say at this point that in later publications, and in response to criticism, Said has modified his position and presented a less homogeneous picture of Orientalism, while he has also downplayed the extent to which it merely constructs and never describes. There is no doubt, however, that *Orientalism*, whatever its shortcomings may have been, revolutionized the way Western scholars and critics looked at representations of non-Western subjects and cultures (just like feminism had somewhat earlier revolutionized the way we look at representations of women and African–American studies had revolutionized the way in which in particular American criticism looks at representations of African–Americans). Said's book also drew attention to the way in which the discourse of Orientalism serves to create the West as well it creates the East. West and East form a binary opposition in which the two poles define each other (see Chapter 5). The inferiority that Orientalism attributes to the East simultaneously serves to construct the West's superiority. The sensuality, irrationality, primitiveness, and despotism of the East constructs the West as rational, democratic, progressive, and so on. The West always functions as the 'centre' and the East is a marginal 'other' that simply through its existence confirms the West's centrality and superiority. Not surprisingly perhaps, the opposition that the West's discourse about the East sets up makes use of another basic opposition, that between the masculine and the feminine. Naturally the West functions as the masculine pole – enlightened, rational, entrepreneurial, disciplined – while the East is its feminine opposition – irrational, passive, undisciplined, and sensual.

Race, ethnicity, and the dominant position of the *metropolis* were already well established on the literary-critical agenda when *Orientalism* appeared, as was the study of Commonwealth writing in English and the study of English literature dealing with colonial relations (E.M. Forster's *A Passage to India* (1924), for instance). Said, however, was the first to draw on the new French theory and on the recently discovered Gramsci (parts of whose work had been published in English in 1971 – see Chapter 4) in dealing with these issues. *Orientalism* offered a challenging theoretical framework and a new perspective on the interpretation of Western writing about the East (and other non-Western cultures) and of writing produced under colonial rule – which might be read both for signs of complicity with Western hegemony and for a possibly counterhegemonic stance. (Just like Gramsci, Said makes room for intentionally counterhegemonic moves.) *Orientalism* put the role of the West's cultural institutions (the university, literary writing, newspapers, and so on) in its military, economic, and cultural domination of non-Western nations and peoples firmly on the agenda and asked questions that we still ask concerning literature's role in past and present racial, ethnic, and cultural encounters. As a matter of fact, our questions have since 1978 only proliferated. Can we really see all Western writings about Said's East, and, by implication, the non-West in general, as more or less indistinguishable from each other as far as their representations of the non-Western world are concerned? Mary-Louise Pratt's *Imperial Eyes* from 1992, for instance, argues that travel writing by women about the non-West is rather different from travel writing by men. Said himself would be the first to admit that such differences are real enough and postcolonial criticism is still busy mapping them.

## Colonized and colonizer

One of the questions that Said does not address but that is central to the work of Homi Bhabha is what actually happens in the cultural interaction between colonizer and colonized. In earlier writings on colonialism, such an interaction had often been denied. Aimé Césaire, for instance, claimed in his 1955 *Discourse on Colonialism* that between colonizer and colonized there is '[n]o human contact, but relations of domination and submission which turn the colonizing man into a classroom monitor, an army sergeant, a prison guard, a slave driver, and the indigenous man into an instrument of production' (Césaire 1997: 81). British and French accounts of colonial life had standardly presented a wholly different, and benign, view of colonialism, but had seen as little interaction between colonizer and colonized as Césaire. The colonizers remained their civilized and disciplined European selves even in the most trying circumstances. The West has always been convinced that its presence overseas greatly affected the 'natives' (to the point that it told itself that the smartest and most sensitive of them immediately started scrambling to adopt Western ways and values), but has never been comfortable with the idea that its sons and daughters might in their turn be affected by the cultures they encountered. It is mostly in literature that we find alternative perspectives. In Joseph Conrad's *Heart of Darkness* (1899) the colonial experience has the effect of turning the ivory collector Kurtz into a megalomaniacal barbarian and in E.M. Forster's *A Passage to India* (1924) two British women also pay a price for leaving familiar territory and suffer permanently unsettling experiences in India.

For Bhabha, the encounter of colonizer and colonized always affects both. Colonialism, with the displacements and terrible uncertainties that it brings, is such a radically unsettling 'affective experience of marginality' (Bhabha 1992: 438) that the colonized subject's plight can be seen as prefiguring poststructuralist indeterminacy and fragmentation. But the colonial experience also affects the colonizer. More specifically, for Bhabha the colonizer cannot escape a complex and paradoxical relationship with the colonized. Drawing on Lacan's views of the way identity gets constructed, Bhabha offers us analyses in which the identity of the colonizer – in Bhabha's work the British colonizer of India – cannot very well be separated from that of the colonized, or at least from the supposed identity of the colonized. As in Lacan, identity is inherently unstable. Instead of being self-sufficient with regard to his identity ('his' because colonialism is an almost exclusively male enterprise), the colonizer at least partly constructs it through interaction with the colonized. The colonizer's identity has no 'origin' in himself and is not a fixed entity, but is differential, a 'meaning' generated by difference. Although that difference has in a sense been constructed beforehand – by Western discourses about the East – the 'British' or 'English' identity of the colonizer can only become a 'reality' after the colonial contact which truly confirms it. As in Lacan, identity is constructed in interaction with 'others' and with 'the Other' (see the section on Lacan in Chapter 6 ).

Bhabha sees signs of the colonizer's partial dependency on none-too-friendly 'others' – and the resulting inherent uncertainty – in a whole range of phenomena. Racial stereotyping, for instance, first of all repeats this process of identity-creation in that it construes not only those who are stereotyped, but also the stereotyper himself – in opposition to the stereotyped. It functions to construe or confirm the stereotyper's identity. However, the repetitiveness of acts of stereotyping points to a continuing uncertainty in the stereotyper: apparently the stereotyper has to convince himself over and over again of the truthfulness of the stereotype – and thus, by extension, of his own identity. The self-confidence of the colonizer is further undermined by what Bhabha calls *mimicry* – the always slightly alien and distorted way in which the colonized, either out of choice or under duress, will repeat the colonizer's ways and discourse. In mimicry the colonizer sees himself in a mirror that slightly but effectively distorts his image – that subtly and unsettlingly 'others' his own identity. In their recent *Key Concepts in Post-Colonial Studies*, Bill Ashcroft, Gareth Griffiths, and Helen Tiffin – three prominent postcolonial critics – cite an example of mimicry from a significantly titled novel – the Trinidadian author V.S. Naipaul's *The Mimic Men* (1967):

> And for Mr Shylock ... the possessor of a mistress and of suits made of cloth so fine I felt I could eat it, I had nothing but admiration. ... I thought Mr Shylock looked distinguished, like a lawyer or businessman or politician. He had the habit of stroking the lobe of his ear inclining his head to listen. I copied it. I knew of recent events in Europe; they tormented me; and although I was trying to live on seven pounds a week I offered Mr Shylock my fullest, silent compassion.
>
> (cited in Ashscroft *et al.* 1998: 141)

This is a deeply ironic passage, especially if we know that the narrator pays Shylock 'three guineas a week' for the room he lives in and take into account Shakespeare's Shylock – which, given the reference to the Holocaust, we clearly are supposed to do. The narrator's seemingly deferential and admiring but watchful attitude must to Shylock be as enigmatic as it is to the reader. More in general, the colonizer's discourse, his most effective weapon in the cultural encounter, is less stable and secure than he thinks. One reason is that stereotyping is a basic element of colonial discourse. Because it is one of its mainstays, colonial discourse cannot possibly be as self-confident and authoritative as it would like to be (and as it presents itself). Apart from this, the colonizer's language is always subject to the effects of Derridean *différance* and is therefore never fully under his control. Colonial power is thus always under the threat of destabilization. Its lack of complete control is partly due to reasons that have nothing to do with either colonizer or colonized. The way the colonizer's identity is always constructed in interaction with 'others' and with 'the Other'; the mimicry that, even if it is wholly sincere, still always presents a distorting mirror; and the effects of *différance* are fundamental givens within the colonial situation. But colonial power's lack of complete control is also the result of acts of conscious resistance on the part of the colonized. In the physical encounter between colonizer and colonized the latter may for instance refuse to meet his oppressor's gaze and in so doing reject 'the narcissistic demand that [he] should be addressed directly, that the Other should authorize the self, recognize its priority, fulfill its outlines' (Bhabha 1994a: 98).

Perhaps the most influential of Bhabha's contributions to postcolonial theory is his notion of *hybridity*. While Said's *Orientalism* keeps the spheres of colonizer and colonized rather firmly apart, Bhabha, with his interest in their interaction, sees important movements going both ways. Shifting his focus from 'the noisy command of colonial authority' and 'the silent repression of native traditions', to 'the colonial hybrid', Bhabha argues that the cultural interaction of colonizer and colonized leads to a fusion of cultural forms that from one perspective, because it signals its 'productivity', confirms the power of the colonial presence, but that as a form of mimicry simultaneously 'unsettles the mimetic or narcissistic demands of colonial power' (Bhabha [1985] 1994b: 112). Hybridity 'intervenes in the exercise of authority not merely to indicate the impossibility of its identity but to represent the unpredictability of its presence' (114).

Like most of Bhabha's notions, hybridity and hybridization thus get positive connotations. In fact, Bhabha's application of post-structuralist theorizing (mostly Derrida and Lacan) to colonial and, later in his career, neo-colonial and internally colonial relations has more generally optimistic overtones. Poststructuralist theory leads him to see the identity and position of the colonizer as inherently precarious. Some critics have objected that this is armchair theorizing – even if it is theoretically correct – and cannot have much relevance in the analysis of the everyday practice of colonial rule. The gun you are carrying as a fledgling colonizer may not fundamentally strengthen your identity, but it may give it enough of a boost to disregard all signs of mimicry that you are likely to encounter. Another point of critique concerns the level of abstraction at which Bhabha's work often operates. Marxist and feminist critics have argued that there can be no such thing as a generalized encounter between colonizer and colonized. To them a theory that addresses the colonial situation without paying serious attention to the differences between men and women and between social classes cannot do justice to the heterogeneity of the colonial encounter. However, Bhabha's focus on interaction and his notion of hybridity have very fruitfully sharpened our awareness of what actually happens (or may happen) in the colonial situation and, by extension, in any encounters between a dominant and an oppressed group. Whereas Said prompts us to question Western representations of the East (and, again by extension, of one culture's representation of an other), Bhabha asks us to submit the actual encounter between West and East – in his case India – to the closest scrutiny.

## The subaltern

Postcolonial Marxists such as Aijaz Ahmad have suggested that Bhabha and other 'Westernized' non-Europeans are hardly in the best position to speak for the colonized and neo-colonized masses. The third postcolonial theorist I will consider here, Gayatri Chakravorty Spivak, has no trouble admitting that her position as an academic working in the West separates her from the masses of India, her country of origin. At the same time, however, she has drawn our attention to that large majority of the colonized that has left no mark upon history because it could not, or was not allowed to, make itself heard. Millions and millions have come and gone under the colonial dispensation without leaving a trace: men, but even more so women. Since colonized women almost by definition went unheard within their own patriarchal culture, they were doubly unheard under a colonial regime. Spivak can be said to be the first postcolonial theorist with a fully feminist agenda. That agenda includes the complicity of female writers with imperialism. 'It should not be possible to read nineteenth-century British fiction without remembering that imperialism, understood as England's social mission, was a crucial part of the cultural representation of England to the English', Spivak tells us in her 1985 essay 'Three Women's Texts and a Critique of Imperialism' (Spivak 1995a: 269). Noting that '[t]he role of literature in the production of cultural representation should not be ignored', she goes on to analyse Charlotte Brontë's *Jane Eyre* (1847) and the way in which it presents the 'Creole' Bertha Mason – Rochester's mad wife – in terms of cultural representation. Spivak's insistence on the importance of feminist perspectives is part of a larger role that she has perhaps unintentionally played over the last two decades: that of the theoretical conscience of postcolonial studies. Her work has as much addressed theoretical shortcomings in postcolonial theorizing as it has focused on postcolonial issues itself.

Spivak represents the voice of difference among the major postcolonial theorists. In spite of their poststructuralist sources of inspiration, Said and Bhabha virtually ignore the question of difference. I have already pointed out how Said's analysis of Western representations of the East has been charged with gender-blindness and how feminist scholars have argued that female representations are different from male ones. This is in fact rather plausible on purely theoretical grounds. If Western representations routinely set up a binary opposition 'West versus East' in which the West is superior and masculine and the East inferior and feminine one might indeed expect female authors to deviate from the pattern. Any female author who is aware of what she is doing will seek to express the East's inferiority – if she indeed subscribes to that essentially male judgement – not by indirectly referring to her own inferiority but in rather different terms. Bhabha, too, makes no difference between men and women in his theorizing of the interaction between colonizer and colonized. Said and Bhabha also largely ignore cultural difference. Said makes no difference between the various European cultures – Protestant or Catholic, liberal or authoritarian – he puts on the rack in *Orientalism* and Bhabha writes as if the interaction of colonizer and colonized can be completely separated from the cultures involved. Spivak, however, tries to be attentive to difference or *heterogeneity*, even within feminism itself: she has taken Western feminism to task for operating within a horizon determined by white, middle-class, and heterosexual preoccupations.

As we might expect from a theorist who is as sensitive to difference as Spivak is, social class – which also plays no role of any significance in Said or Bhabha – is one of her major analytic categories. Of all postcolonial theorists, Spivak has most consistently focused on what in postcolonial studies has come to be called the *subaltern*: literally, the category of those who are lower in position or who, in the military terms that are always appropriate to the colonial situation, are lower in rank. Spivak employs the term (which derives from Gramsci) to describe the lower layers of colonial and postcolonial (or, as many would say, neo-colonial) society: the homeless, the unemployed, the subsistence farmers, the day labourers, and so on. She is aware, however, that categorizations by way of class, too, tend to make difference invisible: 'one must nevertheless insist that the colonized subaltern *subject* is irretrievably heterogeneous' (Spivak 1995b: 26). One result of this attentiveness to difference is Spivak's focus on the female subaltern, a very large – and of course differentiated – category among the colonized (and neo-colonized) that, she argues, has traditionally been doubly marginalized: 'If, in the context of colonial production, the subaltern has no history and cannot speak, the subaltern as female is even more deeply in shadow' (Spivak 1995b: 28).

This focus does not mean that she speaks for – or has the intention of speaking for – the female subaltern. Rather, she is motivated by the desire to save the female subaltern from misrepresentation. In a famous essay from 1988, 'Can the Subaltern Speak?', Spivak, in the wider context of a critique of what she sees as poststructuralist appropriations of the colonial subject, examines the nineteenth-century controversy between the colonized Indians and their British colonizers over what she calls 'widow-sacrifice': the burning of widows on the funeral pyre of their deceased husbands. Spivak concludes that neither party allowed women – the potential victims of this practice – to speak. The British texts construct a position for the woman in which she is made to represent Western individualism and, by implication, a superior Western civilization that emphasizes modern freedom, while the Indian ones present her as choosing for duty and tradition. Although both parties claim that they have them on their side, the women themselves remain unheard.

Spivak combines a Marxist perspective – the emphasis on class as a differentiating factor – with a deconstructionist approach to texts and to identity. In dealing with colonialist texts she tries to demonstrate how they attain their coherence by setting up false oppositions between a supposed centre and an equally fictive margin and how their language invariably deconstructs the coherence they try to establish. Given this deconstructionist perspective, Spivak cannot very well escape the conclusion that our identity is without a fixed centre and inherently unstable. In one way such a decentred identity (or decentred subject) serves Spivak's purpose well: it radically undermines all essentialist pretensions on the part of colonizer and neo-colonizer and it equally undermines the postcolonial fundamentalism that she has little political patience with. In her analyses of, and attacks on, forms of renascent essentialism she also acts as postcolonial theory's theoretical conscience. On the other hand, decolonized nations and cultures, just like the political movements of the decolonized, arguably need some sort of identity that does not immediately deconstruct itself and announce to the world that it is ungrounded and decentred. A political platform that takes itself apart in public cannot be very effective. Spivak's solution to this dilemma is what she calls a *'strategic* use of positivist essentialism' that clearly signals its political agenda. In other words, it is all right to project a stable political or cultural identity as long as we are aware that it is a construction that is always under deconstructionist erasure.

Although Spivak cannot be said to advocate such a development, this lets even a rethought and sceptical humanism in by the back door – if, that is, it is and remains aware of its provisional nature. Edward Said has in his recent publications moved towards such a revised humanist position, once again allowing agency and intentionality to play a substantial role. Like the other offshoots of the poststructuralist revolution, postcolonial theory currently negotiates that very difficult terrain defined by two pairs of opposites: anti-humanism (Foucauldian or Marxist) versus revisionist forms of humanism, and total difference (or total sameness) versus forms of difference shot through with sameness (or sameness shot through with difference). Recognizing this confusing state of affairs postcolonial studies, that is, theory *and* criticism, now generally emphasizes plurality, differentiality, and hybridity without the exaggerated totalizing claims that marked its earlier phase.

## Summary

Postcolonial studies critically analyses the relationship between colonizer and colonized, from the earliest days of exploration and colonization. Drawing on Foucault's notion of 'discourses', on Gramsci's 'hegemony', on deconstruction, and, as the case may be, on Marxism, it focuses on the role of texts, literary and otherwise, in the colonial enterprise. It examines how these texts construct the colonizer's (usually masculine) superiority and the colonized's (usually effeminate) inferiority and in so doing have legitimated colonization. It is especially attentive to postcolonial attitudes – attitudes of resistance – on the part of the colonized and seeks to understand the nature of the encounter between colonizer and colonized with the help of, for instance, Lacan's views of identity formation. With regard to literature, it argues that 'English literature' and 'American literature' have in the postwar period been replaced by 'literatures in English', a term that captures the multicultural and multiethnic nature of current writing in English. It is especially, although by no means exclusively, interested in postcolonial rewritings of English classics – Marina Warner's *Indigo, or Mapping the Waters* (1992), Coetzee's *Foe* (1987) – that contest the ideological thrust of the original, and in texts that in other ways critically analyse the colonial relationship. Given the fact that most of Western Europe's nations – and, arguably, the United States – have been involved in imperialist projects that culturally, and often physically, displaced 'native' populations, postcolonial studies covers a large period of Western history and a vast geographical area.

## Suggestions for further reading

The importance of postcolonial criticism within contemporary literary studies is reflected in the number of good introductions that have appeared in recent years. Elleke Boehmer's *Colonial and Postcolonial Literature* (1995) provides a very readable historical overview of literary writing from both the colonial and the postcolonial period that in one way or another is concerned with imperialism. *Postcolonial Criticism* (1997) edited by Bart Moore-Gilbert, Gareth Stanton, and Willy Maley, has a very useful and relatively brief introduction and presents essays and excerpts from a broad range of postcolonial critiques plus numerous suggestions for further reading. Moore-Gilbert's *Postcolonial Theory* (1997) is an excellent introduction to postcolonial studies' major theorists and to the tensions between theory and criticism. Ania Loomba's *Colonialism/Postcolonialism* (1998) complements these studies because of the attention that she pays to questions of gender and sexuality. Ato

Quayson's *Postcolonialism* (2000) is excellent on current post-colonial discussions, but perhaps not the first text on the subject that a student should read. An older but still useful guide to the field is the famously titled *The Empire Writes Back* (1989) by Bill Ashcroft, Gareth Griffiths, and Helen Tiffin.

*The Post-Colonial Studies Reader* (1995), edited by the same critics, is the standard reader in the field and contains a wealth of material on the major issues. *Key-Concepts in Post-Colonial Studies* (1998), again by Ashcroft *et al.*, offers brief and lucid discussions of not just the key concepts, but of a whole list of minor terms as well. Finally, Edward Said's *Orientalism* ([1978] 1991) still offers one of the best opportunities to see an important form of postcolonial analysis in action.

# Chapter 9

# Sexuality, literature, and culture

In the previous chapters we have repeatedly seen how exclusion and marginalization are basic to the organization of Western culture. Differences that are in themselves wholly neutral become the starting-point for binary oppositions that privilege one of the poles of the opposition at the expense of the other. The centres and margins that are created by this process together constitute a structure that underlies the culture that seems so 'natural' to us and that governs our 'natural', commonsensical assumptions.

Until fairly recently critical interest was primarily focused on the three areas of difference, those of gender, race, and class, that seemed to be most central in the way Western culture has over the ages structured itself. Gender, race, and class were shown to have provided abundant sources for cultural self-definition through a whole range of binary oppositions that always privileged the same social group, that of white males. Feminism and feminist-inspired cultural studies for instance demonstrated how gender pervades Western culture – with its standard privileging of 'masculinity' – and even invades categories such as 'race' that are at first sight totally unrelated to the gender issue. A great many colonial texts contrast the masculine white colonizer to equally male colonial subjects that are presented in feminine terms. Gender and race have traditionally gone together in organizing the West's response to non-Western peoples and in establishing an exclusively Western identity.

Since the 1980s a fourth area of difference, that of sexuality, has gained prominence as an important principle of social and cultural organization. The exclusions and marginalizations that we see with regard to sexuality – think for instance of the stigmatization of, and violence against, homosexuals – are seen by a number of influential theorists as equally pertinent to the way Western culture is organized as other structural exclusions. In fact, some theorists, following Michel Foucault's lead, even see sexuality as the *central* principle of social organization. Before I get around to that, however, I will first sketch some of the developments that led up to this relatively new theoretical angle which, although it emerged within literary studies, was strongly interdisciplinary from its beginnings and has in the course of the 1990s shifted in the direction of cultural studies.

## Lesbian and gay criticism

Sexuality and literature first became an issue within the feminist movement. In its early stages, feminism spoke, or at least seemed to speak, on behalf of all women. A common female front against what looked strongly like a common oppression seemed only natural. In the course of the 1970s, however, various groups within the feminist movement began to express their dissatisfaction with a collective feminism that they increasingly saw as shaped by the interests of the dominant group within the movement: white, middle-class, college-educated, and heterosexual women. As a result, the groups that did or could not identify with this mainstream image gradually broke away to formulate their own feminisms. These breakaway communities included groups of black feminists, Chicana feminists, and, most important for this chapter, lesbian feminists. For a good many lesbian feminists the subversiveness of mainstream feminism did not extend to sexuality. While mainstream feminists questioned traditional views of gender, they failed to question similarly traditional views of same-sex relations. As a result, lesbian feminism turned away from mainstream feminism to pursue its own, separate path.

Lesbian feminism in turn led to lesbian literary criticism. In 1975 Jane Rule published her pioneering *Lesbian Images* and with Lillian Faderman's comprehensive *Surpassing the Love of Men: Romantic Friendship and Love Between Women from the Renaissance to the Present* (1981) lesbian criticism definitively established itself. However, the vanguard of critics that tried to lay out the ground rules for a specific lesbian criticism found that a focus on lesbianism in literature runs into serious practical problems. In the words of a recent commentator:

> What is a lesbian text? Is it one describing lesbian relationships? Is it one written by a lesbian author? Is it one in which hidden kinds of pleasure are offered to an implied lesbian reader? Are texts lesbian if neither author nor content are *explicitly* lesbian? How much of a text has to be about lesbianism to be regarded as 'lesbian'?
>
> (Humm 1995: 162)

And what, for that matter, exactly is a lesbian? The answer might seem fairly straightforward, but it is easy enough to ask questions that complicate the picture. Are for instance sexual acts a necessary condition? Should we consider a woman who has felt a strong and lifelong attraction to other women but has never acted upon it as a lesbian? If not, we will disqualify a good many women who in their own time never had an opportunity to follow their sexual preference, but who, if they were alive today, would openly live with a female lover. This problem leads us to two important issues. The first is the issue of sexual identity. With my rather off-hand introduction of 'a woman who has felt a strong and lifelong attraction to other women' I have in fact taken sides in the controversial issue of what constitutes a lesbian identity. The phrase 'lifelong attraction' strongly implies that this woman's erotic orientation towards other women was already firmly in place at birth, even though it might only have begun to manifest itself during or after puberty. Lesbianism, or, as the case may be, homosexuality, is from this perspective simply programmed into some of us, just as a heterosexual orientation is programmed into the rest. But is that really the case? For many radical lesbians of the early 1970s, lesbianism was a matter of choice – a political anti-patriarchal choice. Or is lesbianism a matter of socialization – of the individual experiences that some of us go through and that turn us into lesbians? The same questions may of course be raised with regard to homosexuality. In fact, a definition of homosexuality would have to take care of an extra complication. Anthropologists tell us that there are cultures, both past and present, in which males engage in homosexual rites without being homosexual in the usual sense of the term. How to classify such acts and the males who are involved in them? I will come back to the problem of lesbian and gay identities below, but it will be clear that there is room for a considerable variety of opinions.

The other issue that is raised by my introduction of the woman who does not act upon her lesbian inclinations is that of visibility – or, rather, invisibility. Gender and race are visible and recognizable categories. There are exceptions, of course. There are men who choose to dress like women and every racial minority has members who can 'pass', that is successfully pose as members of the majority. But on the whole gender and race are obvious. Sexual orientation, however, is not visible. What is more, since it is only really visible at those moments when it is actively acted upon, it can be kept hidden even from one's immediate social environment. So how do we establish which writers have been gay or lesbian when it was impossible for them to reveal their sexual identity in their writings? How can we reconstruct a gay or lesbian literary tradition? I will look here at the answers given by lesbian criticism, not because it is in any way superior to gay criticism, but because it has a longer independent history. As Julie Rivkin and Michael Ryan observed a few years ago, '[m]ore so than Gay Studies, Lesbian Studies has demonstrated a tendency towards separatism, perhaps because as women, lesbians suffer a double oppression' (Rivkin and Ryan 1998: 677). It will be clear, though, that there are many parallels between lesbian and gay criticism.

## Lesbian writing

Lesbian criticism, then, faces a number of very specific and rather intractable problems. One way around them is to opt for lesbian *readings*, that is for interpretations that leave unresolved the question whether a given author, or character, or situation, really *is* lesbian, but instead create the possibility for lesbian recognitions and moments of identification. This does of course not mean that lesbian criticism can make no firm claims and is never more than a reading strategy that could be easily dismissed by people who take a dim view of everything that is not solidly anchored in textual 'evidence'. There is a fast growing body of texts – most of them dating from the last thirty years – that clearly announce themselves as lesbian. But a lesbian reading strategy is a complementary and necessary instrument. Especially in the case of texts published before the twentieth century, when lesbianism was unmentionable, lesbian readings of close friendships between single women have led to often revealing new appreciations of the plays, novels, and poems involved. (The same goes for gay criticism: a well-known example is Alan Sinfield's reading of the poems in which Alfred Tennyson nostalgically remembers his very intimate friendship with a long dead friend (see Sinfield 1986).) Such new lesbian interpretations have led to the identification of texts that together can be said to create a sort of lesbian literary tradition – or at least a tradition of texts that would seem to invite a lesbian reading. Simultaneously, lesbian criticism has drawn our attention to the way that lesbians have traditionally been portrayed in mainstream texts. As might be expected, lesbians (and homosexuals) have standardly been pictured as 'other' and have served to define and confirm the heterosexuality of the centre.

But on what grounds can critics defend a lesbian reading of a text that is in no way explicitly lesbian and that until twenty years ago was never considered within a lesbian framework?

Lesbian critics have been active defining a specific lesbian form of writing on the basis of those texts that are indeed unmistakably lesbian. If there are certain defining characteristics then it should be possible to identify texts from earlier periods as lesbian, or to make at least a case for their hidden lesbian character. It goes without saying that such 'lesbian' characteristics will not be explicit and will therefore not include what is probably the most prominent lesbian theme: the process that leads up to 'coming out' as a lesbian and that functions as the equivalent of the growth towards maturity that we find in many mainstream novels.

Lesbian and gay critics generally agree that lesbian and gay writers work from a special awareness of the constructedness of language and culture and of the fact that the constructions that they see in operation can be contested. After all, lesbian and gay writers have until very recently been forced either to hide their sexual orientation altogether from their audience or to present it so indirectly that only the initiates were in a position to recognize it. À la Recherche du temps perdu, Marcel Proust's early twentieth-century great novel cycle, offers a famous example. The girl Albertine, with whom Proust's novelistic alter ego falls in love, was in the reality of Proust's life a boy. Lesbian and homosexual writers such as Proust saw themselves forced to disguise same-sex relationships as heterosexual ones. Because of such suppressions even the most realistic mode of writing must for lesbian and gay writers always have been more than slightly unreal and false. Naturally, then, we find lesbian writers gravitating away from realism towards a 'romance' mode that often has an utopian dimension. For Terry Castle, writing in 1993, lesbian fiction should never be read as straightforward realism: 'Even as it gestures back at a supposedly familiar world of human experience, it almost invariably stylizes and estranges it – by presenting it parodistically, euphemistically, or in some other rhetorically heightened, distorted, fragmented or phantasmagoric way' (Castle 1993: 90). Moreover, we may expect to find gender ambiguities, role playing that involves gender, and other coded references – such as certain recurrent symbols – to the fact that not everything is what it would seem to be to the unsuspecting reader. More in general, the lesbian (and gay) writer's constant awareness of the gap between their own reality and that of the repressive heterosexual majority, coupled with the necessity – which often still applies – to keep that private reality secret, leads to an all-pervasive sense of irony and theatricality. Here we are moving towards that 'blurring of boundaries between self and other, subject and object, lover and beloved' that by the early 1990s for many lesbian critics had come to constitute 'the lesbian moment' in literary texts (Zimmerman 1992: 11). We are, in fact, moving towards what we now call 'queer theory', in which such exemplary lesbian moments – and their gay equivalent – are accorded a significance that far exceeds specific lesbian or gay conditions.

## The production of sexuality

Queer theory – which has turned a term that traditionally disparages homosexuality into a proud banner – comes in more than one form. All modes of queer theory, however, are indebted to Michel Foucault's multi-volume *History of Sexuality* (1976–1984) and his argument that especially 'deviant', that is non-heterosexual, forms of sexuality play a prominent role in the organization of Western culture. Although 'perversion' is actively marginalized, it is discursively central: the effort to police 'perversion' through a discourse on sexuality that continuously puts it in a negative light paradoxically keeps it in the centre of attention. For Foucault, Western culture has turned sexuality into a cultural construction, into a discourse, that enables it to monitor us constantly and to exercise power: if we do not internalize its sexual rules and police ourselves, then it can step in and force us to conform.

In the first volume of his *History* (originally published in 1976) Foucault argues that homosexuality and homosexuals date from the 1870s (a claim that would seem to be supported by the fact that the term 'homosexual' was coined in 1869). It is easy to misunderstand this. Foucault does not mean to say that sexual acts that we would now call homosexual acts were unknown before the 1870s. In every Western culture they were known and seen as criminal acts punishable by law. What Foucault is saying is that in the later nineteenth century sexual acts between men were no longer seen as incidental to their lives, that is, as other criminal acts like, say, fraud or burglary, that anyone might engage in under certain circumstances, but as expressions of their *identity*. For the first time, Foucault tells us, homosexual acts were seen as part of the essential *nature* of the men involved, as the result of an inclination that was always there. Whereas before that turning-point a man who had sex with another man – a so-called 'sodomite' – was seen in terms of 'a temporary aberration', the homosexual 'was now a species'. The homosexual had come into existence: 'Nothing that went into his total composition was unaffected by his sexuality' (Foucault 1978: 43). What we have here is a crucial shift from behaviour to identity. Although this new homosexual identity naturally predisposed its owners to homosexual activity, men could now be classified as homosexual even if they had never been involved in homosexual acts.

For Foucault, homosexuality and homosexuals were *produced* by a nineteenth-century discourse that claimed new knowledge with regard to sexuality. This 'production' of homosexuality (and of other 'perversions' that were similarly tied to new identities) led to its codification (and condemnation) in legal, medical, psychological, and religious discourses. It led to the fixation of identities (homosexual, heterosexual) and the surveillance of the border between them. In other words, this production of homosexuality is intimately connected with power. Just like other sexual identities, homosexuality is 'a result and an instrument of power's designs'. We should not make the mistake of thinking that what Foucault has in mind is only how homosexuality allowed the various authorities – legal, medical, religious – to tighten the screws of social and cultural repression and to legitimate themselves further, although they certainly availed themselves of the opportunity. As I have noted, 'power' often has a virtually autonomous status in Foucault's work (see Chapter 6). It works *through* us and imprisons us, even if occasionally it may also work to our advantage. In Foucault's view, the 'production' of homosexuality by the human sciences leads to a very general surveillance under whose regime we even regulate and police our own sexuality. As Jonathan Dollimore summarizes Foucault's argument: 'Perversion is the product and vehicle of power, a construction which enables it to gain a purchase within the realm of the psychosexual: authority legitimates itself by fastening upon discursively constructed, sexually perverse identities of its own making' (Dollimore 1991: 106).

## Queer theory

For British queer theorists like Dollimore and Alan Sinfield, that power can be contested. Queer theory questions traditional constructions of sexuality and – especially in its British version – sees non-heterosexual forms of sexuality as sites where hegemonic power can be undermined. In Sinfield's words, subcultures – in which he expressly includes sexual subcultures – 'may be power bases – points at which alternative or oppositional ideologies may achieve plausibility' (Sinfield 1994a: vii). British queer theory, whose political context is 'a general left-wing orientation' (73), takes the assumptions and the interests of cultural materialism into the contemporary debate on sexuality. For Sinfield, sexuality is a faultline (see Chapter 7), a point at which the hegemonic surface may crack and reveal the warring forces underneath: 'Sexuality is an unstable construct in our societies, and hence produces endless textual work. Such an awkward issue has continually to be revisited, disavowed, rediscovered, affirmed. Closure, by definition, is always potentially unsatisfactory' (56). Sexual dissidence – the title of Dollimore's 1991 book – is therefore always at least potentially a political act. As queer theorists, Sinfield and other British queer theorists apply the methods of cultural materialism. They read literary texts against the grain – 'cultural materialists read for incoherence' (38) – in the manner of Pierre Macherey (see Chapter 4) because faultline stories 'hinge upon a fundamental, unresolved ideological complication that finds its way, willy-nilly, into texts' (4). They examine the constructions that a culture has put upon sexually ambivalent texts in order to expose its ideological repressiveness (see Sinfield's *Cultural Politics – Queer Reading* from which I am quoting here for a discussion of the reception of Tennessee Williams's plays). At the institutional level they question 'literature' itself – in particular the ideologically motivated marginalizations and exclusions that have played a crucial role in the creation of the idea of 'literature'. This is not to say that we should turn our backs to the literary tradition. We should, however, approach it from a faultline perspective. As Sinfield tells us: 'successful [texts] are usually risky; they flirt, at least, with the danger that prevailing values might not be satisfactory, or might not prevail' (56).

The queer theory that develops out of cultural materialism draws on Foucault and on the work of Raymond Williams and has strong affinities with British cultural studies. In the United States, however, queer theory has followed a different path. I will focus here on the queer theory that develops out of lesbian feminism, and that is strongly influenced by Derrida, and more specifically on the work of two prominent and highly influential theorists: Judith Butler and Eve Kosofksy Sedgwick.

Lesbian criticism had split off from feminist criticism because lesbian critics felt that mainstream feminism did not do justice to the lesbian presence in literature. Striking out on their own, they assumed that there was such a thing as a lesbian identity – a core identity that all lesbians shared – that expressed itself in certain ways in literary texts. As we would say now, they saw lesbianism in essentialistic terms: as an unchanging condition that is presumably either biologically determined or the result of psycho-social conditioning. However, in the course of the 1990s, and influenced by Foucault and by Derrida's deconstruction, a number of influential lesbian critics began to reject that essentialism and to see sexual identities – not just lesbianism or homosexuality – as social constructions that needed to be deconstructed just like gender and race had been deconstructed to expose the binary oppositions at work within them. Like gender categories, sexual categories now were assumed to be 'regulatory fictions' – instruments of a repressive discourse about sexuality. Any sexual orientation was thought to be a temporary position in a structure of differences (the total field of all possible orientations) that privileged none of them. The obvious social privileging of the heterosexual orientation of the majority at the expense of all other orientations was the work of a centre that defined itself through that what it excluded.

The work of the American critic Judith Butler is a case in point. Butler's Derridean aim is to deconstruct all fixed identities, even our personal identities. They always require 'some set of differentiations and exclusions' so that our identity is always at least partly defined through what it is not. For Butler 'identity categories tend to be instruments of regulatory regimes, whether as the normalizing categories of oppressive structures or as the rallying points for a liberatory contestation of that very oppression' (Butler 1991: 14). The last part of this sentence suggests that if I identify myself as gay because I want to protest the social discrimination of gays there is a good chance that I will indirectly contribute to keeping the anti-gay 'regime' in place. Butler's work, like that of Foucault, allows resistance, but is pessimistic about its effectiveness. As we will see in a moment, the only thing we can really do is perhaps to find a space for ourselves within the existing power structures and to parody power, to make fun of it in a liberating act. But let me look first at how Butler deconstructs identity categories. If we have no fixed identities, then what I consider to be my 'I' is, as Butler puts it, 'the effect of a certain repetition, one which produces the semblance of a continuity or coherence' (18). If that is the case, then my gender, or my sexual orientation, must likewise be the effect of repetition, of the fact that I repeatedly *perform* certain sexual acts or repeatedly *present* myself as gendered in a specific way. In other words, a string of identical or similar performances takes the place of identity. It should be clear that this reverses the historical process that Foucault described: we return from, for instance, a lesbian identity in the sense of a fixed sexual orientation, to a series of discrete, fundamentally unconnected, lesbian acts. And it also reverses our common sense assumptions about our 'I': instead of an 'I' that exists prior to our actions – sexual or otherwise – we have an 'I' that is the result of repetition. The continuous repetition of a certain set of acts – which of course will differ from person to person – creates what might be called an identity effect: the illusion that we are coherent and exercise our free will in doing what we do.

If identities are the effect of repetition, then heterosexuality, which sees itself as the only authentic form of sexuality, must also be nothing but a string of performances. This allows Butler to claim that heterosexuality is a 'repetition that can only produce the *effect* of its own originality; in other words, compulsory heterosexual identities, those ... phantasms of "man" and "woman," are theatrically produced effects that posture as grounds, origins, the normative measure of the real' (21). (Butler speaks of 'compulsory heterosexuality' because, given her assumptions, the predominance of heterosexuality must be the result of social pressure.) Heterosexual activity (like lesbian and homosexual activity) is then a copy (because it repeats earlier performances) for which there is no original. It can only try to pass itself off as the authentic form of sexuality by suggesting that other forms of sexuality like lesbianism and homosexuality are *in*authentic: by setting up a binary opposition in which it turns itself into the centre by relegating other sexualities to the margins. In other words, it needs non-heterosexual identities and activities to authenticate and validate itself. Heterosexuality and what until fairly recently used to be called 'perverse' forms of sexuality are deeply implicated in each other and they are all equally inauthentic. Like gender, sexuality is a social construction. If that is the case, then what is probably the most fundamental binary opposition of all – the one involving the division of human beings into males and females on the basis of biological sexuality – must be a construction too. It is, however, a fundamentally unstable construction. For Butler, following Lacan (see Chapter 6), identity is built upon a radical lack, an absence:

> In my view, the self only becomes a self on the condition that it has suffered a separation ... a loss which is suspended and provisionally resolved through a melancholic incorporation of some 'Other.' That 'Other' installed in the self thus establishes the permanent incapacity of the 'self' to achieve

self-identity; it is as if it were always already disrupted by the
Other; the disruption of the Other at the heart of the self is
the very condition of the self's possibility.

(27)

In the next section I will examine some manifestations of that
supposedly inherent instability of our (sexual) identity – an
instability that for many queer theorists has profound political
implications because it unsettles traditional views of sexuality.

## Drag and cross-dressing

Because of its political potential, queer theory has come to focus
on the actual practice of sexuality. Here, too, it is interested in
boundaries and, more in particular, on the (for queer theorists)
liberating circumstance that seemingly clear visible boundaries
turn out to be blurred upon closer inspection. Not surprisingly,
queer theory has taken a special interest in cross-dressing, and in
particular cross-dressing by males. Cross-dressing is perfect for
destabilizing generally accepted views of gender and sexuality: a
man in a long evening dress or a pleated skirt will in most places
draw a good deal of attention. Men in drag are so interesting to
queer theorists because they simultaneously position themselves
on the 'wrong' end of two axes (or oppositions): on the gender
axis they identify with the feminine pole, in spite of their maleness, and on the axis of sexual orientation (with its hetero/homo
opposition) they take up the homosexual position. In so doing
they first of all blur the boundary between gender and sexuality
(which the feminists had fought so hard to establish with the
argument that while sexuality is a biological given, gender is
nothing but a social construct). Clearly the act of cross-dressing
– that is, the appropriation of gender characteristics normally
associated with the other sex – has significance beyond gender
and is simultaneously a *sexual* act. In drag gender and sexuality
have become inseparable. From the perspective of queer theory
cross-dressers effectively illustrate the constructed character of
gender and sexuality, while they also draw attention to the enor-

mous difference between sexuality and acts of mere procreation. Human sexuality clearly involves much more than procreation. Drag exposes femininity as a role, as a performance. Cross-dressing undermines the claim to naturalness of standard heterosexual identities and emphasizes a theatrical, perform-ance-like dimension of gender and sexual orientation that our discourses seek to suppress. For queer theory, drag and other unusual intersections of gender and sexuality are, so to speak, sites where the constructedness of sexuality becomes visible and where we are confronted with the fact that there are only ever-shifting differences, even in the field of sexuality. Because of their parodic character, drag and other 'deviant' sexualities thus come to function as the heavy artillery in the war against the fixed categorizations of the 'phallogocentric' centre. They are important instruments in the development of what Judith Halberstam has called 'new sexual vocabularies that acknowl-edge sexualities and genders as styles rather than life-styles, as fictions rather than facts of life, and as potentialities rather than as fixed identities' (Halberstam [1994] 1998: 759).

## Homosexuality as cultural matrix

In its most ambitious manifestations queer theory also claims that sexuality, and in particular the exclusions and marginaliza-tions that are at work within the hetero/homo axis, is central to the organization of Western culture. Of particular importance here is the work of Eve Kosofsky Sedgwick. In her *Between Men* of 1985 Sedgwick argues that in a society dominated by men women are basically instruments with the help of which men establish or confirm specific relations. In a patriarchal society the *real* relations exist between men so that women function primarily within male–male relationships – a relationship of rivalry, for instance, if two males desire the same woman. The structure of such a male-dominated society is therefore *homoso-cial* – a term that should not be confused with 'homosexual', especially not since homosocial societies usually see homosexu-ality in strongly negative terms. 'Homosocial' indicates the true nature of *social* relationships, not of sexual ones. Still, sexual classification in fixed categories is central to a homosocially structured society. For Sedgwick, the homosocial nature of the Victorian society that she focuses on inevitably informs its writings: its literature, too, reveals that the underlying relationships of the Victorian period were relationships between men. Sedgwick reads against the grain to bring to light what might be called a socio-sexual structure that is not immediately apparent.

In a later book, Sedgwick proposes an equally wide-ranging thesis. *Epistemology of the Closet* (1990) begins with a Derridean deconstruction of the heterosexuality/homosexuality opposition (which in Western culture usually takes the form of contrasting naturalness, health, and fertility – in short, everything that stands for 'life' – with artificiality, sickness, sterility, and death):

> The analytic move [this book] makes is to demonstrate that categories presented in a culture as symmetrical binary oppositions – heterosexual/homosexual, in this case – actually subsist in a more unsettled and dynamic tacit relation according to which, first, term B is not symmetrical with but subordinated to term A; but, second, the ontologically valorized term A actually depends for its meaning on the simultaneous subsumption and exclusion of term B; hence, third, the question of priority between the supposed central and the supposed marginal category of each dyad is irresolvably unstable, an instability caused by the fact that term B is constituted as at once internal and external to term A.
>
> (Sedgwick 1990: 9–10)

Since the hetero/homo opposition is a matter of unfounded assumptions, it has in the past led to all sorts of false assertions. However, Sedgwick argues that even our current and more sophisticated understanding of homosexuality is still 'organized around a radical incoherence'. According to Sedgwick, 'most educated people' hold 'the minoritizing view that there is a distinct population of persons who "really are" gay'. Simultaneously, they hold the universalizing view that sexual desire is an unpredictable powerful solvent of stable identities; that apparently hetero-sexual persons and object choices are strongly marked by same-sex influences and desires, and vice versa for appar-ently homosexual ones; and that at least male heterosexual identity and modern masculinist culture require for their maintenance the scapegoating crystallization of a same-sex male desire that is widespread and in the first place internal.

(85)

This contradiction leads Sedgwick to identify a 'crisis of homo/heterosexual definition' in Western culture, with far-reaching consequences. (A more recent manifestation of this 'crisis' – which boils down the fact that we would appear to have conflicting ideas of sexuality and do not really know how to define it – is 'the current impasse within gay theory between "construc-tivist" and "essentialist" understandings of homosexuality' (91).)

Our basic uncertainties with regard to sexuality – which keep on surfacing in our views of same-sex sexuality – and in partic-ular our desire to create manageable categories for sexualities and sexual activities, affect many of the binary oppositions that are central to the way we organize our lives. Let me quote a crucial passage in full:

In arguing that homo/heterosexual definition has been a presiding master term of the past century, one that has the same, primary importance for all modern Western identity and social organization (and not merely for homosexual identity and culture) as do the more traditionally visible cruxes of gender, class, and race, I'll argue that the now chronic modern crisis of homo/heterosexual definition has affected our culture through its ineffeaceable marking particularly of the categories secrecy/disclosure, knowledge/ignorance, private/public, masculine/feminine, majority/minority, innocence/initiation, natural/artificial, new/old, discipline/terrorism, canonic/noncanonic, wholeness/deca-dence, urbane/provincial, domestic/foreign, health/illness, same/different, active/passive, in/out, cognition/paranoia, art/kitsch, utopia/apocalypse, sincerity/sentimentality, and voluntarity/addiction.

(11)

In *Epistemology of the Closet* Sedgwick tries to illustrate the formative influence of 'the homo/heterosexual definition' on these oppositions with detailed analyses of a number of late nineteenth- and early twentieth-century literary texts. However, since most of these texts invite homosexual readings because of what we know of their authors (Oscar Wilde, Marcel Proust, and others), the evidence they yield is perhaps less convincing than it could have been. This is not to say that the homo/heterosexual axis cannot be connected with other oppositions. We all know that fierce homophobia often goes together with racism, hatred of everybody 'foreign', and even an often barely disguised contempt for women. (The homophobia of the German Nazis is a case in point.) It would in fact seem to be central to a loud and self-congratulatory sort of masculinism that with its feminine gendering of homosexuality seeks to affirm its own virility. The homo/heterosexual axis clearly intersects with other oppositions. There is every reason, then, to follow the lead suggested by Sedgwick's thesis that

processes of homosexual attribution and identification have had a distinctive centrality in this century, for many stigmatized but extremely potent sets of relations involving projective chains of vicarious investments: sentimentality, kitsch, camp, the knowing, the prurient, the arch, the morbid.

(63)

Queer theory's contribution to literary and cultural studies lies in its emphasis on sexuality as a fourth category of analysis – next to race, gender, and class – and in its insistence that sexuality and gender cannot very well be separated. In its emphasis on sexuality as an instrument of understanding, queer theory gives a much sharper edge to an earlier lesbian and gay interest in sexuality. It confronts us with the meanings that our culture attaches to the range of sexual identities and sexual activities that we know and to the binary oppositions that it sets up and that serve as conduits of power and instruments of oppression.

## Summary

In the course of the 1980s lesbian and gay critics made sexuality – not to be confused with gender – a category of analysis in literary and cultural studies. Lesbian critics, for instance, sought to establish a specifically lesbian literary tradition and tried to define formal characteristics of lesbian writing. For the queer theory that under the influence of Foucault develops out of lesbian and gay criticism – and, in the United Kingdom, out of cultural materialism – the homo/heterosexual opposition is absolutely central to Western culture. 'Queer' therefore provides a vantage point for a radical critique of liberal humanist ideology. Any deconstruction of the homo/heterosexual opposition will directly affect the self-definition and ideological organization of Western culture. As one of the most prominent queer theorists has put it, from this perspective 'queer' stands for 'the open mesh of possibilities' that presents itself 'when the constituent elements of anyone's gender, of anyone's sexuality aren't made (or *can't be made*) to signify monolithically' (Sedgwick 1994: 8). Some queer theorists use cross-dressing and other non-standard forms of sexuality to question traditional classifications of sexual identity. Others, arguing that sexuality is a matter of *performance* rather than of *identity*, challenge heterosexuality's claim to 'naturalness' on theoretical grounds. In its most wide-ranging form, queer theory tries to illustrate the centrality of the homo/heterosexual axis to the West's cultural matrix and the extent to which it pervades other oppositions that at first sight have nothing to do with sexuality.

## Suggestions for further reading

Annamarie Jagose's *Queer Theory* (1997) is a good overview, while Alan Sinfield's *Cultural Politics – Queer Reading* (1994a) offers a lively account of the major themes of both cultural materialism and of the more leftist-oriented queer theory that we find in the United Kingdom. Eve Kosofsky Sedgwick's *Between Men* (1985) and *Epistemology of the Closet* (1990) are classics, but unfortunately not very easy. The opening chapters, however, should be accessible. Judith Butler's books – *Gender Trouble* (1990), *Bodies that Matter* (1993) – also tend to be difficult, but her 'Imitation and Gender Insubordination' (1991), from which I have quoted here, is a very accessible exception. *Novel Gazing: Queer Reading in Fiction* (1997) is massive, wide ranging, but on the whole rather theoretical collection of essays edited by Sedgwick. Marjorie Garber's *Vested Interests: Cross Dressing and Cultural Anxiety* (1992) is a good introduction to the complex fusion of sexuality and gender – and its unsettling cultural effects – that we find in some forms of sexual behaviour.

More traditional and accessible forms of gay and lesbian criticism are to be found in for instance Mark Lilly's *Gay Men's Literature in the Twentieth Century* (1993) and Gregory Woods's excellent and thorough *A History of Gay Literature* (1998). Terry Castle's *The Apparitional Lesbian: Female Homosexuality and Modern Culture* (1993) is a good example of a more traditional, but sophisticated, lesbian criticism (see for instance her interpretation of Sylvia Townsend Warner's *Summer Will Show* [1936]).

Finally, Joseph Bristow's *Sexuality* (1997) is a good introduction to recent theories of sexuality and sexual desire.

# Bibliography

Abrams, M.H. (2000) 'The Deconstructive Angel', in David Lodge and Nigel Wood (eds) *Modern Criticism and Theory: A Reader*, 2nd edn, Harlow: Longman, New York: Pearson [1977].

Achebe, Chinua (1958) *Things Fall Apart*, London: Heinemann.

—— (1977) 'An Image of Africa: Racism in Conrad's *Heart of Darkness*', *Massachusetts Review* 18, 4.

——(1995) 'Colonialist Criticism', in Bill Ashcroft *et al.* (eds) *The Post-Colonial Studies Reader*, London and New York: Routledge [1974].

Ackroyd, Peter (1985) *Hawksmoor*, London: Hamish Hamilton.

Ahmad, Aijaz (1992) *In Theory: Classes, Nations, Literatures*, London: Verso.

Althusser, Louis (1971) *Lenin and Philosophy and Other Essays*, London: New Left Books.

Appiah, Kwame Anthony (1992) *In My Father's House: Africa in the Philosophy of Culture*, New York: Oxford University Press.

Armstrong, Isobel (ed.) (1992) *New Feminist Discourses: Critical Essays on Theories and Texts*, London and New York: Routledge.

Arnold, Matthew (1970) *Matthew Arnold: Selected Prose*, ed. P.J. Keating, Harmondsworth: Penguin.

——(1971) *Culture and Anarchy*, ed. J. Dover Wilson, Cambridge: Cambridge University Press [1869].

Ashcroft, Bill, Gareth Griffiths, and Helen Tiffin (1989) *The Empire Writes Back: Theory and Practice in Post-Colonial Literatures*, London and New York: Routledge.

——(eds) (1995) *The Post-Colonial Studies Reader*, London and New York: Routledge.

——(1998) *Key Concepts in Post-Colonial Studies*, London and New York: Routledge.

Attridge, Derek (1995) 'The Linguistic Model and its Applications', in Raman Selden (ed.) *The Cambridge History of Literary Criticism, Vol. 8 (From Formalism to Post-structuralism)*, Cambridge: Cambridge University Press.

Atwood, Margaret (1979) *Surfacing*, London: Virago [1972].

Auster, Paul (1987) *City of Glass*, New York: Penguin [1985].

Baker, Houston A., Jr (1972) *Long Black Song: Essays in Black-American Culture*, Charlottesville: University Press of Virginia.

——(1984) *Blues, Ideology, and Afro-American Literature: A Vernacular Theory*, Chicago: University of Chicago Press.

Baldick, Chris (1983) *The Social Mission of English Criticism, 1848–1932*, Oxford: Clarendon Press.

——(1996) *Criticism and Literary Theory 1890 to the Present*, London and New York: Longman.

Barr, Marleen S. (1987) *Alien to Femininity: Speculative Fiction and Feminist Theory*, New York: Greenwood.

Barthelme, Donald (1981) *Sixty Stories*, New York: Dutton [1970].

——(1984) *Snow White*, New York: Atheneum [1967].

Barthes, Roland (1972) *Mythologies*, London: Jonathan Cape [1957].

——(1974) *S/Z*, New York: Hill and Wang [1970].

——(1977) *Image-Music-Text*, London: Fontana.

——(1986) *The Rustle of Language*, New York: Farrar, Straus and Giroux.

——(2000) 'The Death of the Author', in David Lodge and Nigel Wood (eds) *Modern Criticism and Theory: A Reader*, 2nd edn, Harlow: Longman, New York: Pearson [1968].

Bell, Michael (1988) *F.R. Leavis*, London: Routledge.

Belsey, Catherine (1980) *Critical Practice*, London: Methuen.

——(1985) *The Subject of Tragedy: Identity and Difference in Renaissance Drama*, London: Methuen/Routledge.

Bennett, Tony (1979) *Formalism and Marxism*, London: Methuen.

Bertens, Hans (1995) *The Idea of the Postmodern: A History*, London and New York: Routledge.

Bertens, Hans and Douwe Fokkema (eds) (1997) *International Postmodernism: Theory and Literary Practice*, Amsterdam and Philadelphia: John Benjamins.

Bhabha, Homi K. (ed.) (1990) *Nation and Narration*, London and New York: Routledge.

——(1992) 'Postcolonial Criticism', in Stephen Greenblatt and Giles Gunn (eds) *Redrawing the Boundaries: The Transformation of English and American Studies*, New York: MLA.

——(1994a) *The Location of Culture*, London and New York: Routledge.

——(1994b) 'Signs Taken for Wonders', in H.K. Bhabha (1994a) *The Location of Culture*, London and New York: Routledge [1985].

Boehmer, Elleke (1995) *Colonial and Postcolonial Literature*, Oxford and New York: Oxford University Press.

Booth, Wayne (1961) *The Rhetoric of Fiction*, Chicago: University of Chicago Press.

Bowie, Malcolm (1991) *Lacan*, London: Fontana, Cambridge, MA: Harvard University Press.

Brannigan, John (1998) *New Historicism and Cultural Materialism*, Basingstoke and London: Macmillan, New York: St Martin's Press.

Brathwaite, Edward (1974) *Contradicting Omens: Cultural Diversity and Integration in the Caribbean*, Mona: Sacavou Publications.

——(1984) *History of the Voice: The Development of Nation Language in Anglophone Caribbean Poetry*, London: New Beacon Books.

——(1995) 'Nation Language', in Bill Ashcroft *et al.* (eds) *The Post-Colonial Studies Reader*, London and New York: Routledge [1984].

Bremond, Claude (1966) 'La logique des possibles narratifs', *Communications* 8.

Brennan, Teresa (ed.) (1990) *Between Feminism and Psychoanalysis*, London and New York: Routledge.

Bristow, Joseph (1997) *Sexuality*, London and New York: Routledge.

Brooks, Cleanth (1968) *The Well-Wrought Urn: Studies in the Structure of Poetry*, London: Methuen [1947].

——(1972) 'The Language of Paradox', in David Lodge (ed.) *20th Century Literary Criticism*, London and New York: Longman [1942].

Brooks, Cleanth and Robert Penn Warren (1976) *Understanding Poetry*, 4th edn, New York: Holt [1939].

Brooks, Peter (1994) *Psychoanalysis and Storytelling*, Oxford: Blackwell.

Butler, Judith (1990) *Gender Trouble: Feminism and the Subversion of Identity*, New York and London: Routledge.

——(1991) 'Imitation and Gender Subordination', in Diana Fuss (ed.) *Inside/Out: Lesbian Theories, Gay Theories*, London and New York: Routledge.

——(1993) *Bodies that Matter: On the Discursive Limits of 'Sex'*, New York and London: Routledge.

Carby, Hazel (1987) *Reconstructing Womanhood: The Emergence of the Afro-American Woman Novelist*, New York: Oxford University Press.

Castle, Terry (1993) *The Apparitional Lesbian: Female Homosexuality and Modern Culture*, New York: Columbia University Press.

Césaire, Aimé (1997) 'From *Discourse on Colonialism*', in Bart Moore-Gilbert, Gareth Stanton, and Willy Maley (eds) *Postcolonial Criticism*, London and New York: Longman [1955].

Chatman, Seymour (1990) *Coming to Terms: The Rhetoric of Narrative in Fiction and Film*, Ithaca: Cornell University Press.

Christian, Barbara (1985) *Black Feminist Criticism: Perspectives on Black Women Writers*, New York: Pergamon.

Cixous, Hélène (1981) 'The Laugh of the Medusa', in Elaine Marks and Isabelle de Courvitron (eds) *New French Feminism: An Anthology*, Hemel Hempstead: Harvester Wheatsheaf [1974].

——(2000) 'Sorties', in David Lodge and Nigel Wood (eds) *Modern Criticism and Theory: A Reader*, 2nd edn, Harlow: Longman, New York: Pearson [1975].

Cohn, Dorrit (1978) *Transparent Minds: Narrating Modes for Presenting Consciousness in Fiction*, Princeton: Princeton University Press.

Collier, Peter and Helga Geyer-Ryan (eds) (1990) *Literary Theory Today*, Cambridge: Polity.

Collins, Patricia Hill (2000) *Black Feminist Thought: Knowledge, Consciousness and the Politics of Empowerment*, 2nd edn, New York and London: Routledge.

Connor, Steven (1997) *Postmodernist Culture: An Introduction to Theories of the Contemporary*, 2nd edn, Oxford and Cambridge, MA: Blackwell.

Culler, Jonathan (1975) *Structuralist Poetics: Structuralism, Linguistics and the Study of Literature*, Ithaca: Cornell University Press, London: Routledge & Kegan Paul.

——(1982) *On Deconstruction: Theory and Criticism after Structuralism*, Ithaca: Cornell University Press.

Davis, Robert Con (ed.) (1983) *Lacan and Narration: The Psychoanalytic Difference in Narrative Theory*, Baltimore: Johns Hopkins University Press.

Derrida, Jacques (1976) *Of Grammatology*, trans. Gayatri Chakravorty Spivak, Baltimore: Johns Hopkins University Press [1967].

——(1982) *Margins of Philosophy*, Chicago: University of Chicago Press.

——(1987) 'Devant la Loi', in Alan Udoff (ed.) *Kafka and the Contemporary Critical Performance: Centenary Readings*, Bloomington: Indiana University Press.

——(1996) 'From *Différance*', in Kiernan Ryan (ed.) *New Historicism and Cultural Materialism: A Reader*, London: Arnold, New York: Oxford University Press [1982].

Dollimore, Jonathan (1984) *Radical Tragedy: Religion, Ideology and Power in the Drama of Shakespeare and his Contemporaries*, Hemel Hempstead: Harvester Wheatsheaf.
——(1991) *Sexual Dissidence: Augustine to Wilde, Freud to Foucault*, Oxford: Oxford University Press.
Dollimore, Jonathan and Alan Sinfield (eds) (1985) *Political Shakespeare: New Essays in Cultural Materialism*, Manchester: Manchester University Press.
Drakakis, John (1985) *Alternative Shakespeares*, London: Methuen.
Eagleton, Terry (1976a) *Marxism and Literary Criticism*, London: Methuen.
——(1976b) *Criticism and Ideology*, London: Verso.
——(1991) *Ideology: An Introduction*, London and New York: Verso.
Eichenbaum, Boris (1998) 'Introduction to the Formal Method', in Julie Rivkin and Michael Ryan (eds) *Literary Theory: An Anthology*, Malden, MA, and Oxford: Blackwell [1926].
Eliot, T.S. (1969) *Selected Essays*, London: Faber and Faber.
——(1972) 'Tradition and the Individual Talent', in David Lodge (ed.) *20th Century Literary Criticism*, London and New York: Longman [1919].
Erlich, Viktor (1981) *Russian Formalism: History-Doctrine*, 3rd edn, New Haven: Yale University Press.
Faderman, Lillian (1981) *Surpassing the Love of Men: Romantic Friendship and Love Between Women from the Renaissance to the Present*, New York: Morrow.
Fanon, Frantz (1965) *The Wretched of the Earth*, New York: Grove [1961].
——(1997) 'On National Culture', in Bart Moore-Gilbert, Gareth Stanton, and Willy Maley (eds) *Postcolonial Criticism*, London and New York: Longman [1955].
Felman, Shoshana (1982a) 'Turning the Screw of Interpretation', in Shoshana Felman (ed.) (1982b) *Literature and Psychoanalysis: The Question of Reading: Otherwise*, Baltimore: Johns Hopkins University Press.
——(ed.) (1982b) *Literature and Psychoanalysis: The Question of Reading: Otherwise*, Baltimore: Johns Hopkins University Press.
Fink, Bruce (1996) 'Reading Hamlet with Lacan', in Willy Apollon and Richard Feinstein (eds) *Lacan, Politics, Aesthetics*, Albany: SUNY Press.
Foucault, Michel (1972) *The Archaeology of Knowledge*, London: Tavistock [1969].
——(1977) *Discipline and Punish*, London: Allen Lane [1975].
——(1980) *Power/Knowledge: Selected Interviews and Other Writings*, ed. Colin Gordon, London: Harvester Wheatsheaf.
——(2000) 'What Is an Author?', in David Lodge and Nigel Wood (eds) *Modern Criticism and Theory: A Reader*, 2nd edn, Harlow: Longman, New York: Pearson [1969].
Frow, John (1986) *Marxism and Literary History*, New Haven: Yale University Press.
Fuss, Diana (ed.) (1991) *Inside/Out: Lesbian Theories, Gay Theories*, London and New York: Routledge.
Gallagher, Catherine (1989) 'Marxism and the New Historicism', in H. Aram Veeser (ed.) *The New Historicism*, London and New York: Routledge.
Gallagher, Catherine and Stephen Greenblatt (2000) *Practicing New Historicism*, Chicago: University of Chicago Press.
Garber, Marjorie (1992) *Vested Interests: Cross Dressing and Cultural Anxiety*, New York and London: Routledge.
Garvin, Paul (ed. and trans.) (1964) *A Prague School Reader on Esthetics, Literary Structure and Style*, Washington, DC: Georgetown University Press.
Gates, Henry Louis, Jr (1987) *Figures in Black: Words, Signs and the 'Racial' Self*, Oxford: Oxford University Press.
——(1988) *The Signifying Monkey: A Theory of African-American Literary Criticism*, Oxford: Oxford University Press.

——(ed.) (1990) *Reading Black, Reading Feminist*, New York: NAL.

——(1992) 'African American Criticism', in Stephen Greenblatt and Giles Gunn (eds) *Redrawing the Boundaries: The Transformation of English and American Studies*, New York: MLA.

——(1998) 'The Blackness of Blackness: A Critique on the Sign and the Signifyin' Monkey', in Julie Rivkin and Michael Ryan (eds) *Literary Theory: An Anthology*, Malden, MA and Oxford: Blackwell [1989].

Genette, Gérard (1980) *Narrative Discourse*, Oxford: Blackwell [1972].

Giblett, Rod (1996) *Postmodern Wetlands: Culture, History, Ecology*, Edinburgh: Edinburgh University Press.

Gilbert, Sandra M. and Susan Gubar (1979) *The Madwoman in the Attic: The Woman Writer and the Nineteenth-Century Literary Imagination*, New Haven and London: Yale University Press.

Gordon, Colin (ed.) (1980) *Power/Knowledge: Selected Interviews and Other Writings*, London: Harvester Wheatsheaf.

Graff, Gerald (1987) *Professing Literature: An Institutional History*, Chicago and London: University of Chicago Press.

Gramsci, Antonio (1998) ' "Hegemony" (from "The Formation of Intellectuals")', in Julie Rivkin and Michael Ryan (eds) *Literary Theory: An Anthology*, Malden, MA and Oxford: Blackwell [1971].

Greenblatt, Stephen (1980) *Renaissance Self-Fashioning: From More to Shakespeare*, Chicago and London: University of Chicago Press.

——(1981) 'Invisible Bullets: Renaissance Authority and its Subversion', *Glyph* 8.

——(1989) 'Towards a Poetics of Culture', in H. Aram Veeser (ed.) *The New Historicism*, London and New York: Routledge.

——(1990) 'Resonance and Wonder', in Peter Collier and Helga Geyer-Ryan (eds) *Literary Theory Today*, Cambridge: Polity.

——(1991) *Marvellous Possessions: The Wonder of the New World*, Oxford: Oxford University Press.

Greenblatt, Stephen and Giles Gunn (eds) (1992) *Redrawing the Boundaries: The Transformation of English and American Studies*, New York: MLA.

Greimas, A.J. (1983) *Structural Semantics*, Lincoln: Nebraska University Press [1966].

Halberstam, Judith (1998) 'F2M: The Making of Female Masculinity', in Julie Rivkin and Michael Ryan (eds) *Literary Theory: An Anthology*, Malden, MA and Oxford: Blackwell [1994].

Handke, Peter (1977) *Three by Peter Handke*, New York: Avon [1970].

Haslett, Moyra (1999) *Marxist Literary and Cultural Theory*, Basingstoke and London: Macmillan, New York: St Martin's Press.

Hawkes, Terence (1977) *Structuralism and Semiotics*, London: Methuen.

Hawthorn, Jeremy (1998) *A Concise Glossary of Contemporary Literary Terms*, 3rd edn, London: Arnold, New York: Oxford University Press.

Hoban, Russell (1982) *Riddley Walker*, London: Picador [1980].

Hoggart, Richard (1971) *The Uses of Literacy: Aspects of Working-Class Life with Special Reference to Publications and Entertainments*, London: Penguin [1957].

Holland, Norman M. (1991) *Holland's Guide to Psychoanalytic Psychology and Literature-and-Psychology*, New York: Oxford University Press.

hooks, bell (1982) *Ain't I a Woman? Black Women and Feminism*, London: Pluto [1981].

——(1992) *Black Looks: Race and Representation*, Boston, MA: South End Press.

——(1997) 'Revolutionary Black Women: Making Ourselves Subject', in Bart Moore-Gilbert, Gareth Stanton, and Willy Maley (eds) *Postcolonial Criticism*, London and New York: Longman [1992].

Humm, Maggie (1987) *An Annotated Critical Bibliography of Feminist Criticism*, Boston: Hall.

——(ed.) (1992) *Feminisms: A Reader*, Hemel Hempstead: Harvester Wheatsheaf.

——(1995) *Practising Feminist Criticism: An Introduction*, London and New York: Prentice Hall/Harvester Wheatsheaf.

Hutcheon, Linda (1988) *A Poetics of Postmodernism: History, Theory, Fiction*, New York and London: Routledge.

——(1989) *The Politics of Postmodernism*, New York and London: Routledge.

Jagose, Annamarie (1997) *Queer Theory: An Introduction*, New York: New York University Press.

Jakobson, Roman (1988) 'Closing Statement: Linguistics and Poetics', in David Lodge (ed.) *Modern Criticism and Theory: A Reader*, London and New York: Longman [1960].

Jameson, Fredric (1981) *The Political Unconsciousness: Narrative as a Socially Symbolic Act*, Ithaca, NY: Cornell University Press.

——(1984) 'Postmodernism, or the Cultural Logic of Late Capitalism', *New Left Review* 146.

——(1989) 'Marxism and Postmodernism', *New Left Review* 176.

Jefferson, Ann and David Robey (eds) (1986) *Modern Literary Theory: A Comparative Introduction*, 2nd edn, London: Batsford.

Johnson, Barbara (1980) *The Critical Difference*, Baltimore: Johns Hopkins University Press.

Kesey, Ken (1962) *One Flew over the Cuckoo's Nest*, New York: Viking.

Knight, Stephen (1980) *Form and Ideology in Detective Fiction*, London: Macmillan.

Kristeva, Julia (1984) *Revolution in Poetic Language*, New York: Columbia University Press [1974].

Lacan, Jacques (1977) 'Desire and the Interpretation of Desire in *Hamlet*', in *Yale French Studies* 55–56, reprinted in Shoshana Felman (ed.) (1982b) *Literature and Psychoanalysis: The Question of Reading: Otherwise*, Baltimore: Johns Hopkins University Press.

Lawrence, D.H. (1972a) 'Morality and the Novel', in David Lodge (ed.) *20th Century Literary Criticism*, London and New York: Longman [1925].

——(1972b) 'Why the Novel Matters', in David Lodge (ed.) *20th Century Literary Criticism*, London and New York: Longman [1936].

——(1972c) 'The Spirit of Place', in David Lodge (ed.) *20th Century Literary Criticism*, London and New York: Longman [1924].

Leach, Edmund (1996) *Lévi-Strauss*, 4th edn, revised and updated by James Laidlaw, London: Fontana.

Leavis, F.R. (1932) *New Bearings in English Poetry*, London: Chatto and Windus.

——(1936) *Revaluation: Tradition and Development in English Poetry*, London: Chatto and Windus.

——(1962) *The Great Tradition*, Harmondsworth: Penguin [1948].

——(1967) *English Literature in Our Time and the University*, London: Chatto and Windus.

Lévi-Strauss, Claude (1982) *The Way of Masks*, Seattle: University of Washington Press.

Lilly, Mark (1993) *Gay Men's Literature in the Twentieth Century*, New York: New York University Press.

Lodge, David (ed.) (1972) *20th Century Literary Criticism*, London and New York: Longman.

——(ed.) (1988) *Modern Criticism and Theory: A Reader*, London and New York: Longman.

Lodge, David and Nigel Wood (eds) (2000) *Modern Criticism and Theory: A Reader*, 2nd edn, Harlow: Longman, New York: Pearson.

Loomba, Ania (1998) *Colonialism/Postcolonialism*, London and New York: Routledge.

Lorde, Audre (1984) *Sister Outsider: Essays and Speeches*, Freedom, CA: Crossing Press.

——(1998) 'Age, Race, Class, and Sex: Women Redefining Difference', in Julie Rivkin and Michael Ryan (eds) *Literary Theory: An Anthology*, Malden, MA and Oxford: Blackwell [1984].

Lukács, Georg (1972) 'The Ideology of Modernism', in David Lodge (ed.) *20th Century Literary Criticism*, London and New York: Longman [1957].

Lyotard, Jean-François (1984) *The Postmodern Condition: A Report on Knowledge*, Minneapolis: University of Minnesota Press.

Macherey, Pierre (1978) *A Theory of Literary Production*, London: Routledge [1966].

Marshall, Brenda K. (1992) *Teaching the Postmodern: Fiction and Theory*, London and New York: Routledge.

Martin, Wallace (1986) *Recent Theories of Narrative*, Ithaca: Cornell University Press.

McHale, Brian (1987) *Postmodernist Fiction*, London and New York: Methuen.

Miller, J. Hillis (1976) 'Stevens' Rock and Criticism as Cure, II', *Georgia Review* 30.

——(2000) 'The Critic as Host', in David Lodge and Nigel Wood (eds) (2000) *Modern Criticism and Theory: A Reader*, 2nd edn, Harlow: Longman, New York: Pearson [1977].

Millett, Kate (1970) *Sexual Politics*, Garden City, NY: Doubleday.

Mills, Sara, Lynne Pearce, Sue Spaull, and Elaine Millard (1989) *Feminist Readings, Feminists Reading*, Hemel Hempstead: Harvester Wheatsheaf.

Montrose, Louis (1983) ' "Shaping Fantasies": Figuration of Gender and Power in Elizabethan Culture', *Representations* 1, 2.

——(1989) 'The Poetics and Politics of Culture', in H. Aram Veeser (ed.) *The New Historicism*, London and New York: Routledge.

——(1992) 'New Historicisms', in Stephen Greenblatt and Giles Gunn (eds) *Redrawing the Boundaries: The Transformation of English and American Studies*, New York: MLA.

——(1994) ' "Eliza, Queene of Shepeardes", and the Pastoral of Power', in H. Aram Veeser (ed.) *The New Historicism Reader*, London and New York: Routledge [1980].

Moore-Gilbert, Bart, Gareth Stanton, and Willy Maley (eds and intro.) (1997) *Postcolonial Criticism*, London and New York: Longman.

Morrison, Toni (1982) *Playing in the Dark: Whiteness and the Literary Imagination*, Cambridge, MA: Harvard University Press.

Mulhern, Francis (1979) *The Moment of 'Scrutiny'*, London: New Left Books.

Muller, John P. and William J. Richardson (eds) (1988) *The Purloined Poe*, Baltimore: Johns Hopkins University Press.

Munt, Sally R. (1994) *Murder by the Book? Feminism and the Crime Novel*, London and New York: Routledge.

'Newbolt Report' (1921) *Report to the Board of Education on the Teaching of English in England*, London: HMSO.

Norris, Christopher (1982) *Deconstruction: Theory and Practice*, London: Methuen.

Peck, John and Martin Coyle (1995) *Practical Criticism*, Basingstoke and London: Macmillan.

Perkins, George, Sculley Bradley, Richmond Croom Beatty, and E. Hudson Long (eds) (1985) *The American Tradition in Literature, Vol. 2*, 6th edn, New York: Random House.

Powers, Richard (1985) *Three Farmers on their Way to a Dance*, New York: Morrow.

Pratt, Mary Louise (1992) *Imperial Eyes: Studies in Travel Writing and Transculturation*, New York and London: Routledge.

Pynchon, Thomas (1967) *The Crying of Lot 49*, New York: Bantam [1966].

Quayson, Ato (2000) *Postcolonialism: Theory, Practice or Process?*, Cambridge: Polity, Malden, MA: Blackwell.

Rabinow, David (ed.) (1984) *The Foucault Reader*, New York: Random House.

Ransom, John Crowe (1972) 'Criticism, Inc.', in David Lodge (ed.) *20th Century Literary Criticism*, London and New York: Longman [1937].

Richards, I.A. (1926) *Science and Poetry*, London: Routledge & Kegan Paul.

——(1972a) 'Communication and the Artist', in David Lodge (ed.) *20th Century Literary Criticism*, London and New York: Longman [1924].

——(1972b) 'The Four Kinds of Meaning', in David Lodge (ed.) *20th Century Literary Criticism*, London and New York: Longman [1929].

Rimmon-Kenan, Shlomith (1983) *Narrative Fiction: Contemporary Poetics*, London: Methuen.

Rivkin, Julie and Michael Ryan (eds) (1998) *Literary Theory: An Anthology*, Malden, MA, and Oxford: Blackwell.

Robbins, Ruth (2000) *Literary Feminisms*, Basingstoke and London: Macmillan, New York: St Martin's Press.

Rule, Jane (1975) *Lesbian Images*, Trumansberg, NY: Crossings Press.

Ryan, Kiernan (ed.) (1996) *New Historicism and Cultural Materialism: A Reader*, London: Arnold, New York: Oxford University Press.

Said, Edward (1991) *Orientalism*, Harmondsworth: Penguin [1978].

Saussure, Ferdinand de (1959) *Course in General Linguistics*, New York: McGraw-Hill [1915].

Scholes, Robert (1974) *Structuralism in Literature: An Introduction*, New Haven: Yale University Press.

Sebeok, Thomas (ed.) (1960) *Style in Language*, Cambridge, MA: Technology Press/MIT and New York: John Wiley.

Sedgwick, Eve Kosofsky (1985) *Between Men: English Literature and Male Homosocial Desire*, New York: Columbia University Press.

——(1990) *Epistemology of the Closet*, Berkeley and Los Angeles: University of California Press.

——(1994) *Tendencies*, New York and London: Routledge.

——(ed.) (1997) *Novel Gazing: Queer Readings in Fiction*, Durham, NC: Duke University Press.

Selden, Raman (ed.) (1995) *The Cambridge History of Literary Criticism, Vol. 8 (From Formalism to Poststructuralism)*, Cambridge: Cambridge University Press.

Shklovsky, Viktor (1998) 'Art as Technique', in Julie Rivkin and Michael Ryan (eds) (1998) *Literary Theory: An Anthology*, Malden, MA, and Oxford: Blackwell [1917].

Showalter, Elaine (ed.) (1985) *The New Feminist Criticism*, New York: Pantheon.

——([1979] 1985) 'Towards a Feminist Poetics', in Elaine Showalter (ed.) *The New Feminist Criticism*, New York: Pantheon.

Sinfield, Alan (1986) *Alfred Tennyson*, Oxford: Blackwell.

——(1992) *Faultlines: Cultural Materialism and the Politics of Dissident Reading*, Oxford: Oxford University Press.

——(1994a) *Cultural Politics – Queer Reading*, London and New York: Routledge.

——(1994b) *The Wilde Century: Effeminacy, Oscar Wilde and the Queer Moment*, London: Cassell.

Skura, Meredith (1992) 'Psychoanalytic Criticism', in Stephen Greenblatt and Giles Gunn (eds) *Redrawing the Boundaries: The Transformation of English and American Studies*, New York: MLA.

Smith, Barbara (1985) 'Towards a Black Feminist Criticism', in Elaine Showalter (ed.) *The New Feminist Criticism*, New York: Pantheon [1977].

Spivak, Gayatri Chakravorty (1995a) 'Three Women's Texts and a Critique of Imperialism', in Bill Ashcroft *et al.* (eds) *The Post-Colonial Studies Reader*, London and New York: Routledge [1985].

——(1995b) 'Can the Subaltern Speak?', in Bill Ashcroft *et al.* (eds) *The Post-Colonial Studies Reader*, London and New York: Routledge [1988].

Steiner, Peter (1984) *Russian Formalism: A Metapoetics*, Ithaca: Cornell University Press.

Stepto, Robert (1979) *From Behind the Veil*, Urbana: University of Illinois Press; 2nd revised edition 1991.

Striedter, Jurij (1989) *Literary Structure, Evolution, and Value: Russian Formalism and Czech Structuralism Reconsidered*, Cambridge: Harvard University Press.

Todorov, Tzvetan (1975) *The Fantastic: A Structural Approach to a Literary Genre*, Ithaca: Cornell University Press [1970].

——(1977) *The Poetics of Prose*, Oxford: Oxford University Press [1971].

Udoff, Alan (ed.) (1987) *Kafka and the Contemporary Critical Performance: Centenary Readings*, Bloomington: Indiana University Press.

Veeser, H. Aram (ed.) (1989) *The New Historicism*, London and New York: Routledge.

——(ed.) (1994) *The New Historicism Reader*, London and New York: Routledge.

Viswanathan, Gauri (1989) *Masks of Conquest: Literary Study and British Rule in India*, New York: Columbia University Press.

Wall, Cheryl (ed.) (1989) *Changing Our Own Words*, New Brunswick: Rutgers University Press.

Warhol, Robyn R. and Diane Price Herndl (eds) (1991) *Feminisms: An Anthology of Literary Theory and Criticism*, New Brunswick: Rutgers University Press.

Washington, Mary Helen (ed.) (1989) *Invented Lives: Narratives of Black Women (1860–1960)*, London: Virago [1987].

Webster, Roger (1990) *Studying Literary Theory*, London: Arnold.

Williams, Linda Ruth (1995) *Critical Desire: Psychoanalysis and the Literary Subject*, London: Arnold.

Williams, Raymond (1961) *Culture and Society, 1780–1950*, Harmondsworth: Penguin [1958].

——(1977) *Marxism and Literature*, Oxford: Oxford University Press.

——([1980] 1996) 'Base and Superstructure in Marxist Cultural Theory', in, Kiernan Ryan (ed.) *New Historicism and Cultural Materialism: A Reader*, London: Arnold, New York: Oxford University Press.

Willis, Susan (1987) *Specifying: Black Women Writing the American Experience*, Madison: University of Wisconsin Press.

Wimsatt, W.K., Jr and Monroe C. Beardsley (1972a) 'The Intentional Fallacy', in David Lodge (ed.) *20th Century Literary Criticism*, London and New York: Longman [1946].

——(1972b) 'The Affective Fallacy', in David Lodge (ed.) (1972) *20th Century Literary Criticism*, London and New York: Longman [1949].

Woods, Gregory (1998) *A History of Gay Literature: The Male Tradition*, New Haven, CT: Yale University Press.

Wright, Elizabeth (1998) *Psychoanalytic Criticism: A Reappraisal*, 2nd edn, Cambridge: Polity.

BIBLIOGRAPHY

Wright, Will (1975) *Sixguns and Society: A Structural Approach to the Western*, Berkeley: University of California Press.

Zimmerman, Bonnie (1985) 'What Has Never Been: An Overview of Lesbian Feminist Criticism', in Elaine Showalter (ed.) *The New Feminist Criticism*, New York: Pantheon.

——(1992) 'Lesbians Like This and That: Some Notes on Lesbian Criticism for the Nineties', in Sally Munt (ed.) *New Lesbian Criticism: Literary and Cultural Readings*, Hemel Hempstead: Harvester Wheatsheaf.

# Index

More, Thomas 178–9
Morrison, Toni 102, 104
Mukařovský, Jan 46
music 167
myths 61, 67

Naipaul, V.S. 197; *The Mimic Men* 208–9
narrative: Lyotard's view 142–3; search for 'grammar' of 67–70; *see also* fiction
narratology 71–5
narrator 73–5
national unity, concept of 10–11
negritude movement 105–6, 193
New Criticism 17, 20–7, 34, 39, 137; and form 14, 18–19, 22, 33, 53; influence on Genette 75; limitations 43, 79, 94; persistence of methods 118; similarity to deconstruction 132
new historicism 144, 176–84, 185; criticisms of 178, 181–2, 184, 185
New Left 177
New School of Social Research 32
New Zealand 196, 202
'Newbolt Report' (on the Teaching of English in England; 1921) 10
*Nights at the Circus* (Carter) 42
nineteenth century: fiction 87, 91, 211; homosexuality 223–4, 231; linguistics 55–6; poetry 18
*nom du père* 161
nonverbal signifying systems 167
normality 152–3
*Nova Express* (Burroughs) 42
novels *see* fiction

object 69–70
Oedipal model 158–9, 160
*Omeros* (Walcott) 195
*One Flew Over the Cuckoo's Nest* (Kesey) 152–3, 156
'opposer' 69, 70
opposition *see* binary opposition
Orientalism 112, 203–6
orientation 44–5
*Othello* (Shakespeare) 186
Other (psychoanalysis) 161, 163, 207, 209, 228–9
Ouologuem, Yambo 194
Oxford, University of 9

Pakistani writers 197
panopticism 148–53
Panopticon 150–1
paradox 21–2; Cretan 121–2
*Passage to India, A* (Forster) 205, 207
patriarchy 93, 96, 230; Cixous' view 166; Lacan's view 161
*Peanuts* (cartoon strip) 136
phallocentrism 165–6
phallus 161
'Philistinism' 2
philosophy, Western 136
phonemes 63
Plath, Sylvia 101
poetry: Arnold's view 2–4, 8; defamiliarization 33, 34–5, 36, 40, 41, 42–3, 44, 45–6; devices 34, 35, 40; Eliot's view 12–15; form 14, 15; formalist view 34–5, 40; Jakobson on language of 47–9; Leavis' view 18; lyric, and the individual 6; meaning 14–15; New Critics' view 21–4; Richards' view 16
point of view 73
*Political Shakespeare: Essays in Cultural Materialism* (eds. Dollimore and Sinfield) 185, 187–8
politics 79–80, 177, 187, 188; link with the personal 95–6; *see also* feminism; Marxism; race
postcolonial studies 106, 107, 112, 144, 163, 183–4, 199–215; class and (subaltern) 212–13; cultural interaction 206–10; feminism and 210, 211–14; *see also* Bhabha, Homi; Said, Edward; Spivak, Gayatri Chakravorty
postmodernism 138–44; criticisms of 143
poststructuralism 60, 80, 92–3, 117–38, 147–69; and absence 64; binary oppositions 128–31; and colonialism 201, 207, 210; compared to structuralism 120–2, 126–7, 135–8; and cultural studies 175, 176; feminism and 96, 164–8; and language 120–8; literary deconstruction 131–5; new historicism and 179, 181; race and 107, 109; *see also* deconstruction; Derrida, Jacques; Foucault, Michel; postmodernism; psychoanalysis